Demystifying mentalities

Themes in the Social Sciences

Editors: John Dunn, Jack Goody, Eugene A. Hammel, Geoffrey Hawthorn

Edmund Leach: *Culture and Communication: the logic by which symbols are connected: an introduction to the use of structuralist analysis in social anthropology*

Anthony Heath: *Rational choice and social exchange: a critique of exchange theory*

P. Abrams and A. McCulloch: *Communes, sociology and society*

Jack Goody: *The domestication of the savage mind*

Jean-Louis Flandrin: *Families in former times: kinship, household and sexuality*

John Dunn: *Theory in the face of the future*

David Thomas: *Naturalism and social science: a post-empiricist philosophy of social science*

Claude Meillassoux: *Maidens, meal and money: capitalism and the domestic community*

David Lane: *Leninism: a sociological interpretation*

Anthony D. Smith: *The ethnic revival*

Jack Goody: *Cooking, cuisine and class: a study in comparative sociology*

Roy Ellen: *Environment, subsistence and system: the ecology of small-scale formations*

S. N. Eisenstadt and L. Roniger: *Patrons, clients and friends: Interpersonal relations and the structure of trust in society*

John Dunn: *The politics of socialism: an essay in political theory*

Martine Segalen: *Historical anthropology of the family*

Tim Ingold: *Evolution and social life*

David Levine: *Reproducing families: the political economy of English population history*

Robert Hinde: *Individuals, relationships and culture: links between ethology and the social sciences*

Paul Connerton: *How societies remember*

Demystifying mentalities

G. E. R. LLOYD

Darwin College, Cambridge

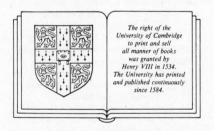

The right of the
University of Cambridge
to print and sell
all manner of books
was granted by
Henry VIII in 1534.
The University has printed
and published continuously
since 1584.

CAMBRIDGE UNIVERSITY PRESS

Cambridge

New York   Port Chester   Melbourne   Sydney

Published by the Press Syndicate of the University of Cambridge
The Pitt Building, Trumpington Street, Cambridge, CB2 1RP
32 East 57th Street, New York, NY 10022, USA
10 Stamford Road, Oakleigh, Melbourne 3166, Australia

© Cambridge University Press 1990

First published 1990

Printed in Great Britain by
Redwood Press Limited, Melksham, Wiltshire

British Library Cataloguing in Publication Data
Lloyd, G. E. R. (Geoffrey Ernest Richard)
Demystifying mentalities. – (themes in the
social sciences)
1. Man. cognition. Psychological aspects
I. title II. Series
153.4

Library of Congress cataloguing in publication data
Lloyd, G. E. R. (Geoffrey Ernest Richard), 1933–
Demystifying mentalities / G. E. R. Lloyd.
p.   cm. – (Themes in the social sciences).
Bibliography.
ISBN 0 521 36661 5. ISBN 0 521 36680 1 (paperback)
1. Belief and doubt – Cross-cultural studies.
2. Evidence – Cross-cultural studies.
3. Cognition and culture. 4. Science – History.
I. Title.   II. Title: Mentalities.   III. Series.
BF773.L66 1990
303.3′72 – dc20 89–9788 CIP

ISBN 0 521 36661 5 hardback
ISBN 0 521 36680 1 paperback

CE

Contents

Note on texts and references

I cite the major Greek and Latin authors by standard editions, for example the works of Plato according to Burnet's Oxford text, the treatises of Aristotle according to Bekker's Berlin edition, the fragments of the Presocratic philosophers according to the edition of Diels, revised by Kranz, *Die Fragmente der Vorsokratiker*, 6th ed. (Berlin, 1952). Greek and Latin medical texts are cited, for preference, according to the *Corpus Medicorum Graecorum* and *Corpus Medicorum Latinorum* editions. Thus for the Hippocratic treatises *On Ancient Medicine, On the Art* I use CMG I 1, for *On Airs Waters Places* CMG I 1, 2, and *On the Nature of Man* CMG I 1, 3. But for Hippocratic treatises not included in that edition I use E. Littré, *Oeuvres complètes d'Hippocrate*, 10 vols., Paris, 1839–61. Thus *On Regimen in Acute Diseases* is cited by chapter and page of vol. 2 of Littré, *On Fractures* similarly from vol. 3, *On Joints* from vol. 4, *On the Places in Man* and *On the Sacred Disease* from vol. 6 and *On the Diseases of Women* from vol. 8.

The translations of Chinese works that I use are cited by the translator's name and the year of the translation. These, together with all the modern books and articles similarly cited, are to be found listed on the bibliography on pp. 157.

Acknowledgements

To acknowledge what this book owes to audiences, correspondents and specialist advisers is no mere matter of formality. Each of the four main chapters originates in lectures and seminars I gave during 1985–7 and my first debt is to those who participated in the discussion on those occasions or who corresponded with me afterwards. I had the honour to be invited to deliver the Rivers lecture in Cambridge in 1985, the Frazer lecture in Oxford, and the Nancy Wilson lecture in Southampton in 1987, and to give a series of lectures and seminars at Peking University and at the Institute of the History of Science of Academia Sinica at Beijing later in the same year. In a real sense this study is a collaborative work, and if I alone take responsibility for its final shape, the ideas it contains largely derive from many different contexts of joint discussion and exploration of the problems.

I have, too, expressly sought, and have most generously been given, advice and criticism both on the overall strategy of my arguments, and on specialised points, from a large number of friends and colleagues. For social anthropological and historical advice I wish to thank Peter Burke, Ernest Gellner, Jack Goody, François Hartog, Mark Hobart, Stephen Hugh-Jones, Caroline Humphrey, the late Sir Edmund Leach, Alan Macfarlane, Rodney Needham, Dan Sperber and especially Tanya Luhrmann (who has allowed me to draw extensively on her unpublished as well as published fieldwork). Among those who have helped me on sinological problems have been Karine Chemla, Christopher Cullen, Jacques Gernet, Catherine Jami, Michael Loewe, Joseph Needham, Nathan Sivin and Donald Wagner in the West, and Zhen Li, Du Shiran, Xi Zezong, Mei Rongzhao and their colleagues and students at Peking University and the Institute of the History of Natural Science of the Academia Sinica at Beijing. To Karine Chemla and to Nathan Sivin especially, both of whom gave me the benefit of particularly detailed comments on earlier drafts of chapter 4, I owe special thanks: their advice

Acknowledgements

both prompted many new lines of inquiry and saved me from many
errors, while of course they bear no responsibility for those that remain. I
have benefited too from the constructive comments on issues to do with
Greco-Roman antiquity from Simon Goldhill, Oswyn Murray, Catherine
and Robin Osborne, and on problems in the interpretation of Sanskrit
materials from Peter Khoroche. Finally it is a pleasure to thank my hosts
and the organising committees of the Rivers, Frazer and Nancy Wilson
lectures, and again my Chinese hosts and Peking University, Academia
Sinica and the British Academy for organising my visit to China in 1987
and for making my stay there so stimulating and enjoyable.

G E R L
Cambridge, March 1989

Introduction

The general problem that this book addresses concerns the validity and usefulness of the notion of mentalities. This has often been used to characterise what is held to be distinctive about the thought processes or sets of beliefs of groups or of whole societies, in general or at particular periods of time, and again in describing the changes or transformations that such processes or sets of beliefs are considered to have undergone. In what circumstances, if any, is it helpful or at least legitimate to invoke the notion of a distinct mentality? How, without some such notion, can major differences not just in the content of specific ideas and beliefs, but between whole networks of them, be described and understood? Yet while the partisans of mentalities, influenced by a variety of arguments, hold that some such notion is indispensable, others have questioned its appropriateness or applicability or condemned its apparent extravagance. How the *explananda* themselves are to be described is as much in dispute as the explanations on offer.

The French sociologist Lucien Lévy-Bruhl secured a wide diffusion for the notion of mentalities, in particular in connection with his ill-starred hypothesis of a *prelogical* mentality. This was supposed to be a feature of much primitive thought and one that helped to establish a contrast between it and the logical or scientific mentality to be found in advanced civilisations and especially in his own society. As is well known, Lévy-Bruhl himself came to renounce that hypothesis explicitly in the Notebooks written towards the end of his life in 1938–9.[1] However it is important to note how much of his earlier positions he retained even when doing so. He continued to talk, throughout the Notebooks, of differences in *mentalities*, and in particular continued to wrestle with the problem of defining and refining his ideas about what he still calls the *primitive mentality*. But where in his earlier work he had differentiated this by means of two criteria, that is as (1) prelogical and (2) mystical, in the Notebooks he abandoned the first while retaining the second. Thus he

1

wrote that the prelogical 'appears henceforth as another aspect or rather as a natural consequence of' the mystical (Lévy-Bruhl 1975, p. 37, cf also pp. 101, 126).

Two further important features of Lévy-Bruhl's discussion of this issue in the Notebooks should also be remarked. First he insisted on 'the fundamental identity of the structure of all human minds', a belief he maintains he had always held (p. 39). What precisely this encompassed was left rather vague, and the illustrations he gave showed that he had in mind very general characteristics indeed. All human minds, he went on, are 'capable of reasoning, of speaking, of counting, etc.' and elsewhere he put it that 'the logical structure of the mind is the same in all known human societies, just as they all have a language, customs and institutions' (p. 49, cf also p. 55).

Secondly, he now conceded that traces of the mystical mentality can be found in societies other than primitive ones. Indeed it is 'present in every human mind', even though it is 'more marked and more easily observable among "primitive peoples" than in our own societies' (p. 101, cf also pp. 104, 125f.).

But although he rejected prelogicality and came to recognise some of the problems connected with demarcating mentalities (pp. 99f.), he still did not abandon the notion of a mystical mentality found especially in primitive societies (let alone abandon talk of mentalities as such) even while he tried various formulations to capture its distinctive characteristics.[2] Thus he modified the claim that it is characterised by a tolerance of contradiction, but retained the idea that it tolerates incompatibilities (pp. 74, 86f. and especially 125ff., 136ff., specifying 'physical', not logical, absurdities). Again he retreated on the matter of the claim that there was some underlying *law* of participation (pp. 60f., 92) though he continued to insist that participation is a fundamental feature of the primitive mentality. Thus he put it that 'for the primitive mentality *to be is to participate*', glossing this with: 'it does not represent to itself things whose existence it conceives without bringing in elements other than the things themselves' (p. 18).

Again while he continued to claim that primitive mentality is affective (pp. 90f., 127ff., 158f.), he modified what he had to say about its lack of concepts. He rejected his earlier statement that 'primitive mentality is not conceptual' as too general (p. 127), and substituted: 'the thought of primitive men is not conceptual like ours [...] Neither the laws of nature, nor the forms of living things play in their thought a role comparable with that which they do in our thought, at least as soon as it is a question of a mystical experience or a magical operation.'[3]

Although Lévy-Bruhl's ideas met with a good deal of criticism,[4] they have proved highly influential. The idea of distinct mentalities has

Introduction

continued to be widely used, primarily but not exclusively in France, in a
variety of contexts, by historians, psychologists, philosophers, social
anthropologists, classicists and sinologists. Among the historians of the
Annales school, for instance, from Lucien Febvre and Marc Bloch onwards,
the study of mentalities has often been contrasted with – and pursued in
preference to – traditional history of ideas or again any history stemming
from a concentration on great men and great texts (see for example
Darnton 1980, pp. 327ff., Chartier 1982, pp. 14, 27, cf Duby 1961, Le Goff
1974, pp. 79f.). Sometimes, too, such a study has been opposed to a focus
on ideologies, though some historians have favoured combining the two
problematics (Vovelle 1982, cf. Darnton 1980, pp. 332f.). Social anthropologists and philosophers have debated the usefulness of the notion in
tackling such problems as the commensurability or incommensurability of
belief systems and the understanding of apparently irrational beliefs and
behaviour.[5] While an anthropologist such as Lévi-Strauss has made
relatively little explicit use of the concept of mentalities as such, his
discussion of certain fundamental characteristics of *l'esprit humain* and his
accounts of the relations between *concrete* and *abstract* science pick up
points from the debates initiated by Durkheim and Lévy-Bruhl.[6]

But the ramifications of the influence of the notion of mentalities go far
beyond these – as one might say mainstream – examples. Thus, in an
important discussion of the use of symbols in Renaissance art, Ernst
Gombrich wrote of the difficulty that the distinction between representation and symbol posed to the 'primitive mentality' (Gombrich 1972,
p. 125). Again in a study of the interactions between representatives of
different approaches to the inquiry into natural phenomena in the
Renaissance Brian Vickers expressly defended the use of the term in
connection with the traditions with which he was concerned: 'the title of
this book [*Occult and Scientific Mentalities in the Renaissance*], in the word
"mentalities", places the emphasis where I believe it should be put: on
two traditions each having its own thought processes, its own mental
categories, which determine its whole approach to life, mind, physical
reality' (Vickers 1984, p. 6). In French philosophy of science, Brunschvicg,
Reymond and Rey especially were all influenced by Lévy-Bruhl's ideas
(Brunschvicg 1949, book 4, ch. 9f., pp. 89ff., 99ff., Reymond 1927,
pp. 106ff., Rey 1930, pp. 434ff., 1933, p. 151). So too, directly or indirectly,
were sinologists such as Granet (1934a, pp. 14, 23, 1934b) and classical
scholars ranging from Cornford and Harrison in Britain, Snell in
Germany, to Schuhl and Robin in France.[7]

Not surprisingly, much of the talk of mentalities has been vague, much
has been diffuse. This has often been brought as a criticism of those who
have used the idea (a criticism already voiced by Evans-Pritchard 1934,

p. 351, cf also Darnton 1980, p. 346, Vovelle 1982, p. 5), though it should be remarked that for Le Goff (1974, pp. 76, 90) the imprecision or vagueness of the term was one of its attractions in that it allowed the historian to study the residues of historical analysis, *'le je ne sais quoi de l'histoire'*. However three general features of the mentalities approach have been picked out by Peter Burke in a useful recent survey article (Burke 1986). These are (1) the focus on the ideas or beliefs of collectivities rather than on those of individuals, (2) the inclusion, as important data, of unconscious as well as conscious assumptions, and (3) the focus on the structure of beliefs and their interrelations, as opposed to individual beliefs taken in isolation.

It is common ground to most of those who have used the term that more than just an individual's beliefs, and more than just individual beliefs, are in question, and sometimes more even than whole networks of beliefs, attitudes, ideologies or world-views – when a mentality is equated with a whole cast of mind deemed to influence, permeate or determine more or less in its entirety the mental activity of those who share it. Febvre spoke of the mental tools or equipment, *'l'outillage mental'*, of groups (Febvre in Burke 1973, Febvre 1982, cf Le Goff 1974, p. 87, Chartier 1982, p. 18). To employ another analogy that lurks not far below the surface in many discussions, just as physical capacities are circumscribed by the physical characteristics of an individual, so too the mental activity of groups, it is argued, reflects mental characteristics that are in principle no less capable of differentiation.

Three of the principal difficulties that confront us in the task of evaluating the validity of the notion of mentalities should be mentioned at the outset. *First* much of the debate has in the past been at cross purposes because insufficient attention has been paid to the question of precisely what is to count as a difference, or a change, in *mentality* – as opposed to any other differences in the contents of thoughts or knowledge or belief.

Talk of mentalities is often occasioned by what the observer or commentator holds to be distinctive or striking peculiarities in patterns of discourse or reasoning, or again in the implicit beliefs that are inferred to underlie modes of behaviour. But apart from well known problems to do with inference *to* belief from either statements or behaviour (Needham 1972, cf. Jahoda 1982) there are further difficulties of inference *from* belief to what are supposed to be the underlying thought processes (Cole and Scribner 1974, p. 144). More generally still, many differences in styles or patterns of thought may well merely reflect differences in the subject-matter under consideration. This is not just a matter of differences that might reflect those between, say, the transmission of religious instruction on occasions of solemn ritual on the one hand, and joke-telling on the

4

other. Might we not want to say that different styles of thought – not just different literary styles – are exhibited in, for example, Coleridge's poetry and his literary criticism? But if so, there is an evident extravagance in allowing a single individual, even a Coleridge, *several* mentalities. It is true that some historians of mentalities have been prepared to contemplate such a possibility. Thus Le Goff (1974, p. 88) did in allowing for the coexistence of several mentalities not just at a single period but in a single mind (*esprit*): he cited Louis XI as an example. Nevertheless if mentality is to signify more than just inclination or attitude (which to be useful it surely must), then the combination of several in a single individual poses severe difficulties. This point will prove fundamental for my argument and I shall be returning to it later.

Converse problems arise in the attribution of a shared mentality to a group, let alone to a whole society. To begin with, this always risks ignoring or playing down individual variations (cf. Burke 1986, p. 443). Collectivities do not think, only individuals do (cf Jahoda 1982, p. 182), but it is not that *any* group, *any* society consists of individuals with entirely uniform mental characteristics. Moreover to legitimate the generalisation to a mentality needs more than merely isolated perceived peculiarities: at the very least the characteristics held to be distinctive need to be, not just indeed distinctive, but recurrent and pervasive. No doubt just how recurrent and pervasive a set of characteristics has to be in order to be considered evidence of a distinct underlying mentality will be a matter of judgement, but that judgement should, in principle, depend on whether or how far other accounts might appear to offer adequate ways of describing and explaining the data concerned. The burden of proof lies, in other words, with those who would employ the discourse of mentalities.

Secondly, we should be clear that in general to appeal to a distinct mentality is merely to *redescribe* the phenomena that are found puzzling or in need of explanation. The question that immediately arises is how the mentality thus invoked can itself be accounted for.

However one theory in the field is exceptional in offering not merely description but also explanation, while also specifying a strong sense of mentalities as corresponding to well-marked psychological states. Those who have followed Piaget's lead characterise the differences in question in terms of stages of cognitive development, deemed to follow an orderly – and the same – sequence throughout human societies. By far the most sustained attempt to apply a Piagetian thesis to social anthropological issues is that of Hallpike (1979), whose work has, however, been criticised extensively (see especially Shweder 1982 and Jahoda 1982, pp. 224ff.).

Piaget's own researches suggested that, at least for those Western children who were his main subjects, the acquisition of certain concepts to

5

do with space, time, number and causation followed a well-defined sequence. How far these findings can be extended to non-Western children has provoked much heated discussion.[8] Yet difficulties of a different order of magnitude arise when a similar hypothesis is extended (as by Hallpike) to explain differences in *adults'* cosmologies or religions or mythologies in terms of mentalities construed as corresponding to stages of cognitive development. We shall be reviewing in due course examples of changes that have taken place through time in the cosmologies or religions or other sets of beliefs in given societies that can be studied historically. However we may note straight away that none of those we shall be considering bears any resemblance to the transitions that occur within a single individual's development through the early years of childhood.

Thirdly and relatedly, in drawing comparisons and contrasts between systems of belief in general, it is essential to keep the terms of the comparison constant.

There are evident objections, for example, to comparing one society's religion with another's technology or science, objections that have been urged by several critics of Lévy-Bruhl (Bartlett 1923, p. 284, Evans-Pritchard 1934, pp. 10ff., Shirokogoroff 1935, pp. 85ff.). More recently Robin Horton's influential studies comparing and contrasting African traditional religion and Western science (Horton 1967, 1982) have been criticised on similar grounds (Beattie 1970, pp. 259ff., Goody 1977, p. 38). One of Horton's chief theses was that a point of similarity between these two was that both aim at explanation, prediction and control, and both, for that end, provide a theoretical framework that invokes hidden entities. Yet although Horton has recently qualified his position (Horton 1982, pp. 228ff.: cf. further below, p. 37), the substantial objection remains. This is that he treats Western 'mechanistic' science as if it could be excised from Western religion and ideology, including the ideology associated with that science. But if the religion and ideology of the society that practises the science are reintroduced into the discussion, both the comparison and the contrast appear much less clear-cut then he represents them.

The point is of particular importance in relation to those particular phases in the development of Western science that we shall be examining in some detail later, namely ancient Greek science, about which Horton has had little to say in either of his main discussions.[9] So far as ancient Greek science goes, I would argue that so far from it being possible to excise the science and treat it in isolation, that science *needed* its polemic with its opponents to define itself. For now, however, the key methodological point is simply this, that the terms of any comparison or contrast between mentalities must be held constant.

Introduction

The strategy of my investigation in the studies that follow is to take a set of problem areas which may on the face of it seem most amenable to the hypothesis of mentalities. These include, especially, instances of extreme divergence or dissonance in discourse, beliefs or world-views, which it is evidently tempting to refer to differences in mentalities. In chapter 1 I tackle the common phenomenon of certain types of what are, apparently, inordinately paradoxical, self-contradictory or counter-intuitive statements, which have often been the starting-point for the discussion of divergent mentalities, as also of the incommensurability of belief-systems, as well as for many sweeping diagnoses of irrationality.

There and in chapter 2 I consider the particular problems posed by science and by the notion of a mentality that corresponds to it. This involves discussion of the nature of the general opposition between scientific and pre-scientific beliefs and theories, where we have to come to terms with, among other things, the role of the contrast between science and myth, and again of that between science and magic, and more broadly still that of the opposition between the literal and the metaphorical. In each case I argue that it is essential to distinguish firmly between the categories used by those who make the statements or hold the beliefs in question and those *we* may use to describe them. The all-important distinction that has scrupulously to be observed is – to put it in the social anthropologists' terms – that between *actors'* and *observers'* categories. In the evaluation of the apparently puzzling or downright paradoxical, a crucial issue is, I argue, precisely the availability or otherwise of *explicit* concepts of linguistic and other categories. This factor has often been neglected – with seriously distorting effects on the interpretation of the beliefs in question. This is particularly true when the distinctions *we* commonly deploy force issues that are alien to the original actors' contexts of discourse: once *those* contexts of discourse are reinstated, much of the temptation to postulate divergent mentalities in this connection lapses.

The explicit categories *we* commonly use in our highly value-laden descriptions – science, myth, magic and the opposition between the literal and the metaphorical – all, of course, had a history and in most cases derive directly or indirectly from concepts invented by the ancient Greeks. This provides us with an opportunity to study the contexts and the circumstances in which they were first introduced in ancient Greek thought, where we may hope to throw some light both on the way in which new styles of reasoning may emerge, and on the significance of the explicit formulation of particular concepts of linguistic and other categories. What that study will suggest is that the Greek concepts in question were often, even generally, made to play a distinct and explicit polemical role. Once that is taken into account we can appreciate that the contrasts drawn for the purposes of polemic were often *over*-drawn. This is true of the opposition between the literal and the metaphorical, for instance, and again of the contrast between myth and magic on the one hand, and science and philosophy on the other. Certainly what, in practice, emerging Greek science and philosophy continued to have in common with the traditional forms of knowledge that they were aiming to replace is often quite as striking as the points where they diverged from previous modes of thought, even though in one respect, the degree of explicitness and self-consciousness of the inquiries concerned, those differences were considerable.

Here then we have a chance to investigate the applicability of the notion of mentalities both in relation to the understanding of highly paradoxical beliefs and with regard to the transition to science, at least in the phases or modalities of that transition that can be studied in ancient Greece. In this case, at least, the revolution that occurred, if that is the appropriate term, was less a matter of some revolution in mentalities, than one in the self-definition of a style of inquiry, where the self-definition in question depended heavily, at points, on that polemic and on the new, self-conscious, categories introduced for those, polemical, purposes.

That, to be sure, does not explain the changes that occurred in that phase of the development of ancient Greek thought, but merely *relocates the problem*. But it transposes it into the area of the more directly investigable, since we can certainly attempt to identify the factors that contributed to the new style of inquiry, new styles of argument and, especially, to a new self-consciousness in both. The thesis of my first two studies develops a well-known argument,[10] that the key factors at work are to be found in the political circumstances of ancient Greece in the classical period, most notably in the nature and intensity of involvement in political life in the autonomous city-states of that period. In the law-courts and assemblies many Greek citizens gained extensive first-hand experience in the actual practice of argument and persuasion, in the evaluation of evidence, and in the application of the notions of justification and accountability. This experience is all the more relevant to their expectations in other contexts because so much philosophical and scientific discussion too was cast, precisely, in the form of similar debates between opposing points of view. Moreover even when Greek political practice can be seen to diverge from the image it presented of itself – its ideology – that does not make the image any the less significant as an indication of what was believed or at least held up as an ideal – a point that has special relevance, as we shall see, in connection with some features of the ideology of democracy in particular.

Introduction

My third study elaborates and modifies this general hypothesis. Here I investigate the development of yet another important explicit concept, that of proof or demonstration. Again my suggestion is that the existence of some concept corresponding to proof is of considerable consequence in the conduct of argument and debate and in styles of reasoning more generally. Some such concept was certainly not confined to the ancient Greeks. But features of the history of Greek discussions of the notion of proof may serve to throw further light on the importance of the social and political background to the development of Greek philosophy and science – and so, one might hope, on the issues to do with mentalities that that development raises. On the one hand, informal proof in the sense of what carried conviction with a particular audience was both extensively used, in law, in politics and elsewhere, and made the subject of explicit analysis in the study of rhetoric. On the other, the notion of rigorous proof, that is, demonstration by deductive argument from axiomatic premisses, was developed in both philosophy and mathematics in part in explicit opposition to looser, informal techniques of persuasion.

Greek political experience here exerts both a direct and an indirect influence upon the development of science. While some philosophical and scientific proof mirrored the techniques of persuasion used in the broadly political domain, there was also an explicit reaction to that fact in a demand for *more* than mere persuasiveness, a demand, indeed, for incontrovertibility. Yet while the invention of the ideal of an axiomatic, deductive method was precisely that, an *invention*, it shared one general feature with what was already commonly accepted in the legal-political domain in such a way as to warrant the claim of an indirect influence here as well. This was the demand that a point of view should be justifiable – by whatever means of justification might be appropriate, and not limited to reasoned argument. But while in political argument justification was conceived in many different guises, in some parts of Greek science what we find is a demand for ultimate, absolute, impersonal, justifiability.

The focus here too, then, is on recoverable differences in the use of language and in interpersonal exchange. My strategic recommendation in these first three chapters is that for some of the issues discussed under the rubric of mentalities, the problems are more fruitfully construed in – broadly – sociological terms than in more purely psychological ones. In connection with the issues we shall discuss, at any rate, there is no need to appeal to postulated differences in mentalities as such, nor to specific psychological qualities, states, habits, capacities or stages. Rather, the important differences concern styles of discourse, converse, reasoning and the varying contexts in which they were used, where one factor crucial to the evaluation of both the styles and the contexts is the question of the availability and use of explicit concepts of linguistic and other categories.

If in the mentalities debate we simply apply *our* categories to the understanding of so-called primitive thought, we are doubly mistaken. First that risks forcing issues by raising questions that are foreign to the actors' own views and concerns. *They* are not generally concerned with the difference between the literal and the metaphorical, let alone with a concept of myth that opposes it to science. Moreover, secondly, an application of our observer categories tends to direct attention *away* from where important differences in styles of inter-personal exchanges or differences in styles of argument may be real enough. Apart from consideration of the status of the individuals concerned and of the role of tradition in sanctioning beliefs and practices, due attention must be paid to the general rules, implicit or explicit, for the conduct of discussion, to the expectations entertained by the participants concerning the criteria for an adequate performance, and especially to the extent to which, and to the ways in which, a point of view is open to challenge. Where, precisely, challenge is, in the original context, not to be expected, nor is indeed in order, the application of our latter-day categories may well be solecistic.

The historical question of the origin of some of our key categories comes, then, to be of crucial importance, and although there was, of course, far more to their long-drawn-out histories than merely a simple appropriation of some ancient Greek ideas, those ideas were, in several cases, the starting-point. As indicated, my claim is that a study of the circumstances of their introduction shows how they were often used precisely to force certain issues, and to mark off, self-consciously, new styles of inquiry from other more traditional ones. If we try to understand the factors that permitted or stimulated those developments, the social and political background of classical Greece provides some suggestive clues, offering not just in some cases analogues to the developments in philosophy and science, but in others factors that seem to have contributed positively to the development of the styles of debate on which those inquiries so largely depended.

My fourth study takes a different form and attempts to test that last part of my argument especially. Much of the material discussed in my first three chapters concerns ancient Greece and that for more than just contingent reasons relating to my own training and specialisation, but rather for essential ones stemming from the substance of my arguments. But to test some of these arguments concerning both the *explananda* and the possible explanations I embark – however rashly[11] – in my fourth chapter on a comparative study of the problems as they present themselves in ancient China.

Introduction

Ancient China is chosen for three main reasons. First there is the comparative richness of the primary source material,[12] texts that can in some cases be dated fairly precisely even if in others this is only possible within broad limits.[13] Secondly there is now available a sophisticated secondary literature (Sivin 1988), on which I draw heavily. Thirdly there are certain similarities, at least as they appear on a first superficial view, in both the political situation and in some of the intellectual products, at various periods in ancient China and in ancient Greece.

Thus, in ancient China too, a period of intense philosophical activity coincides with the political pluralism of the Warring States period (480–221 B.C.). This was followed by a less strikingly innovative period, a period of some consolidation in intellectual activity, when China came under unified central government in the Qin and Han dynasties, where analogies with the experience of the Greco-Roman world under the dominance of Rome have often been suggested. Moreover like the Greeks, the Chinese developed extensive interests in ethics, in natural philosophy, in mathematics, in aspects of logic and epistemology, and in literary criticism, as well as in medicine and in astronomy. We can exemplify from China at different periods, among many other features, the self-conscious study of arguments, the development of certain critical and sceptical traditions, and of explicitly innovative ones, the practice of proof – and some related concepts – in mathematics, and a concept of metaphor – for example as characterising a type of poetry.

Yet alongside certain similarities there are also important differences, and my argument will be that it is not just some of the similarities, but also some of the differences, in the styles of intellectual activity, that reflect, in either case, corresponding similarities and differences in, broadly, the political background and experience. Thus it is notable that the Chinese interest in modes of argument was rather in their use in dialectic, not in formal logic. There and elsewhere the Chinese did not engage in speculative, abstract theorising for its own sake and favoured studies that were, directly or indirectly, of some practical applicability – in this case to achieving success in argument.

Again in mathematics they were less preoccupied than the Greeks with setting out demonstrations: conversely they may be said to be more concerned with obtaining results (though that was not *all* they were concerned with), and the fact that their proofs here did not normally proceed from explicit (but rather from implicit) axioms may be taken to reflect less self-conscious concern with ultimate foundational questions than we find in Greek mathematics. While a concept of metaphor appears in Chinese literary critical theory as a virtue in poetry of a certain kind, that concept was not made the basis for aggressive claims for the superiority of one style of reasoning (philosophising in the Aristotelian fashion) over all others. Nor was poetry considered to be inferior as a vehicle for expressing the truth precisely insofar as it depends on metaphor. In political philosophical inquiry too the practical orientation of much Chinese writing is evident: they did not embark on the abstract exploration of all theoretically possible constitutional forms and principles.

Correspondingly the actual political experience shows marked differences in important respects in these two ancient civilisations. Thus the actual political pluralism of the Warring States period was quite different from that of the classical Greek city-state in one fundamental respect at least. In the Chinese case it was a matter of a plurality of independent states all *essentially monarchical* in character. While there was considerable diversity in the detailed political arrangements proposed or implemented, the common assumption on which they were based was the need for a unified China under the control of a good ruler. In Greece on the other hand pluralism encompassed also a *variety of different types* of political constitution, ranging from the rule of one man to extreme democracy. The principal features of Greek intellectual activities that appear to relate – as I have remarked – to *their* socio-political experience, namely (1) the preoccupation with justification and accountability, and (2) the adversarial quality of much philosophical and scientific debate, are correspondingly far less prominent in Chinese inquiries.

China thus exemplifies what is, in certain respects, a quite different style of early science from the Greek, but one that is just as diverse as the Greek and that is just as difficult to see as the product of some hypothesised, Chinese, mentality. Rather, some of the important differences between East and West relate more directly to differences in the prominence given to certain leading concepts and categories and to differences in the styles of interpersonal exchange, where, in turn, in each case, socio-political factors may be a crucial influence.

Moreover if this comparison suggests some of the strengths of Greek styles of reasoning, it also bears on their weaknesses, especially the destructiveness of their modes of polemic, the pretentiousness of many of their claims to special knowledge, their recurrent failure to deliver in practice on the promise of their theoretical ambitions. We should not, to be sure, underestimate the theoretical interests of the ancient Chinese too: yet the linkage between theory and practice was generally far stronger there than it was in Greece. Here the great strength of the Chinese focus on practicalities, on what is applicable, on what will work, emerges all the more clearly by contrast with the converse weaknesses of much ancient Greek speculation.

Whatever may be thought about the plausibility of these or other explanatory hypotheses, or indeed about the possibility of any causal explanations in this area at all, I suggest in my conclusion that, if we are to make any progress in understanding, the focus of our inquiry needs to be shifted away from a bid to characterise mentalities as such, whether of a society as a whole or of groups within one. It is indeed true that patterns of speech and behaviour, even single acts and statements, often pose severe problems of intelligibility, across cultures and periods, and indeed within our own contemporary culture. But the first step, if we are not to misjudge the *explananda* themselves, is to consider the contexts of communication, the nature and styles of interpersonal exchanges or confrontations, the availability and use of explicit concepts of linguistic and other categories in which the actors' self-representations are conveyed. We are not limited, to be sure, to the mere redescription, in the actors' own terms, of their ideas, beliefs and behaviour. But it is precisely the peculiarities of the various styles of reasoning and discourse, couched in the actors' own terms, that provide the principal challenge at the first stage of interpretation.

The ambitiousness of the project I undertake here will be apparent from even the summary description in this introduction. To carry out such an enterprise might be thought to demand the fullest possible elaboration in the documentation of detailed points. However the practical impossibilities of even beginning to approach that ideal on as wide-ranging a set of problems as these are clear. I construe my principal task rather to be one of opening up new terrains of investigation and of suggesting possible lines of argument. There is no question of my offering these studies as a comprehensive, let alone a fully documented and annotated, analysis of the issues. Indeed each of them retains many of the marks of the informality of the lectures and seminars from which they originate. The justification for this style of treatment must lie in what the book thus hopes to gain in clarity, concision and accessibility, even if it runs the risk of appearing at points no more than merely suggestive.

1

Mentalities, metaphors and the foundations of science

Two of the contexts in which the notion of mentalities has been invoked are (1) in connection with understanding some apparently extravagantly paradoxical or counter-intuitive statements reported in the ethnographic literature as in such famous cases as that of the Nuer belief that 'twins are birds', and (2) the general contrast between the scientific and the pre-scientific. The aim of my first investigation is to tackle some aspects of these issues as they relate to ancient Greek thought with a view to testing how far the concept of distinct mentalities is needed or appropriate. I do not, of course, assume that Greek thought or Greek society bears specific resemblances to those of the Nuer or indeed of any present-day society, though by that I do not mean, either, to claim special, unique status for the Greeks as has been done so often in the past by classicists for whom *'les Grecs ne sont pas comme les autres'* (cf. the critical remarks of Detienne 1979, ch. 1) let alone by those such as Renan who fantasised over what they thought of as a 'Greek miracle' (Renan 1935, pp. 243ff, 1948, p. 393, cf Peyre 1973). But while the notion of mentalities originated as an ethnographic problem, it is, as we have noted, of very general applicability and concerns the historian, the psychologist and the philosopher of science as much as the social anthropologist. The problems span a variety of common interests and dictate an interdisciplinary approach, despite the difficulties that presents and indeed despite the unpopularity it often evokes from specialists who insist on the sacrosanctity of their own disciplines.

In relation to the first of the two types of context I have mentioned, one line of interpretation that has often been pursued proceeds by discussing whether the statements found to be paradoxical are literal or metaphorical. The argument I shall develop here is that where no such category distinction is available to the actors themselves, to press that question risks forcing an issue alien to the original context of discourse. Indeed that distinction was itself introduced, in ancient Greece, in part with that very

14

aim, namely to force issues. A contrast was thereby set up between different styles of discourse not just to privilege that based on the literal, but also to downgrade those that employed what was then labelled the metaphorical – and that despite the fact that in a wide variety of domains, and not just in religious discourse, a demand for strict literality is, *we* might say, strictly impossible to meet.

The literal/metaphorical dichotomy enabled, and enables, a certain type of challenge to be pressed – in relation to the precise limits of the commitment to a belief. Indeed the exact determination of that commitment may only become possible once some such distinction is available. The all-important contrast, I shall argue, is not one between two or more divergent mentalities, let alone between one that does, and another that does not, observe the law of non-contradiction or show exceptional tolerance of incompatibilities. Rather the contrasts concern situations of communication where certain types of challenge, concerning meaning or belief, are possible and expected, and others where they are not.[1]

This will lead us to consider some more general issues to do with the second type of context mentioned above, namely the contrast between the pre-scientific and the scientific, where one of the chief questions relates to the nature of the transition between the two. Some have seen that contrast in terms of a sharp discontinuity – a Great Divide, to use Gellner's expression (1973, pp. 162ff, 1985, ch. 3, cf Lévi-Strauss 1973, p. 473). Others, however, have emphasised rather the gradualness of the relevant changes, as for example Goody has done in stressing the importance of aspects of the changes that occurred in the technology of communication.[2]

Here my argument will be that so far as ancient Greece is concerned, what marks out the scientific is not only and not so much the content of ideas and theories about natural phenomena as the degree of self-consciousness with which the inquiries are pursued. In Greece that self-consciousness was achieved in large part by way of a polemic in which the new styles of investigation sought to differentiate themselves from the old. The locus of the problem is – again – not so much how some new mentality came to be acquired, as the circumstances or contexts in which a certain rivalry between claimants to knowledge could and did develop.

Ancient Greece will be the chief focus of our discussion in this second part of the chapter too. But let me emphasise at once that ancient Greece in the classical period is far from being the only time and place in which important aspects of the growth of science can be studied. The intellectual outputs of ancient Egypt, Babylonia, India and China especially all have their contributions to make to our understanding of the origins of the scientific enterprise, and all pose their special problems of interpretation – as does the exploration of the crises of successive 'scientific revolutions' in later European history. The experience of ancient civilisations shows that what we may call proto-science took different forms and developed in different ways: the similarities and differences between its ancient Greek and ancient Chinese varieties will occupy us in chapter 4. But certainly ancient Greece presents one opportunity – among others – to test against some historical evidence how far it is appropriate to represent the transition to science in terms of a transformation in mentalities. That evidence is not as comprehensive as one should like, to be sure (when is that ever the case?), but it is far far richer than is often imagined. If the Greek experience is exceptional in the influence it later exerted on the development of Western science, it raises all the more delicate problems of interpretation since, as we said, many of the categories we continue to use to discuss the issues originate there.

We may begin with one of the problems that provided some of the initial stimulus to postulate divergent mentalities. It was in part in reaction to what appeared weird, outlandish, paradoxical, inconsistent or self-contradictory statements or beliefs that Lévy-Bruhl was first led to formulate his primitive principle of participation and suspension of the law of non-contradiction (later modified, as we saw, to a thesis concerning an exceptional tolerance of incompatibilities). As already remarked, in the later social anthropological debate a canonical example is the reported Nuer belief that 'twins are birds' (Evans-Pritchard 1956, pp. 131ff, cf Gellner 1970, pp. 34ff, Lukes 1982, p. 275, Sperber 1985, pp. 59f).

Many instances of a similar general type can be given from ancient Greece. Indeed the first observation to be made in that regard is that there are probably as many examples of extremely counterintuitive or paradoxical statements to be found from *within* Greek philosophy as from outside it.[3] I am not thinking just of some of the higher flights of speculative metaphysics in Plato, Aristotle or Plotinus – as when Plato, for example, talks of the supreme principle, the Form of the Good, as being 'beyond being' in the *Republic* (509b). Several of the early philosophers too produce a rich crop of such dicta. For Heraclitus, for instance, 'war is the father of all and king of all', and again 'war is common and justice strife', and again 'thunderbolt steers all', and again 'the dry soul is wisest and best', and again 'souls have the sense of smell in Hades' and again 'time is a child playing, playing draughts: the kingdom is the child's'.[4] To be sure, Heraclitus had a particular reputation for obscurity. But then one can also cite, from admittedly later sources, a whole series of strange injunctions attributed to Pythagoras or to the early Pythagoreans.[5] 'Do not sit on a bushel-measure'; 'Do not stir the fire with a knife'; 'Touch the earth when it thunders'; 'Abstain from beans.' This last appears in the poet-philosopher Empedocles (Fragment 141) in the form: 'wretches, utter wretches, keep your hands from beans.'

The reactions that such statements have elicited in ancient and in modern times have varied from the scandalised or the dismissive to the most elaborate rationalising apologetics. In his great *History of Greek Philosophy* Guthrie opened his section dealing with the Pythagorean material I quoted as follows: 'Pythagoreanism contains a strong element of the magical, a primitive feature which sometimes seems hard to reconcile with the intellectual depth which is no less certainly attested' (Guthrie 1962, p. 182), and a little later he continued (p. 185), after some comments on the beans prohibition: 'Many of the other examples cited betray their origin in sympathetic magic, which assumes a close, quasi-physical relationship between things that to the civilized mind have no such connexion at all.' If that was meant to explain or to reassure, it merely succeeds in being dismissive.

But more often in antiquity (as Guthrie of course well knew, 1962, pp. 182ff.) the line of interpretation adopted, as already reported by Aristotle, was cryptological. Beans, for example, were to be avoided because they resembled testicles, or were like the gates of Hades or the whole universe, or again they are windy and full of the life-force (or more simply cause flatulence) or they contain the souls of the dead, or if chewed and left in the sun they give off the odour of semen. Or again the hidden message was a political one: beans were used as counters in the democratic process of election by lot, and so – if you could read between the lines – the prohibition was to be understood as pro-oligarchic or at least as anti-democratic.[6]

A first reaction to this proliferation of cryptological readings may be one of their authors' misplaced ingenuity: and it is true that a secure understanding of some aspects of early Pythagoreanism may well have been inaccessible already in Aristotle's day (let alone in ours). Yet the important point is that such material is generally seen as a *challenge to interpretation*[7] – even if in some cases we may lack the essential context even to begin one. What this means may perhaps be seen more readily when we encounter paradox or apparent absurdity in, say, Plato or Aristotle, where it is, after all, more difficult to be simply dismissive on the grounds that they were simpletons or fools, and where Plato especially – like Heraclitus – can often be seen deliberately exploiting paradox for particular effects.

The hunt is on, then, to find a reading or readings to make sense of the Form of the Good being 'beyond being', to re-embed that statement in its context and to relate it to other aspects of Plato's thought *assumed to be* a more or less coherent and well articulated, even if flexible, shifting and developing, whole – and even if we must always be alert to the risks that what *we* make of such an idea is just that, our merely arbitrary fabrication. Evidently in such cases, some principle of charity in interpretation (though not necessarily exactly the one that Davidson has advocated)[8] is exercised. That is not to say that such a principle is to be stretched indefinitely or that it is a matter of indiscriminate charity (as Gellner has put it),[9] and it is certainly not to say that inconsequentiality or incoherence is ruled out *a priori*. But the principle ensures that (wherever he or she may end) the student of ancient philosophy does not *start from* the assumption that the outlandish-seeming, the obscure or the paradoxical are just signs of an underlying incoherence, let alone indications of a separate mentality. No doubt so far as a starting-point goes, a similar principle guides any hermeneutical inquiry, including social anthropology, even if, as the interpreter proceeds, sustaining the principle will be, in varying contexts, subject to varying stresses and strains.

One recurrent mode of interpretation or exegetical device is, however, more problematic than is generally assumed, indeed potentially quite misleading to judge by its application to ancient Greek materials. As we have remarked, in the debates on the 'twins are birds' case and many others like it, opposing schools of thought have been divided on the question of whether the statements at issue are to be taken literally or as metaphors.

Already Lévy-Bruhl illustrates this concern. In the Notebooks he still invoked 'participation' as a feature of the primitive mentality in part on the grounds that primitive people use certain terms in what he judged to be an anomalous, indiscriminate, at any rate non-literal way. Basing himself on certain ethnographic reports from French Guinea he cited a case where despite the fact that a dead child's body had been exhumed, it was claimed that it had been kidnapped and eaten by witches. But 'the incompatibility', he wrote, 'is not flagrant for them as it is for us; the facts do not exclude each other, because they are not on the same level of homogeneous experience perceptible to the senses. Given that, it matters little that in their evidence the self-styled witches recount how they have carried off and killed the child, cooked and ate her, speak of the cooking-pot, and meat put on one side, etc. [. . .] All this, which our positive mind takes literally, has only a figurative sense for the mind of primitive men. We give to the words kidnap, kill, eat only a single, univocal sense. For primitive men the sense is double: that which indicates a well-known action, imperceptible to the senses, and of which witches alone are capable, by reason of the supernatural force at their disposal, and in second place the sense verifiable in the natural world.' (Lévy-Bruhl 1975, p. 43).

The first remarkable point about this passage is the claim made with respect to the univocity of 'our' terms such as kidnap, kill, eat, where Lévy-Bruhl seems to ignore or entirely to discount the frequent figurative senses of the corresponding French terms. But more important, for our purposes, is that while he saw that the problem was one of the meaning of certain terms or statements, he still held that the fact that primitive people used certain terms in a way Lévy-Bruhl himself (rather literal-mindedly) judged to be anomalous could be taken to be symptomatic of their mentality. 'Thus, for the primitive mentality,' he concluded (p. 43), 'far from there being there an incompatibility between two homogeneous facts, there is a correspondence, a figuration by the natural phenomenon of the action of supernatural cause.'

This is all the more striking in that in an earlier passage dealing with the same material he had commented (pp. 20f): 'whether the witches are anthropophagous in the sense with which we are familiar, or in the spiritual sense, makes no difference to the black man.' Yet that way of putting it might have led him to reflect on what I take to be a question of considerable significance, namely whether or how far the actors concerned could or would have drawn some such distinction as that between 'familiar' and 'spiritual' senses. Moreover if indeed 'primitive people' observe no distinction in *senses* in some such cases, that would tend to undermine the claim in Lévy-Bruhl's other, later, comment that 'they' do where 'we' do not. However while in *both* passages Lévy-Bruhl seems intent on diagnosing *some* difference between 'them' and 'us', the prior question that needs to be put concerns the applicability of *our* concepts of the literal and the metaphorical or figurative.

A diametrically opposed line of interpretation has been put forward more recently by Sperber in a far more sophisticated discussion of related issues. Commenting on the Dorze belief that, for instance, 'the leopard is a Christian animal who observes the fasts of the Ethiopian Orthodox Church', Sperber objected to the semiological view according to which such a statement need not be taken literally (Sperber 1975, p. 93). Sperber's counter was that, for the Dorze, such a statement 'is not a manner of speaking: he takes it literally'. Sperber was, however, concerned to criticise a certain line of argument according to which a people's own ideas of rationality (for instance) determine what rationality they exhibit, and he went on immediately to add (p. 94) that the Dorze 'is, nevertheless, not ignorant of the art of metaphor; if he says that a valiant warrior is a lion, he doesn't imagine that he has a mane. The "savages" themselves do not authorise us to confuse the literal and the metaphorical.'

Yet from an ancient Greek perspective, at least, that is very much the wrong question. What we should investigate is not whether there are any grounds to speak of such a confusion: but rather whether or how far those categories, of the literal and the metaphorical, are *explicitly* distinguished by the actors themselves. When Sperber remarks that the Dorze are 'not ignorant of the art of metaphor', that does not, in so many words, attribute an explicit category to them. Elsewhere, however, he claims, for example, that 'when the Dorze like so many others accompany the statement of a belief with "It is the custom", they expressly put this statement in quotes' (p. 148). Yet however much Sperber may maintain that such Dorze references to custom are *equivalent to* what he, Sperber, calls putting a statement 'in quotes', the term *expressly* is open to question. Moreover while we may agree that to remark about a belief that 'it is the custom' is certainly to reflect on the status of the belief and not merely to report it, we should ourselves remark that to claim customary or traditional status is often to *block* further questions – whereas, as we shall see, to press a choice between literal and metaphorical is often to *raise* them.

Again Sperber has analogous comments to make about the Dorze terms *adhe* and *ts'ilo* in connection with his thesis that 'even if we accept that truth is a universal category of thought, the notions that express it in different languages are different and diversified' (p. 104). He notes that in Dorze 'the word *adhe* designates both conformity to facts and conformity to tradition', and again that 'the word *ts'ilo* designates both he [sic] who reports faithfully what he has seen or heard, and he [sic] who speaks and acts conforming to tradition and to his own commitments'. He then proceeds (pp. 104f.): 'this lexical fusion in no way implies that in the exercise of their thought, the Dorze do not distinguish the empirical truth from reported speech'. That no doubt is true: there is no such implication. But if the claim is that the Dorze do *draw* the distinction, and do not merely use it, then the question of the precise terms in which they do so becomes important.

In general much more may hang on, precisely, the question of explicitness and of the available actors' categories for qualifying their statements, for example as 'literal' or 'metaphorical', than many discussions of the interpretation of problematic cases appear to allow. We shall be able to see this more clearly if we explore the circumstances in which some of the categories we still deploy were first explicitly distinguished by the Greeks and if we investigate the motivations for those distinctions.

First as to the circumstances, and this is a case where the historical evidence is reasonably secure.[10] Although Plato has no shortage of terms corresponding (roughly) to our 'likenesses', 'images', 'models' and so on,[11] it is not until Aristotle that we encounter a pair of terms to express the contrast between, on the one hand, a word used strictly or properly (*kuriōs*), and, on the other, its transferred application to another domain.

The original or primary sense of *metaphora* in Greek is, approximately, just that, namely transfer (e.g. Aristotle, *Poetics* 1457b6ff., cf Tamba-Mecz and Veyne 1979). If we put the point just like that, it may seem that there is nothing more to this than a piece of straightforward logical or linguistic analysis. But an examination of the use made of the distinction shows that this was far from the case. Already Plato has some highly critical remarks to make about the use of images and likenesses – though as is well known he continues nevertheless to employ them very extensively himself, and not just for embellishment. Indeed he does so in some of those critical remarks themselves. Thus he tells us in the *Sophist* (231a) that likenesses are 'a most slippery tribe' – where we may wonder how slippery that characterisation itself is. Again when we are told in the *Phaedo* (92cd) that accounts that are based on images are charlatans or imposters, the wary will not fail to observe that Plato uses a likeness to tell us that likenesses deceive.

But in Aristotle the negative evaluation, indeed the outright condemnation, of what he calls *metaphora* in prominent contexts both in his logic and in his natural philosophy are even more clearly marked. He insists, for instance, that metaphor and metaphorical expressions are to be avoided in giving definitions (*Posterior Analytics* 97b37f). More than that, the whole of his syllogistic depends expressly on terms being used strictly and univocally. Similarly in his philosophy of science he stipulates that demonstration depends not just on valid argument from true premises, but on premises that are primary, immediate, better known than, prior to and explanatory of the conclusions, and again only univocal terms will do, indeed only predications that are universal, *per se* and necessary, using such terms (*Posterior Analytics* 71b20ff.: see further below, ch. 3). Insisting on clarity, he rules out metaphor on the grounds that, as he puts it (*Topics* 139b34f.), 'every metaphorical expression is obscure'.

But this is not just a feature of his formal logic and official philosophy of science, for it recurs when he is discussing attempted causal explanations and physical theories in his natural philosophy. In his physical treatises he repeatedly criticises the metaphors and images that he finds used in various contexts in his predecessors' work. Thus Empedocles had characterised the salt sea as the sweat of the earth (though quite what Empedocles' aim was in so doing we cannot now recover with any confidence). But to that Aristotle comments (*Meteorology* 357a24ff.,26ff.): 'Perhaps to say that is to speak adequately for poetic purposes – for metaphor is poetic – but it is not adequate for understanding the nature [of the thing].'

A variety of other images proposed by Empedocles and by other Presocratic philosophers are censured on the grounds that they are obscure or crude or stand in need of qualification or that the similarities they are based on are superficial or indeed that the cases compared bear no similarity to one another at all (*Topics* 127a17ff., *On the Senses* 437b9ff., *On the Parts of Animals* 652b7ff., *On the Generation of Animals* 747a34ff., 752b25ff.). He attacks Empedocles again on the question of the account to be given of milk, which Aristotle holds to be formed by a process of what he calls concoction, not one of putrefaction. So Empedocles was mistaken, or he used a bad metaphor, when he spoke of milk as 'whitish pus' (*On the Generation of Animals* 777a7ff.). In what is perhaps the most striking example of this type of move, this time in his *Metaphysics* (991a20ff., 1079b24ff.), Aristotle dismisses Plato's entire theory of Forms or Ideas, no less, on the grounds that 'to say that [the Forms] are models and that other things share in them is to speak nonsense and to use poetic metaphors' – where again we may remark that the term 'poetic' is used as a mark of censure.

It is true that elsewhere, in his rhetoric and in the *Poetics* especially, Aristotle allows metaphor a positive role. In his literary critical discussions, for instance, he approves of certain types of metaphor, and he praises, in the poet, the ability to deploy metaphor, said indeed to be a mark of natural genius and a skill that cannot be learnt from another (*Poetics* 1459a5ff., *Rhetoric* 1405a4ff., 1407a14ff., 1410b13ff., 36ff.). He is also well aware, in his discussion of various types of dialectical argument, of how useful it may be to exploit similarities in order to deceive an opponent, and at one point he even recommends metaphor as a means of making an account difficult to refute (*On Sophistical Refutations* 176b20ff., cf 174a37ff., *Topics* 156b10ff.) – though that may be thought a backhanded recommendation.

But these concessions should not be overinterpreted. The crux of the matter is that it is essentially in the context of techniques of persuasion and in discussing literary style that he is prepared to allow metaphors some role. They may be acceptable in rhetoric and in poetry, but they are disastrous in scientific explanations and they make a nonsense of syllogistic. How Aristotle thought he could live up to the ideals he set himself for scientific explanation, and how far he actually did so, are another and a longer, indeed a very complicated, story (cf my 1987a, ch. 4). But I am concerned here just to point out what the *ideal* – for science – was.

The association of metaphor with poetry, as in those criticisms of (mere) poetic metaphor, provides a clue, I suggest, to the underlying polemic. Aristotle, like Plato too to some extent before him, was engaged in establishing and validating a new style of inquiry. They were both concerned to recommend the pursuit of philosophy, as they each construed it, and in Aristotle's case that would include also his conception of natural science. But this inquiry into nature had, he believed, to be given a firm foundation. It is for that purpose, especially, that he insists that, at least from the point of view of his ideal, there can be no room for the metaphorical. Yet this new style of inquiry not only set itself high standards – impossibly high ones, we might think – but it also negatively and destructively *ruled out* much of the competition as failing in precision, in clarity, in the direct, the literal.

The situation is analogous to that which Marcel Detienne has recently studied in connection with the invention of mythology, that is to say the explicit category (Detienne 1986), to which we shall be returning in chapter 2. For now we may simply note that one after another, in the fifth and fourth centuries B.C., Greek historians, philosophers, even medical writers, categorise what their rivals – predecessors or contemporaries – do as *myth*, while what they themselves offer are rational accounts, *logoi*. As we shall see (pp. 45ff) Herodotus distances himself from earlier story-tellers such as Hecataeus in that way, for being mere story-tellers, while Thucydides in turn distances himself from his predecessors (including both Hecataeus and Herodotus) in similar terms. In the process, where 'myth' (*muthos*) had originally meant simply 'narrative account', 'mythological' is given the pejorative undertones of fiction.

In Aristotle's case the rejection of mere poetic metaphor is one way in which he contrasts his own philosophising with that of his predecessors and with the efforts of those other repositories of traditional wisdom, the poets.[12] This is not just to distance his own philosophising, of course, but also to claim superiority for it. Empedocles manages to get bad marks on every score. On the one hand his explanations are bad natural science; they are steeped in poetic metaphor. On the other he is not a proper poet either, though he writes in verse. 'There is nothing in common between Homer and Empedocles', Aristotle remarks contemptuously at one point (*Poetics* 1447b17ff.), 'except the metre.' Again when discussing those who deliberately cultivate ambiguity, he comments that such people often write in verse. This is what Empedocles does: he just bamboozles his audience with his elaborate circumlocutions, and he has the same effect on them as diviners do, whose ambiguous statements are greeted with nods of acquiescence – we are to understand uncomprehendingly (*Rhetoric* 1407a32ff.).

My argument is, then, that in origin, the distinction between the literal and the metaphorical – like that between myth (as fiction) and rational account – was not just an innocent, neutral piece of logical analysis, but a weapon forged to defend a territory, repel boarders, put down rivals. Of course the question of the legitimacy of its use in its Aristotelian form raises problems of the greatest complexity (which I shall do no more than allude to shortly). But it can perhaps be seen readily enough how the Aristotelian dichotomy is likely to force an issue and how indeed it was so used. If we encounter in an Empedocles an appeal to a cosmic principle of Love (his two chief cosmological forces were called Love and Strife), the question can be pressed: is this strictly and literally Love? If the answer is yes, how does it relate to more mundane cases of sex? But if the answer is no, what precisely is being claimed and why is a cosmological principle to be termed Love? Or again, to pick up one of Aristotle's own actual examples, when Plato claims that the particulars participate in the Form (a beautiful object in the Form of the Beautiful itself, for instance), is this a literal participation? It had better not be (and Plato points that out for himself in the *Parmenides*, 130e ff., with regard to the Form of the Large, bits of which are not to be said to be found in large objects). But if this is a metaphor, what is it a metaphor for? However, it is of course only if one accepts the Aristotelian demand for the literal rather literally that one will be moved to attempt (impossibly) to do metaphysics without metaphor.

However there were those in the ancient world, as there are some today, whose response to the dilemma was to try to make a virtue out of what Aristotle had deemed a vice. The categories that had been forged in part to foreclose, to reject, to mark a failure, were, by a remarkable act of finesse, used by some – and used self-consciously – as a very present help, a refuge in times of trouble. If 'metaphor' was a charge offered as a term of censure by those who insisted on strict literality, there were plenty of those who did not mind, who turned the other cheek, who gloried in their rejection of the normal canons of logical communication. Eventually issues to do with the literality or otherwise of many items of religious belief were to become a central concern of theology – as they did especially when the question of the precise wording of the creed became a topic of dispute in the Arian controversy.[13] But already in the late second or early third century A.D. Tertullian had famously proclaimed: 'The son of God is dead: this is to be believed since it is absurd. Having been buried he rose again: this is certain, since it is impossible.'[14] Nor was this rejection of normal logic a type of reaction confined just to Christianity, nor even to religion, nor just to late antiquity. Already in Plato's recognition that *logos* is not all-sufficing, that *muthos* must sometimes be employed, we find the beginnings of an acceptance of the limitations of the former. Indeed as we shall see (below, ch. 2, p. 45), not only does Plato make extensive use of *muthos*: there are occasions when he does so deliberately in order to insulate a viewpoint from a literalist-minded brand of criticism.

The metaphorical, the imagistic, the mythical could be and were invoked by some to express disapproval of a discourse that used them. But those very same categories could also be cited explicitly in an attempt to shield views from a certain type of challenge – by directly disowning a commitment to their literal truth. However, unless the Aristotelian dichotomy itself was overhauled and criticised, to invoke the metaphorical in that way would hardly do, for it ran the risk of merely seeming evasive. What was needed, rather, was an alternative theory of meaning, or at least an alternative account of that dichotomy, one that did not treat the metaphorical as deviant in the name of an insistence on ultimate literality.

Yet quite what those alternatives should be remains, as we remarked, as a central problem in the philosophy of language. Obviously the constraints on language that a poet can accept differ from those appropriate in such a domain as the law, and they differ again from those appropriate in natural science. Emancipation from Aristotelian demands for the literal, for precision, for the univocal, comes appreciably more easily in some contexts than in others, though of course the metaphor-proliferating proclivities of speculative thought cannot escape just *every* attempt at scrutiny merely by an appeal to the irreducibility of the metaphorical mode. Meanwhile in antiquity and subsequently, those who remained within the framework of the Aristotelian interpretation of that dichotomy found themselves in a double bind. On the one side, how could the demands for the literal be met? But on the other, invoking the metaphorical, and denying commitment to literal truth, was likely to seem merely to duck the issue and to leave obscure *what* claims were being made.

This takes us back to where we began the discussion of the Greek origins of the metaphorical/literal distinction. The importance of the distinction between actors' and observers' categories has been repeatedly emphasised by social anthropologists. Yet parts of the anthropological debate on the issues that concern us on the question of mentalities are open to the charge of paying that distinction insufficient attention. At least it is often not clear from the ethnographic reports *how far* the distinctions deployed correspond to the actors' *own* linguistic categories. Yet it is evident that where *there are no such explicit categories as these*, statements of ideas and beliefs are less liable to a certain type of challenge – the type that Aristotle issued to Empedocles and to all and sundry. They are not totally immune to challenge, no doubt, insofar as even without any category of the metaphorical as such, certain questions can be put to probe the limits of the commitment to a belief. For example, Evans-Pritchard raised, in order to deny, the possibility that the Nuer thought that a twin has a beak and feathers – although he also put it that they thought that a twin is not just *like* a bird, but *is* one (Evans-Pritchard 1956, p. 131). Nevertheless in the form 'Do twins have beaks and feathers?' the question is surely unlikely to arise in the ordinary experience of the Nuer, but only, maybe,

25

when they are visited by anthropologists. That is, one might conjecture that that question is likely to arise only or mainly in the context of a questioner who already has the literal–metaphorical dichotomy in mind – a questioner who was setting out to explore the issues that, as we said, that dichotomy tends to force.

If we are to get clearer on some of the issues to do with 'mentalities', the question of the availability and use of explicit concepts of linguistic categories (such as in the present case, the literal–metaphorical dichotomy, and others will be suggested as we proceed) may be highly significant. From this perspective we can come to understand how, in any given society, traditional beliefs are maintained, and what types of implicit tension or explicit challenge different kinds of belief, about society or about natural phenomena, may be subject to. For those purposes, whether the society has an explicit category of the metaphorical opposed to a further explicit category of the literal may well be of the first importance.

One reflection that the Greek data prompts is that when those categories were made fully explicit there, that was a move in the debate between rival styles of wisdom and itself led to an intensifying of that debate. They were used as one way of drawing a contrast between the poetic on the one hand, the natural scientific on the other. I do not think it would be too far-fetched to imagine Aristotle commenting on the Dorze statement that the leopard is a Christian animal, that it might be 'adequate, perhaps, for poetic purposes', but was 'not adequate for understanding the nature of the thing'. To which the Dorze might counter that that was not what they were interested in.

While Aristotle might allow a little (not much) to what has been called the social use of metaphor (Sapir and Crocker 1977), he would still resist, in principle, its use in natural scientific explanation. Moreover he would surely not fail to remark that many of the examples cited in the anthropological literature are ones where there is a failure – as *he* would see it – to observe the category distinction between the world of natural phenomena on the one hand and that of human society and cultural phenomena on the other: animals cannot have religions. But then Aristotle had 'nature' and 'culture' as explicit categories too. Indeed in that case that contrast, the contrast between *nomos* (which covers law, custom and convention) and *phusis* (nature) goes back, in Greece, to the century before Aristotle (Heinimann 1945, Guthrie 1969, ch. 4, Ostwald 1986, pp. 250ff., Farrar 1988, pp. 106ff., 115). Once again, however, in the anthropological literature, the extent to which the subjects reported on themselves have and use those as *explicit* categories often remains unclear even while so much anthropological discussion, both in general

26

and in particular cases, is articulated round the nature–culture dichotomy.[15]

The particular importance of having the literal and the metaphorical as explicit concepts may lie in that they enable questions of meaning and commitment to be put more easily and more forcefully. No doubt many differences between different types of discourse are more or less generally acknowledged. At least there is ample evidence from many societies for the existence of explicit categories of the riddle, the oracle, and the sacred text, for instance, each of which marks out a special type of discourse well enough. But none of these leads as directly as does the dichotomy between the literal and the metaphorical to the fundamental question of the way in which language as a whole works, to the relation between words and reality and to the nature of the process of communication. Self-consciousness on those issues certainly goes with a range of differences in the modalities of interpersonal exchanges, and with the possibility of a radical problematising of the question of mutual understanding. Once that possibility and the self-consciousness exist, then that can have far-reaching consequential effects on assumptions concerning the need to meet demands to explain and justify a view.

These observations do not, of course, *remove* the puzzling features in many of the surprising items of discourse or behaviour that provided one initial stimulus to talk of divergent mentalities. On the contrary, whether we are dealing with the Nuer, with the ancient Greeks, or with our own society (to which we shall be returning, ch. 2 pp. 40ff., 67ff.,), the substantive problems of interpretation posed by many statements, assumptions, beliefs and modes of behaviour remain. The Nuer statement that twins are birds and the Dorze one that the leopard is a Christian animal have, no doubt, to be understood, in each case, against a background of a rich and complex set of beliefs that are gradually acquired by the members of the society concerned, a set that contains more and less central, more and less secure, items, some open to doubt, others requiring specialist or learned interpretation, and yet others passing as unquestioned or axiomatic.

Just as much is true also of our own culture. This is so not just of its religious beliefs – as for instance when it is said that God is one and God is three,[16] or again that the sacramental bread and wine are the flesh and blood of Christ. It is also true of many of its political slogans, for example (as for instance how such an expression as 'Forward with the People' is to be taken) and indeed of some of its scientific theories. Certainly the meaning of complex scientific statements can only be grasped against a background of considerable other knowledge. That is true in general, and before we come to particular problematic cases that might be thought to

27

put a particular strain on 'common sense' or usual assumptions. Faced with wave–particle duality in the theory of light, for instance, a latter-day Lévy-Bruhl from Nuer-land (if one could imagine such a person) might well mutter 'tolerance of incompatibility'.

However our study of the topic of metaphor suggests that where there may be important differences distinguishing one *context of discourse* from another is on such issues as the expectations entertained by speakers and their audiences on the status of different types of statement. These differences relate to the degree to which statements may pass unquestioned. They may do so, for instance, either as part of the shared knowledge of the group, or as belonging to a domain where *questioning* is inappropriate. Or again, alternatively, they may be open to challenge and we should then ask of what kind, and expressed by means of what explicit categories. It is not that the differences that we have identified lead us to postulate, or justify our postulating, a distinct mentality, corresponding, that is, to a certain awareness of the possibility of challenge. Rather, given that that awareness may well vary not just generally from one society to another, or from one group to another, but – more precisely – from one *context of discourse* to another, where the very same individuals may participate in a variety of such contexts, we should resist talk of divergent mentalities here on the grounds that we have identified before, namely the extravagance of attributing a plurality of mentalities to the same individual.

Finally it is clear that so far as the converse category of the literal goes, Aristotle's formulation and use of that concept are a manifestation of *his* expectation, his confidence, that literal truth was there to be attained, not least in the explanation of natural phenomena. This was often and maybe generally a simplistic overconfidence, we may say: but at the same time it no doubt provided a powerful incentive to the pursuit of his style of scientific investigation.

This has already taken us to the second of the two topics mentioned at the beginning of this chapter as occasions for appeal to the notion of mentalities, namely the contrast between the pre-scientific and the scientific. We may now attack the question of the Greek evidence concerning this more directly, since, as we said, it offers promising opportunities for the study of purported transformations or revolutions, however they should be described, whether in mentalities, or rather, for example, in modes of thought construed in terms of context-relative styles of reasoning. The origins of science, as I said before, should certainly not be construed as a matter of a single historical event. Rather a whole range of issues would have to be considered, in any full account, in connection with widely separated historical periods, both long before and long after classical antiquity, the Greece of the fifth and fourth centuries B.C.. The difficulties that philosophers of science have encountered in specifying items either of content or of method, either of theory or of practice, as constitutive of science as such as a whole, should just strengthen our resolve in this regard. So too should the work of historians of science who have pointed to the great diversities of practice, and to the tensions, even discrepancies, between principles and practice, even in twentieth-century science.[17] Any attempt to privilege one in the series of relevant transitions, and claim that *it* was decisive, is likely to be arbitrary, even if we chose to argue (a thesis that would at points prove difficult to sustain) that the transitions – in Western science at any rate – were all connected and cumulative.

The qualifications aside, certain investigations that *are* continuous with what is normally included in our term science were initiated in ancient Greece, and by this I mean nothing more sophisticated or more controversial than that *that* is the appropriate rubric to apply to such diverse inquiries as, for example, Greek theoretical astronomy (that is, astronomical model-building), to Archimedes' statics and hydrostatics, to Galen's experimental anatomical and physiological vivisections – and so on.[18] Clearly this is not the *whole* of science as we now understand it (no radio astronomy, no molecular biology, no chemistry even, and the list could be extended), and clearly it was not carried out within the institutional framework – of scientific education and research establishments – that now exists. But they are deliberate and systematic investigations of nature that belong, nevertheless, to the same genus.

The initiation of such investigations takes place in Greece against a background of ongoing traditional beliefs, and the relationship between the new-, and the old-style, wisdom is, or should be, of considerable importance. Thus from the point of view of mentalities we have to pay due attention to the fact that an analysis of that relationship yields quite widely divergent results in different areas of Greek natural science. One recurrent doubly mistaken move is simply to excise what are held to be the progressive developments in ancient Greek thought and to focus exclusively on them – as when some talk about Greek *medicine* when what they are actually referring to is only one part of what must be included under that term, namely Hippocratic medicine, and then probably only to a fraction of that part, namely those Hippocratic authors who advocated a certain brand of rationalistic approach to the subject. This is doubly mistaken, not just because clearly unsound in general methodology, but also because it ignores important points of substance in those interrelations of the new, and the old, wisdom: and if we are to have a reliable basis on which to judge whether there is any call to talk of a transformation of mentalities in this regard, we have first to investigate those interrelations.

Although students of ancient Greek society can, in the strict sense, be no ethnographers, that should not prevent us from emulating, as far as our materials permit, the kind of dense – or as Geertz (1973) would say, 'thick' – account that considers the data concerning belief-systems against the whole background of the geographical, economic, technological, social and political situation of the society under investigation. Moreover, within certain limits at least, that goal is attainable, even if so much discussion of Greek science has failed lamentably to attain it and has often seemed not even to wish to attain it. The myth of the founding of Greek science is recreated as it is retold: but unlike some myths it is not creatively retold. If it loses nothing in the retelling (in the sense that the same grand claims are repeated uncritically), it often fails to gain anything either, fails, that is, to put to good use the results of some serious specialist work.

Let me try to indicate, in the briefest possible compass, what a sufficiently dense account might look like, taking for the moment just the single example of Greek medicine where the evidence is particularly rich. This is not the place to attempt to carry through such a project, but outlining the materials that exist for it will serve my present purpose of drawing attention to the circumstances in which what we identify as certain scientific developments took place.

If we leave aside self-help, and the help available from within the immediate household or community, healing the sick was, in one or other of its aspects, the work of no less than five more or less clearly demarcated groups, even before we include Hippocratic medicine, itself, as already remarked, no homogeneous tradition. Of these five groups, two, the 'root-cutters' (*rizotomoi*) and the 'drug-sellers' (*pharmakopōlai*), were concerned primarily with different aspects of the collection, sale and administration of drugs, especially herbal remedies. There were obvious links between these two, though our evidence suggests some division of labour, even if also some overlap, between those who actually collected *materia medica* – in the fields or on the mountains[19] – and those whose main activity was selling it and whose main base was the market. Then a third category – again poorly represented in our direct sources, but quite extensively in our indirect ones – consists of women healers, who were involved in far more than their principal name, 'midwives' (*maiai*), might suggest to us, for they were evidently called in for many women's ailments unconnected with childbirth. They were associated sometimes with male doctors, though as I have pointed out elsewhere (1983, pp. 70ff., cf. Hanson forthcoming) the male writers of Hippocratic treatises generally cast their female associates in a subordinate role.

The fourth and fifth groups consist of those whose discourse on diagnosis and treatment drew heavily on the categories of the divine and the demonic. There are, however, important differences to be discerned between, on the one hand, the itinerant sellers of purifications we hear about from Plato and the Hippocratics, and, on the other, those who practised religious medicine (involving especially soliciting dreams from god: the practice of incubation) within the confines of increasingly well-established temples, the sanctuaries of Asclepius in particular. Many of these temples yield precious epigraphical evidence, inscriptions set up mostly to advertise the successes of the shrine by recording the cures achieved – and not just the cures. The god could help the faithful not just by suggesting a treatment or carrying one out, but by telling them where to find the treasure, or the child, that had been lost.[20] Just how well-established these temples were, any tourist visiting Epidaurus or Pergamum knows: the earliest of these temples, it is worth remarking, are contemporary with the period to which our chief Hippocratic texts belong (fifth and fourth centuries B.C.) and they continued to flourish down to the second century A.D. and beyond, thereby giving the lie to anyone who might be tempted to represent the history of Greek medicine as one of the triumph of some kind of Hippocratic rationalism leading to the demise of other forms of practice.

Then there is the evidence from those Hippocratic texts themselves, not that they present a united front, let alone an orthodoxy, either on the causes of diseases or on their treatment, or even on the principles and methods that should guide medical practice. On the contrary, they frequently disagree not just with some of the other groups I have mentioned, but also among themselves, and as we shall see (below, pp. 48f.) some of these writers contend in addition with what they represent as the intrusion or infiltration of ideas, including new-fangled methodological recommendations, from outside medicine, from such other fields as natural philosophy.

Now the relations between and within all these groups are a matter of very considerable complexity. Some of the boundaries in question were evidently strongly contested and defended, while others were marked by relations of tolerance, of mutual, though not necessarily symmetrical, respect. Thus we do not find Hippocratic writers launching into an open attack on midwives in the way they do against the itinerant purifiers. Nor is it just the Hippocratic authors (far better represented in the extant evidence than the other groups) who do the attacking. There are implicit criticisms of other healers, including for treatments we actually find being used by Hippocratic writers, in the traditions of temple medicine.[21]

There is, then, a whole series of questions here to be investigated –

31

concerning the areas of influence, rivalries and alliances of these various groups – in the dense account we should aim for. But so far as our immediate concerns go, namely what this evidence can tell us about the problem of emergent Greek science, three points are fundamental. First, contributions to positive knowledge are far from being confined to those who figure among our Hippocratic authors. Greek pharmacopoeia, in particular, was the accumulated achievement of the root-cutters, the drug-sellers and others, as much as of Hippocratic writers. We should not underestimate the powers of sustained observation, in that field and in others, of other kinds of healers besides the Hippocratics. It is true, however, that the Hippocratics do not just provide many excellent examples, for instance in the context of clinical case-histories, but also sometimes accompany these with explicit methodological recommendations: I shall return to that point later.

Secondly and conversely, it would be quite wrong to represent everything that is contained in the Hippocratic Corpus as imbued with a secure sense of how scientific progress is to be achieved in medicine. On the contrary, dogmatism, arbitrariness and wild speculation are features of many of their theories, and many of the therapies they advocated are foolhardy in the extreme – for some of which, indeed, they were in turn duly criticised by other ancient writers themselves (see below, pp. 54f).

But then the third, crucial, point relates to the styles of justification demanded or developed in some contexts and to the degree of self-consciousness attained on the matter of such justification, at least by some of those who participated in the debate. What is distinctive, in this regard, is not so much the variety of Greek medical styles: a similar variety can indeed readily be exemplified in other ancient as well as in modern societies, in ancient Egypt and Babylonia, for instance (Wilson 1962, Oppenheim 1962), as well as in, for example, modern Japan, as finely documented recently by Ohnuki-Tierney (1984). Rather it is the engaging in argument concerning some of the grounds of the divergence.

This is not just a matter of the explicit criticism, in some of our Greek texts, of other styles of healer, named or unnamed. We hear also of direct confrontations between healers who challenged each other, or were challenged by their own patients or clients, to justify their diagnoses or treatments. Moreover we know of open, public debates, often adjudicated by lay audiences, in which theories of diseases, or of the constitution of the human body, or the nature of the medical art itself were discussed.

Some claims to superiority rely merely on assertion, as if greater success in treatment and cure spoke for itself. But some Greek healers did not just agree to differ, but in certain contexts, at least, were led to examine the basis of the disagreement, undermining or exposing the opposition's methods and assumptions, while presenting their own (naturally enough) in the best light possible, as indeed the one true method of the art of medicine. Yet if that suggests the development of a new critical spirit, we have to be careful to note the limitations of its field of application. Many assumptions, much of the vocabulary of health and disease, were common ground, and remained unexamined, across the board of Greek medicine. That included many assumptions concerning the nature of the female body, for instance (King 1983), and about the need for sick patients of either sex to be 'purified' or 'cleansed', even when the type of 'purification' or 'cleansing' offered varied dramatically – from ritual procedures supported by the discourse of the divine all the way to purely physical purgings, blood-lettings or emetics (Lloyd 1979, p. 44, Parker 1983). If the chief context of debate was the nature of the art of medicine itself, there was much that was never subjected to critical scrutiny.

Moreover when we investigate how far some of the more articulate writers lived up to their own expressed ideals, the shortfall often becomes visible. The methodological ideals themselves were in many cases impecc-able, that one should be careful to make the most extensive examination before arriving at a diagnosis, that one should withhold judgement where the issue is uncertain or the evidence insufficient, that in general one should avoid fanciful speculation and stick to what could be verified by observation (Lloyd 1987a, chh. 2 and 3). In practice, however, as I have remarked, they often failed to live up to their principles, sometimes indeed doing little better – *we* might say – than the opponents they singled out for criticism for *their* failures.

At the same time the statement of the principles itself was of the greatest importance, since once they were made *explicit* they could be, and they were, used as a standard by which to judge performance – including, indeed, in some instances, the inadequate performance of the very writers who were responsible for stating the principles. Again, as with the explicit formulation of the metaphorical–literal dichotomy by Aristotle, the methodological and epistemological points formulated by medical writers were often developed, and deployed, in polemic. Not the least important of the categories made explicit in the context of the medical debate, and so deployed, is that of the magical, the Greek term being particularly insulting in Greek polemic, since it associated whatever was so catego-rised with the alien, that is barbarian, Magi: I shall explore this theme in some detail in chapter 2.

Medicine is, to be sure, only one of the domains in which early Greek contributions to the development of science can be studied: more examples from other areas of investigation will be examined in due course. But our brief survey of the data for medicine already suggests how unsatisfactory it would be to attempt to capture the complexities of the issues through the application of the notion of mentalities and their transformation. Such contributions to the development of science as we can associate with early Greek medicine are not confined to a single group. The groups in question can, in any event, hardly be represented as each manifesting some distinct – whether new or traditional – mentality. Rather it is the interactions between groups that are important, for that generated a certain type of rivalry between some of them. The formulation of explicit new methodological principles undoubtedly eventually had far-reaching effects, but if we seek for the original stimulus for that development, much of the answer is to be found in that complex rivalry and the attempts made, within it, to validate one or other competing view of the nature of the art of medicine.

An attempt may now be made, in conclusion, to tie together the main strands of my discussion and to suggest at least some preliminary findings. Talk of mentalities has often veered towards the inflated or the tendentious, to the hopelessly vague, or to both. Certainly it seems quite *in*appropriate, so far as the ancient Greek world goes, to talk of *the* or even of *a* Greek mentality, as if some such were shared by all Greeks, or all the relevant ones (if we could identify them), let alone was peculiar to, or distinctive of, them. When we further take into account ongoing traditional attitudes, patterns of belief and behaviour (from which no one was free in their society, any more than in our own), the 'mentality' we would end with would be not just hybrid, but a monster. But that is not to say that the issues sometimes discussed under the rubric of mentalities are not important ones: rather that the problems have to be relocated.

One such relocation can be suggested in relation to a set of issues concerning the degree to which, and the manner in which, the status of statements or beliefs is open to challenge. An analysis of some of the topics where *observers* often make use of the category of the metaphorical prompts one to question precisely what difference it may make to have some such category. What difference it made for that category to be invented – the historical question – can at least partly be answered. Its introduction was, I said, no mere neutral piece of logical analysis, but a move in the polemic in which the introducers, Aristotle especially, sought to establish the criteria for proper philosophy and science – their kind – and to put down rivals (both poets and other philosophers). In terms of the influence Aristotle's ideas have had on centuries of subsequent discussion, that has been nothing short of amazing. He presented his opponents with a double-bind to escape from which it was essential (I argued) to have an alternative analysis of the literal–metaphorical relation-ship to offer. Even now it is still widely assumed that the metaphorical is deviant, and the permeation of the metaphorical in all natural language, not just in religious or poetic discourse, but right at the heart of science itself, can still not be said to be *fully* appreciated, although one might have thought that the points had been made repeatedly and emphatically enough by philosophers of language and by philosophers of science.[22]

But it is not just in relation to the literal–metaphorical dichotomy that the forging of explicit categories appears to be of fundamental importance. Time and again questions to do with the initiation of Greek scientific inquiries turn on the availability of explicit distinctions, and how they came to be *made* explicit is at least one of the key issues. Talk of the initiation of scientific inquiries there can be as mystifying as any talk of mentalities has ever been, for it might make it appear that the inaugu-rations of Greek natural philosophy, of rationalistic medicine, and so on, were the product of pure thought. Yet an analysis of how they constituted themselves and of what they presupposed shows that that was far from being the case.

We should not expect, nor do we find, total uniformity in the relevant social, cultural and ideological background across *all* the various areas of Greek speculative thought, although the rivalry present in such large measure in medicine is a prominent feature also in natural philosophy, in other areas of natural science, even, to a lesser extent, in mathematics. But one crucial phenomenon we encounter in a variety of fields is the raising of second-order questions, the development of methodological and epi-stemological self-consciousness, an explicit concern with foundations (another ancient Greek preoccupation that has had far-reaching reper-cussions to the present day, though many now of course resist the demand for foundations). Many of the major methodological and concep-tual breakthroughs, which have been hailed as among the triumphs of Greek scientific rationalism, were far from being *just* that. It was not as if the importance of sticking to what can be verified by observation was a principle arrived at as the result of some cool, dispassionate, seminar held by a group of the best minds who had suddenly decided they wanted to turn themselves into good philosophers and scientists. On the contrary, as in the metaphor case, it must be seen as an item in, and the product of, a hard-hitting polemic in which the new-style inquiries fought to distin-guish themselves from rivals, notably but not exclusively from traditional claimants to wisdom. The second-order questions that provided the methodological and epistemological basis for, and in that sense were largely constitutive of, the new inquiries, often spring from, or directly relate to, that rivalry.

35

But if the instigation of a certain type of debate appears to be one key question, that is, of course, just to push the problem one stage further back – as I said, to relocate it. Yet at least we are dealing here with a concrete topic with aspects of which, at least, we can get to grips and where we have some prospect of advancing the discussion.

Two features may be mentioned straight away. First, independently of material that has to do with the beginnings of Greek philosophy and science, we have evidence that throws light on the context and occasions, in Greece, on which actual (and not merely literary) debates were held at physical meetings. Thus we know that this happened, for example, at Olympia and at other great pan-Hellenic games. We have direct evidence also concerning the role of the audience, which was often an active one, especially when they were responsible for deciding who had won. Again we know that there were those (often called 'sophists') who specialised in such debates and in giving competitive or exhibition lectures, including on subjects to do with what we call natural science and including on what gives an inquiry a right to be called a rational one. For those who engaged in such debates, there was often much at stake, their reputations, even their livelihoods. Yet it is clear that some occasions were not *totally* serious. The association between debate and *play* is made, partly, it is true, by those who considered the debaters as no better than entertainers and maybe a good deal worse. But it was also made by some who accepted and even exploited the link on their own behalf and for their own purposes, as most notably by the famous sophist Gorgias. Debates were evidently sometimes engaged in just for their own sakes, and not in the spirit of exploring such topics as the foundations of claims to knowledge in philosophy and science.[23]

Secondly and more importantly still, the development of these contexts of debate in other fields may, indeed must, be understood against the political background of ancient Greek society, especially the very extensive experience that many Greek citizens had of debates in the Assemblies and the law-courts, of evaluating evidence and arguments there in matters both of private legal disputes and of strategic public concern, issues to do with the constitution itself, no less, as well as with decisions between peace and war. The hypothesis that we shall be exploring in some detail in chapter 2 and again in chapter 4 takes its starting-point and inspiration from the work of Vernant, Vidal-Naquet and their associates, who first emphasised the fundamental link between the development of Greek philosophy and science and the political life of the Greek city-state (Vernant (1962) 1982, (1965) 1983, Vidal-Naquet (1967) 1986). Our aim will be to see how far this and other explanatory hypotheses can take us towards an understanding of the distinctive features of styles of inquiry developed in ancient Greece. But for now it is enough merely to note that several ancient authors themselves remark on both the similarities and the contrasts between the purely intellectual debates we have been referring to and those held in the political Assemblies.[24]

What our account, as elaborated so far, has in common with, and where it diverges from, two other current theories, may be stated summarily in conclusion. In *The Domestication of the Savage Mind* Goody rejects the notion of radical discontinuities in developments from the 'Savage' to the 'Domesticated Mind' and stresses that domestication was indeed a gradual process. He acknowledges that a complex of causes is at work and explicitly disavows monocausal explanations on several occasions (Goody 1977, pp. 10, 46, 51). But the most important factors, in his view, relate to the technology of communication, and especially – so far as Greece is concerned – to the spread of literacy made possible by an alphabetic system of writing.

The argument I have proposed here concerning the importance of certain category distinctions being made explicit may be taken to chime with Goody's preoccupations at least insofar as it focusses on problems to do with the nature and contexts of communication. However, while no one can doubt that the availability of written texts and of those able to read them led to far-reaching direct and indirect effects on all aspects of Greek intellectual life, it must still be emphasised that the rivalry I have described between and within competing groups was still one mediated mainly in the *spoken* register. Moreover so far as explanatory hypotheses go, the *political* experience that I shall argue provided the necessary background to, and in some respects positively stimulated, the crucial intellectual developments in *styles of inquiry*, goes beyond factors encompassed by the thesis of the technology of communication.

Finally Horton has recently reiterated a thesis that lays particular stress on differences between consensual and competitive stances or modes of theorising (Horton 1982, pp. 228ff.), where he too has drawn attention to valuable points, even though the thesis needs some nuancing in relation to the Greek material.

Thus in Greece I have remarked that some of the boundaries between different groups of those concerned with healing are marked by relations of some tolerance, even while others are veritable battlefields. With this regard too, then, as so often elsewhere, it would be better not to attempt the grand unqualified characterisation of Greek society *in toto*. Moreover the emergence of the competitive is itself, as indeed Horton recognises, in need of explanation. In that respect, then, the thesis may not go far enough. But in another it may need more serious qualification. As I have

already noted, one point of comparison he finds between African traditional religion and Western science relates to what he now labels 'secondary theories'. But this is to obscure what I have argued to be a fundamental
issue. The question I would press is precisely how far any given secondary
theory – in Africa or anywhere else – is recognised as such – *as secondary*.

Both our account of the *explananda*, and our attempted explanations,
will themselves need modifying in due course. Our next step is to consider
evidence from both the ancient and the modern world concerning two
further fundamental category-distinctions and the effects of their being
made explicit, namely those where magic, on the one hand, and myth, on
the other, are both contrasted with science and philosophy.

2

Magic and science, ancient and modern

If one of the original motivations for invoking the idea of differences in mentalities was somehow to account for what seemed highly counter-intuitive or paradoxical statements of the kind we have discussed in chapter 1, another was certainly provided by the problems in understanding magical practices and beliefs, often associated with 'mystical' or 'mythical' patterns of thought and so with the corresponding postulated mentality.[1] Indeed some time before Lévy-Bruhl a certain preoccupation with the problem of magic is a recurrent feature in writers of different types. In some cases the strategic interest motivating the introduction of the topic is clear. Nineteenth-century evolutionists of different philo-sophical persuasions often invoked magic in developing the theme of the primitivism of archaic times. That theme, variously interpreted, was one shared by philosophers as otherwise divergent as Comte[2] and Hegel.[3] However it was Frazer who was responsible for a particularly clear and influential statement of the view according to which the three states through which human societies have developed are marked by magic, religion and science respectively (Frazer 1911–15).

Some of the reasons for the popularity of the *Golden Bough* have been analysed by Edmund Leach (1961, 1965, cf. Ackerman 1987). As a literary artefact it is highly polished, making liberal use of evocative epithets that reveal both a certain condescension and a certain romanticism. Frazer introduced his readers, at a safe distance, to the 'wild man in the woods', the 'poor savage' with his 'vain fancies'. These were savages who stalked across 'misty mountains' or under 'azure skies', who lived in 'humble cottages', although some of those in the ancient world also had 'stately fanes' in which to perform their 'solemn rituals' (Frazer 1911–15, 1, p. 68). The book publicised a corpus of material concerning magical practices and popular beliefs but did so in a way that not only did not threaten, but positively encouraged, complacent feelings of superiority in an assumed civilised readership. 'Magic', Frazer wrote magisterially (1, p. 53), 'is a

39

spurious system of natural law as well as a fallacious guide to conduct' – while the *real* laws of nature were, by implication, pretty securely under control.

Much of the debate has now moved on from Frazer and his contemporaries. Contributors to fashionable controversies on Rationality and Relativism now more often take Quine or Thomas Kuhn or Richard Rorty as their starting-point. Yet some of that debate has a rather sterile air, or at least it does not address sufficiently directly what we may, with only a little licence, call Frazer's problem, of the relationship between magic, religion and science (though we shall be concerned here mostly with the first and last members of that triad). Much has been written on the problem of understanding alien cultures and on the incommensurability of systems of belief, and certainly valuable points have emerged, concerning the difficulties of translation, the presuppositions of comprehension, the very idea of a system of belief or of a conceptual scheme – valuable, not least, as an antidote to latter-day Frazerian condescension.

Yet quite apart from the difficulties that arise in attempting comparisons *between* societies, Frazer's problem is posed in the sharpest possible terms *within* just *one* society, namely our own.[4] Here there is no barrier interposed by the problems of translation from a native to our own natural language, since we all speak English though of course with considerable dialect and personal variations. Nor will it do to treat magic, religion and science in our own society as three distinct, hermetically sealed subcultures, or to dismiss the first two (in Frazerian fashion) as throwbacks or residua.

That last point needs some immediate elaboration and it is one to which I shall be returning. We have only to glance through the pages of mass-circulation newspapers, for instance, to be reminded of the fact that there are plenty of people, in our own society, who in one spirit or another, with one motivation or another, consult their horoscopes. Yet somehow that is often felt not to count, not to detract from the claim that the society we live in is, if not *just* scientific, nor *totally* scientific, at least predominantly characterisable as scientific. Yet apart from the obvious point that the characterisation might seem to underestimate the extent to which religious beliefs and practices still feature in life in twentieth-century societies, however 'advanced' or industrialised, there are two other problems that have to be faced. One of these comes from the side of the sociology of magic in our own British society (recently the subject of some detailed ethnography by Tanya Luhrmann, 1986, 1989), and the other from the side of the place of science and of the scientist within it.

First from the side of magic, it is important first to register the problems of evaluation that spring from the underground or covert nature of magic, which is itself in part a reaction to the general reluctance, in polite society, to take the subject at all seriously or as anything but an occasion for mild embarrassment. Luhrmann has, however, now provided detailed evidence not just to confirm that magic is extensively practised, in our very midst, in University towns and London suburbs (it is certainly not confined to the wilds of East Anglian fenland, for example) but also to show that the practitioners are simply not all the social or psychological misfits that some popular mythology would have us believe. Many hold down regular jobs as computer engineers, as laboratory technicians or as social workers, many again have graduated from University, and some even hold doctorates in philosophy (Luhrmann 1989). 'Our' magic, to be sure, presents certain differences from that practised in many traditional societies, notably in that it is often the result of a deliberate revival and in having institutionalised science to contend with. We shall return to these points in due course. Yet our magic is magic of a sort nevertheless, by which I mean that for all the contrasts, comparisons are also possible with the magic of traditional societies.

Secondly, from the side of science, it takes no ethnographer to make the point (cf, however, Tambiah 1973, p. 226 and especially Tambiah 1990). While there are many interrelated groups, each with its own traditions, values, buzzwords, to which professional scientists come to belong by a process of learning and social incorporation, the professionals in question do not live lives *entirely* taken up with scientific activity. Many of them are religious; some distinguished scientific acquaintances of mine consult their horoscopes, have their lucky charms, curse their car when it refuses to start and otherwise act in an ordinary human, not necessarily totally rational way. Besides, do not scientists also dream?

Nor is this just a matter of scientists being human beings in, as it were, their spare time. In their very activity as scientists there is clearly more than some self-images of that activity allow – particularly, perhaps, as that activity is represented, for pedagogic purposes, in the classroom, where the emphasis is on the articulation of a body of accepted theories. In the past, belief in the self-sufficiency of the experimental and hypo-thetico-deductive methods to deliver results has been something of an article of faith, as if the results were somehow the automatic outcome of the correct application of the methods. But today, we must say, that will scarcely do. At least we have learnt from work in both the philosophy and the sociology of science by Holton (1973, 1978), Kuhn (1957, 1970, 1977) and many others, that we should not underestimate the ritualistic elements of scientific activity, nor the complexity, even the deviousness, of scientific creativity and of the scientific imagination, nor again the complexity of the factors that come into play when new science supersedes old and scientific revolutions succeed.

So far, then, from magic, religion and science each adequately characterising a stage of social development, or a whole type of society, they coexist, in social practice, in our own society, and pose problems of understanding our own – before we come to any alien – culture. Moreover they pose problems that no simple postulate of differences in mentalities can begin adequately to describe, let alone to explain. Some of the problems discussed under the heading of cognitive dissonance (Festinger 1957) are relevant here. We must try to understand how it is that not just different groups, but sometimes the same individuals, hold in suspended coexistence what at first sight seem incompatible beliefs, and adopt conflicting styles and criteria of evaluation, whether of theories or of behaviour. Can we begin to specify how some such apparently conflicting patterns of belief come to be compartmentalised or insulated from challenge, or how, on the contrary, they become permeable to one another or vulnerable to criticism? Moreover in the clarification of these problems, much that is assumed in the use of the three categories of magic, religion and science themselves comes into question, as indeed does the very framework within which the issues can be discussed.

The way in which science *fits on to* the rest of the culture is problematic in twentieth-century Western societies. But those problems are all the more acute in the ancient world when what we can begin to recognise as science was first initiated. There there were, at least initially, no readily available models, no obvious agreed success stories (whether of intellectual or of practical success) to which appeal could be made in order to legitimate claims for the superiority of the scientific to other approaches. Frazer himself collected some marvellously rich data to do with magic and religion in the Greco-Roman world: but he hardly made any attempt to test his assumptions about science against the evidence that antiquity provides concerning its origins – that is to say concerning at least the Greek episodes in that complex story.

Much of the subsequent debate on magic and science has also lacked a diachronic dimension or a sense of the history of the problems. Yet an analysis of how and where – and even why – the dispute between magic and science originated in the West can be used both to throw light on aspects of the current debate and to take further our inquiry into how some such enterprise as science defined and legitimated itself in ancient Greece in the first place. Let me repeat that by the use of the term science I do not mean to prejudge the issue of just how far the ancient Greeks' investigations tally with one or other view of science that *we* might take. Indeed as we shall see in due course, some strange items were presented

42

as 'physics' (or the inquiry into nature) or as 'mathematics' or as 'medicine' in the ancient world. At the same time, as I remarked in chapter 1, other parts of Greek science, such as astronomical model-building, or Archimedes' statics and hydrostatics, or Galen's experimental vivisections, for example in his investigations of the nervous system, look familiar enough.

The strategy of my discussion in this chapter will unfold as I tackle three main questions. First – following up our inquiry in chapter 1 – what were the key moves in that self-definition of science, at least in its ancient Greek forms? Can we say, secondly, what in the society that produced that science, allowed it to emerge or favoured its emergence? Third, can we draw any lessons from our historical study for issues in the modern debate on Frazer's problem?

The argument I shall present on the first question will be that those moves had less to do with an effective ability in the matter of the control – or even of the understanding – of nature, than with the development of a discourse, or one might say a rhetoric, of legitimation. That makes it all the more important to answer the second question – to see where the attractions of the discourse lay. Here developing the social and political argument I have already adumbrated I shall stress three convergent factors, first the rivalry among those who laid one claim or other to special knowledge in ancient Greece (a rivalry that reflects the well-known agonistic features of Greek culture generally), second the existence of models for the discourse of legitimation in the context of legal and political debate, and thirdly and more controversially the possible influence of ideas associated with the ideology of democracy in particular. Finally, on my third strategic question, I shall explore very briefly what I take to be the consequences of making the category of magic itself explicit.

I shall attempt to keep as close as possible to the ancients' own categories to determine how *they* saw the changes that took place (even if this means the use of a good deal of the original Greek which will require glossing), and it is, once again, fundamental to my argument that the key categories they use to present those changes are *their invention*. In general, of course, Frazer's problem is discussed in relation to *other* societies using *our*, observers', categories of science, religion, magic, not *their*, actors', ones, and quite what category in native thought is being translated or interpreted as magic or religion – let alone science – is often quite unclear: or rather, usually there is no such category and all is interpretation.

But that is not the position we are in, where magic is concerned, in antiquity. The Greeks after all had a word for it. Better still, they might even be said to have invented that category. Within the framework of ancient discussions of *magia* certain simple but important points stand out (cf my 1979, pp. 12ff). First the origin of the label: *magikē* is the sort of thing that the Magi practise. Many of those who use the label may be none too clear about just what kind of practice that was, nor even about who precisely the Magi were. Herodotus, for instance, represents them as a distinct Median tribe who – or members of which – acted as priests and the interpreters of signs and dreams (Herodotus I 101, VII 19, 37ff.), but others had much vaguer ideas on the topic. However for all Greeks the Magi are certainly foreign and therefore potentially threatening and dangerous, potentially the possessors of special powers. For the readiness to attribute special power to foreigners one can refer to a comparable point that Shirokogoroff made in his study of Mongolian shamanism. He remarked on a variety of occasions that in neighbouring groups people tend to consider *other* groups' shamans more dangerous than their own (Shiroko-goroff 1935, pp. 373 on the Biracen, pp. 387ff. on the Tungus generally).

Secondly and relatedly, the term and its cognates generally carry pejorative undertones, and not just in the texts of high literature whether Greek or – with the corresponding terms, *magicus* etc – Latin. It is true that some ancient authors, like some modern ones, show a deep-seated ambivalence on the issue, officially condemning *magikē* but exploiting its frisson, or again themselves approving practices that they are well aware are thought by others to be, or to be no better than, *magikē*. Pliny, to give an obvious example, expresses himself horrified at the shocking behaviour of the magicians, but records some of their practices without condemning them and even endorses others. It is striking that while he often scoffs at the beliefs and practices of the Magi he also records counter-measures, practices that are supposed to 'render the arts of the Magi vain' (e.g. *Natural History* XXVIII 85, 104) – not something that would be necessary if they were all empty fictions (cf my 1983, pp. 135ff, Green 1954). Nevertheless the term and its cognates are often a signal that the idea or practice in question is being, or is going to be, censured.

That might make it seem that 'magic', as used by many ancient authors, is simply the ritual they disapprove of: as if their rituals are other people's magic, and vice versa. That will need qualifying in due course, but we should first broaden the framework of our discussion to consider some of the other category distinctions that were invented and made explicit in part (though it is true only in part) in the development of what were *claimed* as new styles of rationality. The job of work of disapproval that 'magic' does in some contexts, 'myth' does in others (cf. Detienne 1986). Of course the Greek word *muthos*, as is well known, originally just means story or narrative account and as such does not carry the pejorative undertones of mythical in the sense of fictitious. Conversely, the term often used as its antonym, *logos*, may mean no more than word or speech or discourse, though the Liddell-Scott-Jones lexicon, in its six-column entry for the word, also gives, for example, 'reckoning', 'grounds', 'reason' (in the sense of rational faculty) and 'definition' among many other senses. But one well known and recurrent motif in a variety of writers from the fifth century B.C. onwards is to represent what their predecessors or contemporary rivals offer as *muthos*, while what they themselves provide is *logos*.

The range of deployment of this as a contrastive pair is far wider than that of magic itself. It is a favourite with the historians, for instance. Hecataeus had begun by ridiculing the 'many tales of the Greeks' as 'absurd' and in contrasting his own accounts had claimed that they were true (*alēthēs*, Fr. 1). But Herodotus castigates early story-tellers such as Hecataeus indeed as just that, for believing and purveying fantastic tales. For instance, the idea that the earth is surrounded by Ocean is merely laughable (Herodotus IV 36, cf. 42). Herodotus himself in general has seen, has heard, has inquired – or so he claims (Hartog 1988). Nevertheless he receives his own discomfiture in the next generation. Thucydides represents his predecessors, Herodotus – by implication – included, as offering mere entertainment; their accounts are beyond verification or scrutiny (*anexelegkta*), and have, in his striking phrase, 'won their way to the mythical' (*epi to muthōdes eknenikēkota*, I 21). He, by contrast, has laboured to obtain accuracy. He disclaims any certainty about the remote past, and he produces not just something that is immediately attractive, but a 'possession for always'. He defeats the competition, one may say, by claiming that his own work is no mere piece produced *for* a competition, *agōnisma* (I 22).

From the rich material available from Plato on related themes it is enough, for now, to quote the *Gorgias*, where Socrates, introducing his story of rewards and punishments in the after-life, tells Callicles what he calls a fine *logos*, though it is one that Callicles himself will consider a *muthos*, indeed an 'old woman's *muthos*', which he will despise (*Gorgias* 523a, 527a). Yet Socrates himself believes his story to be true, saying at the beginning 'I shall tell you the things I shall tell you as things that are true' (523a) and again at the end (524ab): 'these are the things, Callicles, that having heard I believe to be true'. Note how the same story can be *logos* to one who believes it to be true, *muthos* to one who does not.[5] Aristotle, too, though occasionally allowing a good word for those such as Hesiod who speculated about the gods and the origins of things, often castigates them for obscurantism, for indulging in what he calls 'mythical sophistries' or 'wise-talk' (e.g. *Metaphysics* 1000a5ff., 18f.).

Again from the fifth- and fourth-century medical texts we may cite, for now, a passage from one of the surgical treatises, *On Joints*. There the writer records how some tell a tale, *muthologousi*, about how the Amazons dislocate the joints of their male offspring in early infancy, at the knees or at the hips, to make them lame, so that the male sex will be unable to plot against the female. For my part, the writer goes on (ch. 53, 232 7ff, 12ff), I do not know whether this is true (*alēthēs*): but I do know what would be the effect of dislocating the joints of young infants – and he then goes on to specify the various types of dislocation, both inward and outward dislocation, at the hips, at the knees, and for good measure, at the ankles as well. We have left the fantasies of myth, we are to understand, for the realities of surgical experience.

These contrasts are far from all exactly equivalent, but one theme that runs through the texts I have just mentioned (and many others) is that *muthos* is associated with what is unverifiable, *logos* with what you know, or at least believe, to be true (*alēthēs*). To be sure, untruth, lies and deceit had always been a familiar part of Greek culture, and some of the culture heroes of *mētis*, 'cunning intelligence' or wiles, such as Odysseus himself, were masters of the crafty lie (Detienne and Vernant 1978). But the accusation of mythologising differs from one of lying in part because it fudges the issue of the extent to which there is a deliberate intention to deceive. Often those who tell myths know, as it were, no better. They give you no outright falsehoods fabricated with set intent to mislead, but what may even attempt to be truth, though never a truth that is more than second-rate, judged, that is, from the stand-point of *logos*. For first-rate truth it is *logos* alone – at least according to *logos* itself – that will do. As with the category of the metaphorical, then, which we studied in chapter 1, the *logos–muthos* contrast offered an *explicit* category distinction that could be, and frequently was, invoked in order to downgrade whole classes of discourse. It too provided a way of casting aspersions on those who engaged in such discourse or at least did so exclusively, inappropriately or unselfconsciously, without, that is, recognising what they were doing. Poets in general, for instance, at least in the view of some.[6]

But if it is easy enough to see how such a contrast could be used as an argumentative device, to claim superiority for one type of discourse over another, the question that must now be pressed is this: what justification was there, or could there possibly be, for the often repeated claim to be able to offer *logos* yourself on subjects where all that the opposition – your rivals – could manage was *muthos*, or even just *magia*? An attempted justification might well take different forms in different genres. In a historian it might be that you know the truth because you had conscientiously inquired, had collected and collated different stories, had spoken to and cross-examined eye-witnesses or maybe even (like Thucydides sometimes) been an eye-witness yourself.

The *form* of the justification is easy to discern: yet the questions persist. Thus while Herodotus often goes out of his way to record divergent opinions on events, it is sometimes far from clear on what grounds he himself eventually settles for one view rather than another. It is not always evident that the versions on disputed points that he rejects are blatantly self-serving, for instance, or that their authors were notoriously unreliable. In most cases what is at issue is not a matter of comparatively straightforward fact, but one of motivation or interpretation. But how secure, for example, were the grounds on which he concluded, in the face of alternative accounts, that the view of most Greeks was correct, that Cleomenes' madness was a punishment sent from heaven for his attempt to suborn the Pythia in the matter of Demaratus' paternity, that is to give the judgement that Demaratus was not the son of Ariston (Herodotus VI 75ff.)?

Thucydides, too, for his part, may well insist that he is writing not just to entertain and that he has worked hard at sifting all the evidence, but while some of the grounds for his inferences are set out in the text, not all are exactly transparent. He repeatedly engages in interpretation of the motivations of Greek states, political groups or individuals, and in political analysis of a speculative type – for example concerning the general causes of *stasis* (III 82ff, cf below, p. 64). There is, to be sure, no reason why he should not do so. Of course there is no reason why his history should have been limited to the recording of easily checkable facts. But it also encompasses judgements that are a long way from being in any obvious fashion verifiable, not least concerning the general principle – that history broadly repeats itself – that underpins his claim for it as a 'possession for always'. That does not make his history *myth* (though Cornford's label 'mythistoricus' is not *totally* wide of the mark, Cornford 1907). Yet evidently many of the claims his history makes to give the truth, even to give a justifiable account, are contestable, to put it mildly. As a modern French ancient historian has put it: *'Thucydide n'est pas un collègue'* (Loraux 1980).

When we turn to the evidence for emerging Greek proto-science, the question of the grounds for the claims made by those who represent themselves as on the *logos* side of the *logos* versus *muthos* and/or *magia* divide is often more problematic still. Natural philosophy could be used to illustrate the point, but I shall concentrate on the richer materials from early Greek medicine, where indeed the issue takes a particularly poignant form in relation to claims to be able to achieve *cures*.

That medical theory and practice have – at long last – been put on a new and altogether sounder footing is a recurrent theme in Hippocratic treatises of quite different types. It is true that some of the hyperbole comes from the authors of sophistic exhibition lectures, or *epideixeis*, where the context of performance encouraged ostentation (see my 1987a, ch.2). Yet some of the claims themselves, however intended, are remarkable enough. Thus the writer of the treatise called *On the Art* includes in the definition of medicine the claim that it is able to remove the sufferings of the sick completely (ch. 3, 10 20ff). There are two main classes of diseases, he goes on, those where the signs are easily seen and those where they are not so clear. But in the former group 'in all cases the cures should be infallible, not because they are easy, but because they have been discovered' – and even in the latter group medicine should not be at a loss (chh. 9f, 15 11ff).

But such claims are not confined to those who may have had little or no experience of actual medical practice (as is the case with some of those authors of sophistic lectures). That is certainly not true of the author of the work *On the Places in Man* who nevertheless asserts (ch. 46, 342 4ff.): 'the whole of medicine, thus constituted, seems to me to have been discovered already [. . .] He who understands medicine thus, waits for chance least of all, but would be successful with or without chance. The whole of medicine is well established.'

There is a similar claim in the treatise *On Ancient Medicine* too, a work that has often been held up as a shining example of all that is best in Hippocratic medicine, if not a work by Hippocrates himself (and many have thought that as well).[7] 'Medicine', that treatise says (ch.2, 37 1ff.), 'has long had all its means to hand, a principle and a method that has been discovered, according to which many fine discoveries have been made over an extended period of time.' Moreover 'the rest too will be discovered', and (ch. 8, 41 8ff) 'the whole of this art of medicine could be discovered using the same method of inquiry'. Other theorists are attacked explicitly because what they propose is unverifiable, based on what the author calls 'hypotheses'. In emphatically rejecting the need for such 'hypotheses' in medicine he expresses his disapproval also of what he considers arbitrary speculation on such subjects as 'things in the sky' or 'things under the earth'. If anyone were to speak and declare the nature of these things, it would not be clear either to the speaker himself or to his audience whether what was said was true or not, since there is no criterion to which one should refer to obtain clear knowledge' (ch. 1, 36 18ff).

The self-consciousness of such a methodological statement is, for its time, remarkable and the principle is, no doubt, wholly admirable. One piquant and no doubt calculated feature of his attack is that it strikes at *anyone* who spoke about 'things in the sky' and 'things under the earth' without distinction: the would-be natural philosophers who did so were no better, by implication, than those who told myths about Zeus, Hades and Poseidon. Yet we have to ask how the author himself fares by his own high methodological standards. To meet those criteria his own theories should all be solidly grounded: yet they include an account of diseases as caused by depletion and repletion (ch. 9, 41 17ff.), and a theory that the elementary substances in the body are the bitter, the sweet, the astringent, the insipid, the acid and so on (ch. 14, 45 26ff.). Evidently these are supposed to be no arbitrary hypotheses. Evidently the author would wish us to believe that in these cases 'it would be clear' 'to the speaker and his audience' 'whether what was said was true or not'.

The topic of element theory attracts the wildest speculations from both medical writers and natural philosophers, often with no recognition, on their part, that their proposals are just that, for the most part wildly speculative (cf my 1979, pp. 139ff). In some cases, indeed, it is explicitly claimed not just that the theory is correct, but that it can be, or has been, *proved*. Thus the treatise *On the Nature of Man*, which we shall be considering in greater detail in this connection in chapter 3, first criticises various opponents who put forward monistic theories without proof: they add to their speeches 'evidences and proofs that amount to nothing' (ch. 1, 164 14). The writer then goes on to claim that he himself will 'produce evidences and declare the necessities' for his own theory. His view of the fundamental constituents of the body turns out to be that they are the four humours, blood, phlegm, yellow bile and black bile, but his vaunted evidence and proof depend chiefly on the observation that all four are found in the excreta. That shows well enough, perhaps, that all four are present in the body, but singularly fails to deliver on the promise to demonstrate that these are the *elements* of which the body is composed (chh. 2–7, 170 3ff.).

To be sure, to try to evaluate the claim made with regard to medical *practice* is generally a desperately tricky affair. To investigate where Hippocratic remedies differed from those of their rivals and how effective they were would require a lengthy digression. But some points are, broadly, clear. The main areas of innovation were in surgical practice and in dietetics, including drug therapy.[8] But in both cases some of the new techniques introduced were drastic and may well have done more harm than good. Thus one new-fangled dietetic fad was a reducing diet, but according to critics of the treatment among the Hippocratics themselves that sometimes amounted to seriously weakening the patients or even starving them. The excessive or inopportune use of fasting is criticised by the writer of *On Regimen in Acute Diseases* (ch. 11, 310 1ff, 316 9ff.) for instance. Again some of the surgical procedures described appear to be little more than adaptations of standard Greek instruments of torture: forcible straightening on the so-called Hippocratic bench, described at *On*

Joints chh. 72f, 296 6ff, and *On Fractures* ch. 13, 462 7ff. bears an uncanny resemblance to the rack. Several writers exhibit a certain ambivalence about what they call 'mechanical methods'. Dealing with attempts to reduce humpback by succussing the patient, the treatise *On Joints* (ch. 42, 182 13ff.) condemns the practice as being merely spectacular, carried out just 'to make the crowd gape' – at the bedside, indeed – 'for to such it seems marvellous to see a man suspended or shaken or treated in such ways; and they always applaud these performances, never troubling themselves about the result of the operation, whether bad or good. Yet this same treatise then goes on to endorse and recommend a modified version of succussion in some cases itself (chh. 43f. and 70, 184 5ff., 288 11ff.).

Yet although there are exceptions, in the main most of the Hippocratic doctors depended on the same traditional therapies that had been available for centuries in ancient Greece. Some may – but then again some may not – have been more cautious in their use of those therapies, and certainly many developed impressive diagnostic skills. But on the whole they relied very much on the same techniques of cure. We can be fairly confident, from what some of the more unassuming and modest medical authors themselves say, that those remedies were largely ineffective in the treatment of the more severe or 'acute' diseases. Many references in the *Epidemics* and elsewhere testify honestly to the helplessness that many physicians felt when confronted with what they call pneumonia, pleurisy and the like. Indeed the need to watch out for intractable cases, and the advice *not* to take them on, are recurrent themes, although to be fair it should be added that some doctors insist that even incurable cases should not be abandoned.[9]

The treatise *On the Sacred Disease* provides an opportunity to take stock of several of the points I have made so far. This author engages in all-out polemic against those who thought of the sacred disease (that is, epilepsy) as indeed caused by divine or demonic forces, people he labels 'vagabonds' 'charlatans' 'purifiers' and – precisely – 'magicians' (ch. 1, 354 12ff., cf my 1979, pp. 15ff.). This disease is like any other, he claims: it has its own nature and its specific natural causes. What he offers in place of the 'magic' of the purifiers is, then, a naturalistic account, and there is no doubt that he does a remarkable hatchet job on the opposition – though I shall come back to them in a minute. He attacks them not just for their ignorance, but also for deceit, fraudulence, inconsistency and even impiety. Yet when we press the question of how well-grounded the Hippocratic writer's *own* theories are, the admiration we may feel for his no-nonsense, anti-mumbo-jumbo stance has rather to be qualified.

As I pointed out in *Magic, Reason and Experience* (pp. 20ff.) many of this author's own anatomical theories are quite fantastical. What is particularly striking is that he is one of the few Hippocratic writers who refer to the possibility of carrying out a dissection to check a theory. To show that the sacred disease has natural causes, he suggests a post mortem exam-ination of the brain of a goat purportedly suffering from the same disease. 'If you cut open the head,' he says (ch. 11, 382 8ff.), 'you will find that the brain is wet, full of fluid and foul-smelling, convincing proof that disease and not the deity is harming the body'. At the same time it evidently did not occur to him to use this method to check his own anatomical descriptions of the courses of the veins leading to the brain – and this despite the fact that they play a crucial role in his own naturalistic explanation of epilepsy, which he believes to be caused by bile and phlegm blocking the veins. He directs some well-aimed blows at the purifiers who 'diagnosed' one type of epilepsy as the work of the Mother of the Gods, a second that of Poseidon, a third that of Enodia and so on (ch. 1, 360 13ff.). Yet his own talk of bile and phlegm coursing round the body, and his own account of the vascular system by which they are conveyed, while different in *style*, to be sure, are also very largely a product of his imagination.

To prefer the Hippocratic approach to that of the purifiers you needed already to be persuaded in advance that the former was at least on the right lines. The claim for superior rationality had to rely on the notion that bile and phlegm are visible substances and *the sort of* substances that could cause disease – whereas the Gods (you assumed *a priori*) could not or would not. Again it might be conceded that the *actual* description of the courses of the blood-vessels may not be accurate, but it was never-theless *the kind of* account that could be got right – by using the very method, post-mortem dissection, that the author of this treatise refers to, but does not then exploit to check his own anatomical theories. However as far as that Hippocratic work itself goes, the author does little to inspire confidence that his own approach *had* actually begun to deliver results.

Moreover we can press a similar set of questions with regard to his claims to be able to treat epilepsy and indeed to cure it. To suggest that purifications, charms and incantations do any good, he says (chh. 1 and 18, 354 12ff., 396 5ff.), is mere bluff and deception. But his own claim in ch. 18 (396 5ff.) is that 'a man with the knowledge of how to produce by means of regimen dryness and moisture, cold and heat, in the human body, could cure this disease too, provided that he could distinguish the right moment for the application of the remedies'. Nor is it just epilepsy that he thinks he can diagnose and control. An earlier chapter gives an equally confident account of the different kinds of *madness*, some caused by bile and others by phlegm (ch. 15, 388 12ff). These too, he implies, are curable by controlling temperature and humidity by regimen, for the

51

therapeutic principles he sets out in ch. 18 (394 19ff.) are claimed to be valid for *every* kind of disease.

But who, we might ask, is bluffing now? The claims that this writer makes for the art of healing as he practises it are hardly less extravagant than any his opponents can have made. It might look, on this basis, as if this is not a confrontation between science (even proto-science) and magic, but between one kind of magic and another, or at least between one kind of rhetoric and another – one (that of the purifiers) that sticks close to traditional patterns of belief concerning the power of the gods, the importance of purification and so on, and another (that of the would-be rationalists) that offers an alternative discourse, but that is just as hopelessly overoptimistic in what it asserts it can achieve.

The case for the Hippocratic approach depended, we said, on the promise of *eventual* delivery: correct naturalistic diagnosis and effective treatment of epilepsy and madness – as of other less serious sicknesses – would one day be possible. The purifiers attacked in *On the Sacred Disease* themselves have no chance to answer back (though we do have some later articulate ancient defenders of temple medicine, such as Aelius Aristides: Behr 1968). But what arguments might be adduced on behalf of those who used the discourse of the divine or demonic in their medical practice? One possible defence that might be used derives from the Malinowskian thesis that magic is generally used in cases beyond the technological control of the society concerned (Malinowski 1922, 1935, Evans-Pritchard 1937, Horton 1967, cf. Tambiah 1973, p. 226). Charms and incantations, it might be pointed out, were here being employed in just such a case. Yet while that suits the particular case of *epilepsy* very well, it will not do as a general argument. For we know that temple medicine, at least, was far from confining itself to intractable diseases, but claimed to be able to deal with everything from cases of headache and insomnia to non-medical misfortunes, such as losing some valuables.[10]

Another line of argument is more promising, though it too needs qualifying. The proper way to judge the main categories of ritual activity that are labelled as magic – it has been said – is not in terms of efficacy, but in terms of felicity – where the issue is not whether the behaviour achieves a practical result, but whether it has been carried out correctly, in a way that accords with social expectations.[11] Thus to take an example from our own culture, much of the ritual of a wedding ceremony in a Christian Church – the bride standing to the left of the groom, or having the ring put on the fourth finger of the left hand, or wearing white – should be judged not by canons of efficacy, but by those of appropriateness. It is not as if it is seriously believed that by showering the bride with confetti her fertility is promoted: though those who expect confetti-throwing at weddings might feel that without it, it had not, somehow, been a proper wedding.

That has, to be sure, been a most fruitful distinction to introduce. But two reservations are needed. First, to judge from the claims recorded in the inscriptional evidence for ancient temple medicine, as also from those attributed to the purifiers, these used the language of efficacy, not just that of felicity. However, secondly, what will count as efficacy can be far from straightforward. Effective treatment and cure will sometimes not be open to much doubt, any more than what counts as success in the matter of a lost piece of jewelry will be. But in such a case as epilepsy, we might ask, what is the *best* that could be hoped for? Where the patients themselves, or those around them, were liable to be alarmed at the devastating character of the onset of the sacred disease, the purifiers might argue that their symbolic diagnoses of which god is responsible and their recommendations about how to remove pollution offered worthwhile psychological support.

The distinction that Gilbert Lewis and others have insisted on, between disease and illness, is helpful here (Lewis 1975, pp. 148ff., cf. Frankel 1986, p. 5). The category that concerns the healer is much wider than the recognisable cases of people being sick; the healer has to do with anything that conflicts with *being*, including *feeling*, well. But then behaviour that stressed the social incorporation of the individual, or that helped to reintegrate him or her within society, would be more use – the temple healers as well as the purifiers might argue – than hardbitten talk of naturalistic causation backed up by lectures on physiology. To be sure, a Hippocratic might reply, in similar vein, that his naturalistic explanations at least removed the anxiety generated by a belief that an illness had been sent because you had offended some deity: but that too, of course, would be a matter of influencing the attitudes of the patients and of those around them, not of producing a cure.

Where, as with epilepsy, some kind of psychological support was the *most* that could be hoped for, then everything would depend on the prevailing attitudes of those to whom that support was being offered. The Hippocratic approach might suit one type of clientele. But the temple healers, for their part, and the purifiers, for theirs, might argue that their treatments drew on a more deeply rooted set of traditions and assumptions and so would be more helpful, where most ancient Greeks were concerned, than the Hippocratic brand of rationalism. The temple healers and purifiers might, then, justify their treatments in terms not *just* of felicity, but also of efficacy, but efficacy, here, that was, precisely, a matter of what was felicitous or appropriate.

These are arguments and considerations that *we* might supply. Moreover they presuppose concessions that the temple healers could not afford to make, at least not too publicly. In public – as is clear from the inscriptional evidence again – their stance was that the god can do anything. The strength of the consolation they offered depended on their – or at least their patients' – belief in that proposition. But even in direct confrontation with the self-styled rationalists, and on the grounds on which those rationalists themselves chose to fight the battle (namely efficacy), they had possible lines of defence and of attack. Meanwhile to their contemporaries – to the Greeks who, we should recall, continued to flock in great numbers to the shrines of Asclepius throughout the classical and Hellenistic periods – it is not that temple medicine seemed to them in an untenable position, for all the intellectual onslaughts of the Hippocratics and others.[12]

The puzzle may be, rather, to see where the attraction of the self-styled rationalists' approach lay and that leads us back to the question of how well grounded their attacks on *muthos* and *magia* were. Caution, on three separate scores, must be expressed. First, much of *muthos* is not a matter of what can or should be verified, and much of *magia* is in any case a matter of felicity, not one of efficacy. Over large areas of belief and behaviour there need be, or should be, no question of myth, magic and ritual being in direct conflict with science or unable to coexist with it (cf Tambiah's idea of the 'multiple orderings of reality', Tambiah 1990). Secondly, even in the matter of efficacy, what will count as such is often fuzzy-edged, unclear and open to negotiation – though sometimes, to be sure, there will be little room for such negotiation and in such cases or areas a conflict between alternative approaches *may* arise *if* there are alternatives. Thirdly, so far as being able to deliver on their *own* promises of understanding and effective control goes, the Hippocratic doctors sometimes seem to be on ground that is as shaky as that of their opponents.

That last caution represents a point that was already well taken in the ancient world. Later ancient medical writers themselves occasionally berated the Hippocratics both for their fanciful treatments and for their fantastic theories. As an example where both were criticised, there is the belief that the womb moves around inside the female body causing all kinds of disruption and disorder. This idea is found in several of the Hippocratic gynaecological and pathological treatises such as *On the Diseases of Women* II (chh. 123–31, 266 11ff), as well as in a famous text in Plato's *Timaeus* (91c, cf my 1983, pp. 83f., King 1983). However it gets short shrift from the second-century A.D. gynaecological writer Soranus, who indeed repeatedly criticised Hippocrates or his followers (I ch 45, III ch. 29, IV chh. 13–15). It is nonsense to suppose, Soranus says (III ch. 29, 112 10ff., 113 3ff.), as some people have, that the womb is like some living creature and that it can be persuaded to return to its proper place in the body by being coaxed by sweet-smelling fumigations applied below, at the vagina, and repelled by bad odours administered above, at the mouth. 'For the womb is not like a wild animal, issuing forth from its lair, delighted by fragrant odours and fleeing bad smells.' The situation in medicine is, then, analogous to that which we found in the writing of history. You might accuse your opponents – according to genre – of mere story-telling, or mumbo-jumbo, or superstition (*deisidaimonia*). But the counter-charge, the come-uppance, that you yourself were doing no better, could also often be made, and often was, if not in your own generation, then in subsequent ones.

When due weight is given to those three points, we may wonder what basis was left for the would-be rationalists' assault on what they disapproved of, even while there can be no mistaking their disapproval. A natural reaction would be to dismiss most of what I optimistically called 'proto-science' as not even 'proto', as no better than the 'myths' and 'magic' that these same writers spent so much time and energy combatting and refuting. Certainly some extraordinary theories and practices were advocated by the self-styled proponents of rationality. But that was not all there was to it. First there are exceptions to the rule of exaggerated or over-optimistic claims. Besides, this very feature of much Greek proto-science, the elements of bluff and exaggeration, itself may provide important clues concerning the situation within which that proto-science itself developed. Finally the differences between the rhetoric of *logos* and the practice of *muthos* altered the very framework within which a debate could take place.

To illustrate the first point very briefly: of course qualifications need to be made to the thesis of bluff and counter-bluff that I have presented, and the eventual results of Greek science are not as impoverished as I might be taken to have implied, at least in the matter of the understanding achieved, even if less often in that of any increased control of nature to which that understanding led. There are contexts where the claims made by the scientists are not obviously excessive, and where a method, for instance, was not just imagined to be applicable, but actually came to be applied, and applied successfully to yield what can only be described as new discoveries and insights in cases where there could be little room for doubt as to what counted as an advance in understanding.

The nature of those successes differs in different fields. There were not so many clear-cut discoveries in medicine proper, for instance, as in anatomy. But even in medicine one important advance in Greek diagnostic procedures came with the discovery of the value of the pulse in that regard, an achievement attributable to Praxagoras in the late fourth century B.C. In anatomy, however the successes of the fourth and third centuries were considerable. First Aristotle actually applied the method of dissection fairly extensively to animals, and then shortly afterwards the Hellenistic biologists Herophilus and Erasistratus dissected human subjects as well. Indeed according to our chief source, Celsus (*On Medicine* I Proem 23f, 21 15ff.), they practised not just human dissection but also human vivisection (on criminals obtained from the kings, i.e. the Ptolemies). How extensive the latter was is not at all clear, but Herophilus and Erasistratus were certainly responsible for some major advances in anatomy, for the discovery of the nervous system, for example, as well as for the first detailed descriptions of the valves of the heart, of the ventricles of the brain, and of the ovaries (von Staden 1989).

Again in mathematics and the exact sciences, the ancients were impressed – and with reason – by the results obtained in the systematic study of harmonics, for instance, in optics (in the study of reflection and refraction especially) and in the development of geometrical models providing a framework for astronomical theory. Some of the results obtained in these fields depended on empirical research and on the development of experimental methods (see Lloyd 1964 and 1979, ch. 3, von Staden 1975). But more often the advances came from the application of mathematics to physical problems and the development of axiomatic, deductive demonstration (which we shall be analysing in chapter 3). It would, however, be a mistake to think that it was *just* in argument that the Greeks (even the chief spokesmen of *logos*) excelled. Nor did *all* the applications of mathematical notions produce durable results. Certainly in many cases such a claim can be made, as in statics, in hydrostatics and in parts of harmonics, optics and astronomy. We may also note that greater importance came to be attached to exactness both in the formulation of theories and in the data used to support them: we can trace not just how measurement came to be used in different inquiries, but also how the concept came to be made explicit (Lloyd 1987a, ch. 5). Yet in other cases the search for the quantitative – in ancient as in modern times – led to nothing more than spurious precision or even mere *ad hoc* numerology. We shall be coming back to the variety of studies that passed as some kind of mathematisation of physics in chapter 3.

My second reason for not being too hastily dismissive of even what seem the flawed features of this proto-science was that the very weaknesses of early science may help to reveal significant factors relating to its first beginnings – that is, so far as ancient Greece is concerned. Where we associate science with the delivery of confident results, in Greek proto-science we sometimes have the theory of how the results *might be* delivered without any *actual* concrete delivery. How did that happen?

How did the theory of methods and procedures sometimes develop in advance, as it were, of their effective implementation?

We have already mentioned, in chapter 1, the competitiveness of the situation within which many of the Greek proto-scientists worked, and this may provide us with our first clue. The suggestion would be that one consequence of that situation was the development of a certain methodological self-awareness, at least in certain quarters. That the situation was intensely competitive has by now perhaps become sufficiently clear. If you were a Hippocratic, as we said, you had not just purifiers and temple healers and, come to that, other Hippocratics to contend with, but quite a few other groups who claimed in one way or another to be able to heal or help the sick, the root-cutters, the drug-sellers and the midwives. The relations between these various groups were, we noted, far from all or always polemical – although criticism of others was not confined to the literate spokesmen of Hippocratic rationalism.

Negatively that competitive situation manifests itself in the elements of stridency and bluff that we have remarked. However, positively, it may be seen as contributing to a certain self-awareness, at least in some writers. One recurrent phenomenon, not just in medicine, but also in philosophy and even in mathematics, is the attempt at explicit self-definition, the concern to state what, in the eyes of the authors in question, marks out *their techne* (art, craft or science) from others, or *their* approach to that *techne* from other approaches. But the purpose of that exercise was often, of course, implicitly or explicitly to claim superiority for the writer's own procedures.

Thus the author of the treatise *On the Art* whose exaggerated claims we remarked before, began with an attempted *definition* of medicine (ch. 3, 10 19ff): 'first of all I define what I take medicine to be'. We have noted his – over-optimistic – answer: the infallible cure of diseases with visible signs and the alleviation of the rest. With greater sophistication the writer of *On Ancient Medicine*, as we saw, differentiates not just between competing theories of diseases, for example, but between different *methods*, his own, supposedly based on long experience, and that of his opponents who adopt arbitrary hypotheses. Indeed in this case the writer is concerned not just with different approaches to medicine, but with the relationship between medicine and natural philosophy. It is in the latter domain that the method he objects to is most used (ch.1, 36 15ff.) and he explicitly attacks Empedocles among others for holding that the inquiry into nature in general is prior to medicine (ch. 20, 51 6ff.).

It certainly could not be claimed that the type of internecine rivalry that existed between intellectuals of various kinds in the fifth and fourth centuries in Greece *inevitably* led to the raising (by some of them) of second-order questions about the nature, status and methods of the various branches of the inquiry concerning nature and of other types of investigation. On the other hand it is surely likely that that rivalry *stimulated* interest in those questions; a claim to overall superiority could be given all the greater scope by being grounded in a fundamental contrast between *methodologies*. As for the importance of those second-order questions themselves, that can hardly be doubted. If we ask where the distinctive *Greek* contributions to early Western science lie, it is in that area that one of the most important parts of the answer is to be found. It is certainly not the case that the Greeks invented medicine, or mathematics, or astronomy. On the other hand, in the West at least [13] they were, so far as we know, the first to engage in self-conscious analysis of the status, methods and foundations of those inquiries, the first to raise, precisely, the second-order questions.

The rivalry that obtained in speculative thought may be seen as just one aspect of the well-known agonistic traits that are so widespread in Greek culture generally. But we can be more specific. The particular type of *agōn* or contest that repeatedly serves as a model in early Greek philosophy and science is – as many before me have said – that of the law-suit or political debate, and the question we should now investigate is how far the distinctive features of Greek philosophical and scientific activity may be thought to reflect the social and political circumstances of the society that produced it.

First it is important to distinguish between different types of connection that might be posited. Of course we can *infer* certain features of the social and political circumstances from the very nature of the intellectual debates that occurred in early Greek speculative thought. Thus the rivalry we have spoken of in speculative thought, where new-style claimants to knowledge emerged to challenge those traditional repositories of wisdom, the sages, poets and religious leaders, tells us something about the society in question, notably the lack of a rigid authoritarian structure controlling those who wanted to set themselves up whether as teachers for example, or as healers. There was certainly no such authoritarianism in early Greek religion. Indeed the competitiveness of Greek culture was sanctioned by religion, in the sense that one of the chief contexts for official competitions, not just in athletics, but also in poetry and music, was provided by the festivals held in celebration of one or other deity.

Again we can point to *parallelisms* between features of intellectual inquiry and aspects of political life, as when we remark on the similarities in the form of debates in various areas of speculative thought and those in the legal or political arena. But apart from parallelisms, how far does it seem possible to trace *direct influences* or *causal connections* between features of the political and social situation and the development of those early scientific inquiries? How far do political and social factors help to explain the rise of science in Greece, that is of the particular types and styles of inquiry initiated there?

It is prudent to enter an immediate disclaimer. Evidently there can be no question of anything approaching a simple, let alone a single, causal explanation of the highly complex and heterogeneous phenomena we refer to under the rubric of the emergence of Greek science. Necessarily many other factors besides the political and social would have to be brought into consideration in any attempt at a comprehensive account. The aim of my discussion here is rather to see *how far* we can take the hypothesis of social and political influences on the development of Greek science.

Let us take up first some of the parallelisms I mentioned. The representation of philosophical and scientific inquiry as essentially a *contest* between opposing points of view is no merely literary figure of speech. Throughout Aristotle's *Topics* the discussion of dialectical method presupposes a context of opponents in argument striving for victory, by fair means or, we might add, by foul – provided you are not found out, though the reasoner who *just* exploits appearances is dubbed eristic or contentious. Similarly in the *Rhetoric* the recurrent preoccupation is with persuading an audience and having your point of view prevail. Dialectic and rhetoric are, of course, in Aristotle's view, of general use and applicability across the board in any domain of human reasoning. But in the specific field of cosmological inquiry he notes at one point (*On the Heavens* 294b7ff.) that there is a general tendency for theorists to pursue an investigation only up to a point. 'This is a habit we all share, of relating an inquiry not to the subject-matter itself, but to our opponent in argument.' Again the author of *On the Nature of Man* (ch.1, 166 2ff.), criticising his monistic opponents, refers to the debates they hold and counts it as a bad mark against them that 'the same man never wins three times in succession', but now one, now another, whoever happens to have – as he puts it – 'the glibbest tongue in front of the crowd'.

More generally, the evidence that the Greeks appealed to in science as well as in the law-courts and in history, are witnessings, *marturia*.[14] Some of the proofs, *tekmēria*, they aim for are what will persuade an audience, though eventually (as we shall see in chapter 3) demonstration, *apodeixis*, came to be given a rigorous technical definition in Aristotle's formal logic. Again several of the terms for testing and scrutiny, *elenchos, dokimazein, basanizein*, have technical, often primary, uses in the legal/political domain, of the examination of witnesses, of the testing of a candidate's eligibility for office, of the torture to which slaves had, in principle, to be submitted when called as witnesses.[15]

We saw that much of the use of the vocabulary of verification, accountability, testing, evidence, proof, in *scientific* debate outran the substantial points actually being made by those who used that vocabulary. Yet over and above the occasions when such discourse *had* some justification in those debates, we should recognise that its attraction lay, in part, in the already acknowledged role of that same discourse in the context of litigation and political argument. Indeed the legal procedures that that vocabulary reflects themselves had origins that can be traced back, in some cases, into the archaic period,[16] even while our direct evidence for the use of the terms themselves, in law and politics, becomes appreciably richer in the fifth century. Those terms were not necessarily just *borrowed* from those other domains and then grafted on to science; but their intelligibility and popularity *there* may (I suggest) owe something to their deployment *elsewhere*. The suggestion then would be that the style and sophistication of much early Greek philosophical and scientific debate presuppose an audience who were experienced judges of argument, and if we ask where they gained that experience, the political and legal domain supplies a large part of the answer.

But over and above the general considerations I have so far adduced – the agonistic features of Greek culture, the extensive political experience of many Greek citizens, and the importance of the legal institutions of the Greek city-state – a further specific, but admittedly far more speculative line of argument is worth exploring in connection with a particular feature of the way in which the political alternatives were presented or imagined in classical Greek debate. How far, we may ask, does it seem possible to connect the emergence of Greek scientific rationality with the ideology of democracy in particular? That is not a new idea either, of course: yet it seems possible to refine and modify, and so strengthen, the argument.

I note immediately, however, two possible difficulties to meet which we shall have to introduce some preliminary qualifications. First the thesis might be thought to fail on the straightforward chronological grounds that early Greek philosophy and science antedate the institutions of democracy and so the latter cannot be held to have been a factor contributing to the development of the former. Secondly it might be objected that if the thesis had something to it, it would prove too much, since, after all, early Greek philosophy and science are certainly not confined to the democracies.

To take the chronological objection first, its force depends entirely on what are thought to be the key moves in the two developments (1) of philosophy and science, and (2) of democracy. So far as actual dates go the first two Ionian philosophers, Thales and Anaximander, are roughly contemporary with Solon and Pisistratus in the early and mid sixth centuries respectively.[17] If, as can plausibly be argued, the institution of the full democracy at Athens was the result of the reforms of Cleisthenes in 508 B.C., then there can be no question of saying that they could have influenced the first Ionian philosophers. However, if that is undeniable, that is far from being the end of the matter, for both the developments in question are more complex than that argument allows to appear. First, so far as philosophy and science go, what I have taken to be *chiefly* constitutive of these are the second-order questions, and these only begin to be raised some time later than Thales, that is to say in the epistemological debate that begins with Heraclitus (at work around 500 B.C.) and more especially with Parmenides (who was born between 515 and 510 B.C. and whose work therefore dates from the early fifth, not late sixth, century). As for the most important medical and mathematical writers with whom we are concerned, they were active in the mid or late fifth century, when indeed they do not belong to the fourth, and there can be no question of *their* not being well aware of what, in those centuries, democracy was held to stand for.

Moreover, secondly, while it was Cleisthenes who was responsible for establishing the full democracy at Athens, we should not forget that to some ancient writers it was Solon who *initiated* the democracy there, viz. with his reforms in 594. One of our most important sources is the Aristotelian *Constitution of Athens*, though whether it is an authentic work of Aristotle himself or composed by one of his pupils or associates is disputed. The view that text expresses (41.2) is that the democracy had its starting-point (*archē*) with Solon. The most democratic features of his reforms are specified, namely the prohibition of loans secured on the person, the ability to seek redress on behalf of any injured party, and the right of appeal to the jury-court (9.1). That last was the crucial factor, for it was said to have the consequence that 'being master of the vote, the people became master of the constitution'.

So while Cleisthenes' constitution was recognised as being *more* democratic than Solon's (41.2), three features that form (as we shall see) an important part of the later democratic ideology are already present in Solon's work. These are (1) the importance of the access of all (all citizens, that is) to justice, (2) a certain policy of openness, manifest in his promulgating his reforms publicly and in explicitly justifying them in the poems that have come down to us,[18] and (3) the possibility of radical constitutional change, though in Solon's case his opportunity for reforms came as a result of the crisis in Athenian public life. Our reaction to this first objection, then, is to insist *both* that Greek philosophy and science are gradual developments (where the most important work was done in the fifth and fourth centuries) *and* that democracy itself *also* was.

Then to the second objection – that philosophy and science are not confined to democracies – a two-part answer can be given, one part in terms of *ideas*, the other in terms of *practice*. So far as the influence of ideas goes, the point is simple: you did not, of course, have to be pro-democratic or to live in a democracy to be influenced directly or indirectly by ideas associated with its ideology. Secondly so far as practice goes, even though democracy and oligarchy were regularly *defined* as antonyms of one another, on the key issue of the extent of political involvement and participation the differences between the two, in practice, can be represented as matters of degree rather than of kind. The essential point is that in both types of constitution discussion and deliberation on the important political issues took place: it is just that in the oligarchies those who participated, those with whom the final decision rested, were a smaller proportion of the total population. A balance must then be struck: the democracy is an extreme manifestation one may say of certain principles exemplified by the city-state, the *polis*, itself; but that should not lead us to underestimate the point that much of the advocacy, or propaganda, for those principles belonged to the democratic ideology.

With those provisos duly entered, the positive point I wish to explore is the recurrent theme of the potential ability of everyone (again to be understood as every citizen) to participate in the political process, to be, if not themselves initiators of political proposals, at least responsible judges of those put forward by others. They needed to be – or at least they needed to be represented as such – since in their hands lay the ultimate decisions right across the spectrum of political life. Theirs was the deciding voice in the law-courts, where as dicasts they combined the functions we would associate with both jury and judges. In the assembly they voted on peace and war, strategy and tactics, on the constitution itself. The decisions they made, moreover, directly affected themselves. If the vote was for war, it was those who were there voting who then formed the army and navy that had to fight it.

At Athens, as Loraux (1986) especially has shown, one of the most important vehicles for the expression of the ideology of the democracy was the Funeral Speech, the best known example of which is the one Thucydides puts into the mouth of Pericles (II 35ff.). There the emphasis could hardly be stronger on the point that *all* have equal justice, *all* partake in the affairs of state, in the formation and implementation of policy (II 37, 40). The man who does not participate in political life, Pericles is made to say, is not considered – as by implication he might be in other states – merely an *apragmōn*, a man who quietly minded his own business. In Athens he was considered positively useless (II 40, cf. 63: Carter 1986, Farrar 1988, pp. 103f.). Moreover what that Funeral Speech *praises* corresponds well enough to what Plato so often *condemns*, in his vivid descriptions of the chaos of political life when everyone thinks he can have a say, where there are no experts, let alone the kind of ruler Plato himself hoped for, the philosopher-kings of the *Republic*.[19]

Now the argument I would mount does not concern the *realities* of democratic life, but rather, as I said, its *ideology*; that is the crucial modification to be made to some theses concerning Greek science and Greek politics. The realities of the decision-taking process in fifth-century Athens were no doubt very different from the image Thucydides makes Pericles present, and in any case that image is in stark conflict with Thucydides' own descriptions of the Athenian assembly in action – of its fickleness, irresponsibility and lack of judgement, especially once Pericles was dead.[20] No doubt in practice the political clout exercised by different citizens varied enormously. At many points we have direct evidence of the influence of wealth, birth and connections, and elsewhere the question is not whether, but how, they were at work.

The realities of the society that has often been held up as a paradigm of openness were, no doubt, nothing like as open as its propaganda presented. At the same time it *was* a propaganda of openness. Even if in the often grim realities of actual political life some citizens were definitely more equal than others, the ideology of the democracy provided a powerful statement of one point that is fundamental for other areas of Greek self-conscious rationality, namely the principle that in the evaluation of an argument it is the argument that counts, not the authority, status, connections or personality of its proponent. Of course it is no more true of Greek intellectual debates in other fields, than it is of Greek political life, that those who evaluated arguments discounted who it was who proposed them. Plato had already referred in the *Phaedrus* (271a ff.) to the theme of fitting speeches to audiences, and Aristotle goes further. He makes explicit allowance for that factor in his *Rhetoric*, where he identifies the *character* of the speaker as contributing importantly to his being or not being persuasive and offers advice about how to *seem* to have the right kind of character (*Rhetoric* 1356a1ff., 1366a23ff., 1377b21ff.). Nevertheless in principle that factor should, at least in the view of some, be discounted, and in the process much that had been sanctioned merely by traditional authority became open to challenge and was in fact challenged.

Acountability, evidence, proof, all had acknowledged roles, we said, in the general discourse of political and legal life. But for one further principle that is important to the new rhetoric of science it is not enough to refer to these general models. In the law-courts, at least, opposing litigants had to take the existing laws as given (however much they might seek to reinterpret them for particular argumentative purposes). So too in politics, for sure, the constitution was in some sense given. Yet it was part of the ideology of the Athenian democracy, at least in the fifth century, that the people's assembly is plenipotentiary. It could decide whatever it liked, including to change the constitution.[21] Indeed in 411 B.C., remarkably, it was the democratic assembly that, according to Thucydides (VIII 67f.), voted itself for a time out of existence.[22]

Now it could not be claimed that this (theoretical) possibility of radical political revisability *directly produced* the radical questioning of accepted beliefs (about nature, causation, the origins of things and so much else) that is characteristic of much early Greek speculative thought. But several considerations suggest that there may be more to this than *mere* analogies or parallelisms. To begin with, it might be conjectured that the possibility of radical questioning in the political sphere may have released inhibitions about such questioning in other domains (nor can a feedback effect in the reverse direction be ruled out). That cannot be directly shown. On the other hand this much can be confirmed that there were many Greeks – and not just spokesmen representing the democratic ideology – who believed that the radical questioning of tradition in politics had particularly far-reaching repercussions on attitudes generally.

Three texts will serve to illustrate the point. First there is Thucydides' famous general account of the devastating effects of *stasis* – political faction – in the Peloponnesian War (III 82f). The upheavals in political fortune and the instability of government were accompanied not just by terrible cruelties and by an unprecedented cynicism in the political domain, but by a general moral degradation and by what Thucydides saw as the total perversion of the language used to express moral judgements. 'Unreasoning rashness', (*tolma alogistos*) for instance came to be judged to be 'courage favouring partisans' (*andreia philetairos*), while 'delay that was inspired by forethought (*mellēsis promēthēs*) was considered 'cowardice under a specious name' (*deilia euprepēs*). The traditional sanctions were all undermined, piety and oathtaking came to count for nothing, and there was a total absence of any foundation on which trust could be based (III 82.6, 82.8, 83,2).

Secondly, as we again learn from Thucydides, it was indeed part of the democratic ideology that the character of the constitution affects the lives of the citizens through and through. Pericles, as Thucydides represents him (II 37, 40), repeatedly juxtaposes the freedom and openness of Athenian politics with the freedom and openness the Athenians show in their conduct more generally. The greatness of Athens depends upon its constitution (*politeia*), its pursuits and customs (II 36). Although when he puts it, in the famous phrase, that 'we philosophise without softness', he does not mean, of course, that the Athenians all engage in philosophical speculation, it is nevertheless a claim in the more general and basic sense of the word that they 'love wisdom' (which leaves, to be sure, what counts as 'wisdom' quite indeterminate).[23]

Thirdly, and from a quite different standpoint, Aristotle records an argument that indicates that the connection between attitudes in politics and in other branches of knowledge had been drawn. This is to the effect that in every art – not just in politics, but also, for example, in medicine – the pursuit of what is good takes precedence over merely following tradition, and although Aristotle then goes on to criticise the argument, his grounds for doing so are also revealing. Politics is unlike other arts in one crucial respect, that law and custom depend, ultimately, for their acceptability, on habituation, and that takes time: so that to alter laws and customs too frequently is to weaken their authority. For Aristotle, too, as for so many others, the political domain is paramount and the key to people's attitudes. If the authority of tradition is open to challenge there, it is likely also to be elsewhere, and it is precisely because innovation in the political field has such far-reaching effects that particular caution is needed (in Aristotle's view) concerning the degree to which it should be permitted.[24]

The realities of political life were, we said, one thing, the imagination of possibilities in the ideology something rather different. Yet the final feature of the ideology that should be remarked is its limited capacity to deliver, not as much openness as it professed, for sure, but maybe more openness than might have existed but for the ideology. Here was a propaganda that was, to some extent, the prisoner of its own rhetoric – just as some high-minded scientific methodological statements also were. Of course reneguing on the fine-sounding political principles you claim to live by is always possible and often evidently happened in ancient democracies. Yet once the principles were as clearly and emphatically set out as those of the democratic ideology were, there was some dis-advantage in ignoring them completely. One disadvantage certainly was that it gave your political opponents (in your own or other states) an argumentative point to use against you. *They* could and would point to any failure to live up to the principles as evidence not just of your inconsistency and unreliability, but perhaps also of the impracticality of the principles themselves.

To illustrate the *risks* that the ideology of democracy took, the *actual* openness that stemmed in part from that ideology, and the *limits* to that openness, we may refer to a literary genre that while not totally confined to Athens is a distinctive product of its culture, namely tragedy. While tragedy is the genre, *par excellence*, that uses and reworks myth, it is easy to see that classic Athenian tragedies are much influenced by features of the social and political background that we have been discussing and not just in the well-known way in which Antigone and Creon, Electra and Clytemnestra and many others, reproduce, in their carefully balanced speeches, the antiphony of law-court speeches measured by the water-clock.[25] A number of scholars have recently posed the questions of whether, how, or how far, tragedy serves the ideology of the city-state, more strictly that of the democracy, more strictly still that of Athens itself (Vernant and Vidal-Naquet 1988, Goldhill 1986, 1987a, 1987b). On the one hand many of the circumstances that framed tragic performance in the theatre of Dionysus are ideologically loaded. Before tragedies were performed at the Great Dionysia, the war-orphans who had been educated and armed by the city were paraded before the spectators as they passed into the ranks of citizens, and this was also the occasion when the tribute received from Athens' allies was put on display. On the other hand the tragedies themselves question, undermine, subvert, as much as, or more than, they reaffirm the institutions of democracy, not least in their representations of heroes – from Oedipus to Antigone, from Philoctetes to Heracles – who passed as anything but model democrats.[26]

Yet perhaps at a second level the questioning of institutions, including those of the democracy itself, is a possibility that the democracy prides itself on permitting: in principle, that is, since in practice there were limits to how far even the democracy tolerated criticism of itself. The claim was that the democracy stood for free speech, *parrēsia*,[27] but those who took that claim too literally or imagined it extended indefinitely could find themselves in trouble – as Socrates discovered at the cost of his life. Comedy too illustrates both the freedom to criticise and the limits to that freedom. We hear from various sources of moves made against the comic poets,[28] and Aristophanes himself tells us in the *Acharnians* (502ff.) that Cleon indicted him for defaming the state in the presence of foreigners – though that did not put an end to Aristophanes' attacks on Cleon himself, at least according to Aristophanes. But the fact that the most concerted effort to curb free speech came when Athens was under the rule of the Thirty Tyrants, and that that freedom – including in the theatre – was restored when the democracy itself was, illustrates the value the democracy set on it not just in principle but also to some extent in practice.

For tragedy and comedy in their different ways, and with greater or less seriousness, to question, implicitly or explicitly, some of the institutions and beliefs of the democracy did not itself threaten, but even confirmed, the openness of those institutions. Not that it is enough to represent tragedy or comedy as mere permitted safety valves for public opinion, or as a recognised means of mediating conflicts (cf. Murray 1987) – for such views quite underestimate the complex nature of the real challenge they could and did present. Pericles, in the Funeral Speech (Thucydides II 38) is made to speak with pride about the Athenians' *agōnes*, their competitions, including undoubtedly those in the theatre of Dionysus. But the double-bind inherent in the democratic ideology was that, priding itself on its very openness, it had to include itself in what it allowed to be challenged, questioned, and even subverted and attacked.

The third and final question I mentioned at the outset concerned how far any historical study of the Greek contributions to science and to the category of magic can throw light on the framework within which they may be understood today. In Greek antiquity, I have argued, science needed, or at least it used, the contrasts with *muthos* and with *magia* (to a lesser extent also one with religion)[29] in its bid to define and legitimate itself. But now, with science not struggling to be born, but supplying the dominant model of rationality in our culture, it is rather the converse that holds. It is magic, in our society, that sometimes defines itself by contrast with science and religion: indeed some magicians claim that theirs is the true science, the true way not just to understanding but also to control, since it is not just felicity that is invoked as criterion (whether a ritual, for example a path-working, has *felt* right, for instance) but also *efficacy*, although the way in which magic is held to *work* will sometimes be glossed with the metaphor that it does so at a different level, on a different plane (I draw once again on Luhrmann's work, Luhrmann 1989). The level or plane metaphor allows head-on conflict to be avoided or deferred, securing at least a first-stage (even if fuzzy) defence for magic and some insulation to challenge on the score of efficacy. But with or without recourse to those metaphors, our remarks about the ancient purifiers illustrate that what counts as *working* – in the matter of healing, at least – often depends on what is *worked on*: it is one thing to change a person's temperature, another just their feelings, yet another just your own.

The situation once the category of magic as such became available exhibits certain analogies with the one we described in chapter 1 once the category of metaphor had been made explicit. The metaphorical–literal dichotomy was originally used by Aristotle in a way that clearly showed *his* preferences and value judgements; for science and philosophy, as for logic generally, only the literal will do. Yet the very same category of the metaphorical was used, and used self-consciously, already in later antiquity, in an attempt to protect certain ideas and beliefs from attack – except that, as we said, that defence was hardly satisfactory without overhauling the Aristotelian dichotomy itself, since the challenge could always be mounted, to give the literal account of which the supposed metaphor was a metaphor.

Analogously the self-conscious use of the category of magic sometimes discounts the pejorative undertones the terms in question generally carried in antiquity and in certain contexts still carry in English. Faced with what may be intended as labels of censure, if not of abuse, those called magicians – today at least – may accept the title with equanimity, even with some relish – except that for them to do so without redefining the terms in which the contrast between science and magic is generally construed will again hardly do. At least it runs the risk of expressing no more than a rejection of science, leaving the grounds for magic's claim for some special status quite undisclosed. Indeed those who insist on the ineffability of magic will insist further that they are in principle undisclosable.

Once again there is double-bind. For magic to compare itself directly with science and to claim to outdo it is in any case implicitly to acknowledge, even while it contests, the dominant role of science as a model of rationality in our culture: and for the claim to be sustained some response must be given to the demand to cash out the metaphors of planes and levels. But for magic to protest that that comparison is inappropriate still leaves unclear what claim is being made for it. It is true that our culture supplies other models besides science which can provide a framework within which magic can be understood, art, drama and not least religion itself. They too can be and have been exploited as ways of conceptualising the activities of magic: but again in those cases, too, the question arises of *how* magic is to be construed as art, drama, religion – of what *kind* of art, drama, religion it is. When 'magic' first became visible as such in Greece, it was cast in the role of an antonym of rational inquiry, of *logos*. In our own society, where much of the background of tradition against which the activities of 'magic' were understood has been eroded or has disappeared, it has to *create* its traditions and indeed the very context within which it can be understood, using for that purpose the resources provided by the dominant culture but very much dependent on the models it offers.

In early antiquity, however, before the loaded designations, magician, magic, had come to be in common use, those who would eventually be called by them – the ancient purifiers, for instance – proceeded and had to proceed in a way that was very different from their modern counterparts. The purifiers could not use *science*, at least, as a marker, and claim that somehow or other, on some 'plane' or other, what they did was the real thing of which the science we know in mundane life is just a poor reflection. They just got on with the job, of making more or less socially acceptable use of more or less traditional religious categories, certainly working within that traditional framework even if that framework was not so static and inflexible as to inhibit all possible creativity. But clearly their self-understanding, and the understanding that others in their culture had of them, depended on that relationship with tradition.

The questions, then, of how the actors themselves perceive their own activity, or the conventions within which it fits or from which it deviates, the traditions that do or do not sanction it, are prior to and independent of the question of the existence of some such category as magic itself. But once that category exists, it can hardly fail to change the perception. In that sense – as with the category of the metaphorical – the question of the availability of the explicit category is a crucial one: for the category enabled the challenge to justify the activity to be pressed. Once again an issue was forced, by that challenge, and the activity could no longer remain, or could not do so so easily, an unquestioned item invisible – or indistinctive – against the background of the traditions to which it belonged. Conversely it is also clear that, in the absence of the category, the answers to the questions of the relationships between the activities and beliefs that *we* might label 'magic' and the culture within which they fit will inevitably be multifarious and diffuse. This is not to say, any more than in the metaphor case, that the *substantive* problems of understanding many varieties of puzzling ideas, beliefs and behaviour thereby disappear, for they certainly do not. But it is to point out that a *general* theory of magic (including, that is, magic in the pre- or non-explicit situation) would be as chimerical as a general theory of tradition itself. *A fortiori* the need to invoke some mentality that corresponds to the phenomenon of magic *in general* lapses, even while specific patterns of belief and behaviour, and the way they are represented by the actors themselves, continue to pose problems of interpretation.

When science is rejected nowadays in the name of something different (and not just by magicians) that is in part a reaction to some of the continued aggressions committed in the name of rationality. These include, for instance, the demand for accountability, for verification (or falsifiability), for transparency, for pragmatic results, in contexts where they are *not* appropriate – as if *we* can get by *entirely* without myth, without symbolism, without metaphor and some of these at the heart of science itself. Certainly we have found – and for reasons I have tried to elucidate – that some extraordinary aggression was displayed in the name of *logos* in the early days of Greek science and that those who championed *logos* were often very bad at practising what they preached. Yet what they preached was not just more *muthos*, or *magia* in a different guise. In the field of natural science *some* of the confidence that was expressed – that the problems were soluble and on their way to being solved – had *some* basis, in the application of certain methods, whether of argument or of research. Eventually much of what the Greeks just *imagined* science could deliver, in terms of understanding and control, was indeed delivered, though usually not in ancient science. The surprise is that the Greeks developed much of the discourse of the methods before those methods had *in practice demonstrated* anything like their full potential. But if that is a surprise, one line of argument would be that reference to the social, legal and political background helps to explain *some* of the attractions that that discourse had for the ancient Greeks even before their science itself had chalked up any very considerable list of indisputable successes.

It is true that *in a sense* many of the methods the Greek proto-scientists applied are not new at all, but those that any human being uses in practical contexts or when faced with problems of understanding. Empirical methods of research develop from ordinary, common-or-garden observation, and no reader of Lévi-Strauss is likely to underestimate the extraordinary capacities for observation in what he calls concrete science (Lévi-Strauss 1966). What those Greek scientists who advocated *historia* did was just that, to *advocate* empirical research self-consciously. Again informal testing procedures and techniques of argument are, we might say, as old as the human race. What the Greeks did was to insist explicitly on testing and verifiability, and to carry out the first explicit formal analysis of schemata of argument.

But this making of methods, arguments, categories *explicit* was no trivial matter. The weapons the proponents of *logos* self-consciously deployed against others – in some cases invented to use against others – could be, and were, turned against themselves. Once the explicit ideal was that of being able to give an account, withstand scrutiny, let alone deliver practical results, the stakes being played for were higher. They might anticipate – some as we saw, certainly got – their come-uppance. Where what counted was just felicity, that was a matter of what corresponded to the expectations of society or a group, an essentially conservative or inward-looking criterion. Even though no tradition can afford totally to inhibit innovation, and in practice within the magical traditions there is much that is innovative, curiosity, even research and the beginnings, as Lynn Thorndike (1923–58) wanted it, of experimental science, nevertheless the appeal, implicit or otherwise, to tradition for validation looks backwards to the old not forwards to the new. The Hippocratic doctor who paid lip-service to the ideal of verification and to the test of experience might *only* be paying those ideals lip-service (and conversely, without any explicit methodology, a purifier or a temple-healer might *in practice* pay a lot of attention to experience). Yet the methodology, once made explicit, could guide the practice and it could help build into it an openness towards development.

Much of the ancient attack on magic appears misguided, and the criticisms narrow-minded, even bigoted. Yet there was something to disagree about, about criteria, methodology, aims, if not always also in practice/praxis. The rhetoric of science, even of proto-science, differs from that of magic, and differs too from the security of the traditional ways or of what Socrates called the unexamined life (Plato, *Apology* 38a). For whether or not the practitioners live up to the ideal, the ideal invokes examination and scrutiny and it leads – if not inexorably – outwards.

To emphasise, as I have done, the excesses committed in the name of rationality in the early days – and more recently – is not to say that the claims made were *all* excessive. To insist that there is much that lies – and may always lie – beyond its limits (as well as those of science) is not to be confused with some councils of despair. Certainly the celebration of the incomprehensible has often taken even more alarming forms that the tacit refusal to acknowledge its existence. But there are two dangers, not just one. The mistake the Greeks themselves often made was to believe in the imminent triumph of reason, as when the Hippocratic treatise *On Ancient Medicine* confidently predicts the future discovery of the whole of medicine (see above, p.48), or when Aristotle states his belief that nearly all possible discoveries and knowledge have been achieved already (*Politics* 1264a1ff., cf *Metaphysics* 981b20f.). That came partly from an optimism about the potentialities of methodical inquiry: though it was not just optimistic, but hopelessly over-sanguine, to imagine that the problem of the elementary constituents of physical objects, let alone all diseases, would soon be brought within the compass of scientific understanding and control. As for those who claimed they had already been, that was part of the tactics of persuasion, in the bid of the new-style wisdom to replace the old, but part also of the modes of self-deception that characterise that bid.

But conversely there is the mistake of an attempt to collapse, after all, the distinctions that those Greeks forged and made explicit in part in the rhetoric of persuasion. There is, to be sure, some truth in the claim that science is, as has been said, white mythology (cf. Derrida 1982). The ideological grip of science, its pretensions to unchallengeable status in certain contexts, its uncritical acceptance of questionable or downright inexcusable means for uncertain ends, have all to be debunked, and so too the mystifications perpetrated in the name of demystification. But that is not to deny, but rather to assert, that demystification here should be attempted, without believing that *ultimate* demystification can be achieved. The sources of inspiration, as Plato said (*Phaedrus* 244a ff.), in love, in poetry, in religion and in prophecy (and we can add to his list science too) are divine, under the aegis of the Gods. What was it to say this? Would it not be wise not to rush to assume that we can comprehend the problems to which that dark saying alludes? At the same time, the *results* of inspiration, as Plato also said (*Timaeus* 7le ff.), have generally to be evaluated by a 'man in his right mind', by *logos*. For the results of science, at least, we may agree that there is eventually no other way – even if we should also acknowledge that much else in human communication fails by the strictest tests of accountability that science would demand.

3

The conception and practice of proof

Our first two studies have explored the consequences of making the dichotomy between the literal and the metaphorical and the categories of myth and magic explicit. The argument has been that in each case, in origin, they played an important role in an ancient Greek polemic during which science and philosophy defined and legitimated themselves in contrast to the existing more traditional repositories of knowledge. Moreover the availability or otherwise of such explicit categories is one general criterion relevant to the analysis of differences within styles or modes of reasoning and argument. On the one hand there appears to be no justification, in these contexts at least, to talk either of divergent mentalities or of transformations in them. On the other the differences introduced by the use of explicit concepts of linguistic and other categories are reflected in important differences in styles of reasoning and of interpersonal exchange.

A further concept that offers a similar possible field of investigation is that of proof. The aim of the present chapter is to explore the evidence relating to the way in which that concept was first made explicit in ancient Greece, and the difference it made or the repercussions it had once it was available *as* an explicit concept. The practice of proof – in whatever area of thought – is of course far from confined to the Greeks, even among ancient civilisations: but the practice is one thing, having the explicit concept another. We shall see that in Greece two different and to some extent competing ideas come to be formulated during the fifth and fourth centuries B.C. and we shall also see that while the concept of rigorous proof had momentous consequences in a whole variety of domains of Greek thought – logic, mathematics, natural sciences, philosophy and medicine, for instance – not all those repercussions can be represented straightforwardly or unreservedly as positive ones. Finally the frequent use of both the practice and the notion of proof in the field of politics and the law will enable us to elaborate, and in one significant respect to modify, our thesis about the relationship between the development of intellectual inquiry and the social and political background in ancient Greece.

At the outset we must be clear that 'proof' and 'proving' may signify a variety of more or less formal, more or less rigorous, procedures. In some domains, such as law, proving a fact or a point of law will be a matter of what convinces an audience as being beyond reasonable doubt. Again in some contexts, including in mathematics, 'proving' a result or a procedure will sometimes consist simply in testing and checking that it is correct. Both of these are quite informal operations. But to give a formal proof of a theorem or proposition requires at the very least that the procedure used be exact and of general validity, establishing by way of a general, deductive justification the truth of the theorem or proposition concerned. More strictly still Aristotle was to express the view that demonstration in the fullest sense depended not just on deductive (he thought specifically syllogistic) argument but also on clearly identified premises that them-selves had to fulfil rather stringent conditions (see below, pp. 76f.). He was the first not just in Greece, but so far as we know anywhere, explicitly to define strict demonstration in that way.

Two crucial distinctions have, then, to be observed, (1) between formal proofs and informal ones, and (2) between the practice of proof (of whatever kind) and having an explicit concept corresponding to that practice, a concept that incorporates the conditions that need to be met for a proof to have been given.

That second distinction has, in my view, been ignored or badly underplayed in recent attempts to see the notion of proof as originating long before even the earliest extant Egyptian and Babylonian mathema-tics. The distinguished Berkeley mathematician Seidenberg has recently published a series of articles aiming to show that some highly sophisti-cated mathematical concepts, including the notion of proof, originate in Vedic ritual.[1] Now admittedly any attempt to interpret the exceptionally obscure and fragmentary evidence in Vedic texts is bound to be fraught with difficulty. Let us concede, however, the first step in Seidenberg's argument, which is that this evidence implies that Vedic ritualists had a mastery of certain geometrical procedures, of two kinds especially: (1) they could solve such problems as that of constructing an altar with an area in a given relationship to that of another altar by the application of certain rules, and (2), relatedly, they could evaluate correctly the areas of a variety of geometrical figures. Now as regards (1), to carry out a geometrical construction by itself is not to prove anything. But as regards (2), even if the Vedic ritualists knew how to get the right results in this type of case as well, viz., in establishing the areas of complex

74

figures that would still not give them any explicit notion of what proof is.

Of course, given the problems of interpreting this literature, and the difficulty, in any event, of establishing a negative proposition, we could not rule out that the Vedic ritualists had some such idea, even though there is no mention of it in our extant sources. That cannot be ruled out. But it must be held to be extremely unlikely. First there is an argument from within the Vedic evidence itself (the problems are set out in the Supplementary Note at the end of this chapter, pp. 98–104). This is that in the key texts we find no distinction observed between *exact* procedures and *approximate* ones. Both are used apparently indiscriminately, and that suggests that their authors were not concerned with *proving* their results at all, but merely with the concrete problems of altar construction.

Secondly the Greek evidence we shall be analysing in detail shows that notions of proof only came to be made explicit there at the end of a long and quite complex development. The practice of proof, in Greece, antedates by several generations the first explicit formal definition (first given by Aristotle in the fourth century B.C.) and the process whereby such notions as that of the starting-points or axioms came to be clarified was both hesitant and gradual. That long and complex development, in Greece, belongs to and is a further instance of the gradual heightening of self-consciousness we have exemplified before, when second-order questions came to be raised concerning the nature, status, methods and foundations of different types of inquiry. None of the attendant circumstances surrounding these developments, and none of the steps by which the various interrelated key notions came to be made explicit, can be paralleled in Vedic literature or in the evidence for Vedic society. If we cannot ourselves *prove* the negative, it remains, as I have said, an extremely *un*likely proposition.

A brief look at some other evidence will serve to drive home these points. If we turn to the far more abundant and more secure evidence for ancient near-Eastern mathematics, the importance of the two contrasts we have drawn, (1) between more and less formal proof, and (2) between the practice of proof and having the concept, becomes clear. The results obtained in both Egyptian and Babylonian mathematics are enormously impressive, and informal proof, both the practice and the concept, can occasionally be exemplified. But as for attempts to make the rigorous notion of proof explicit, they simply do not figure in our extant evidence. While again we cannot be sure that our evidence is not lacunose at just that point, that again seems improbable. We do find, however, in Egyptian arithmetic, for instance, a use of a notion of proof in the loose sense of the confirmation or checking of a result. In the Rhind Mathematical Papyrus, problems 32ff., for instance (Chace, Bull and Manning 1929, cf. Peet 1923, pp. 67ff), the scribe is represented as working through to the solution of a problem. Then he checks that his result is correct, in what is often translated into English, legitimately enough, as the 'proof'. At this point, then, we have an explicit notion corresponding to a regular mathematical procedure. However this is not proof in the formal sense we have defined (let alone an Aristotelian-style demonstration). What we have is, at most, a notion of the need for checking a result.

If we turn to other domains outside mathematics, and to modern societies rather than ancient ones, we can again confirm the relevance of our two distinctions. Interesting ethnographic evidence is available concerning a number of societies where skill in argument is highly developed and much prized, for example in the context of litigation. Gluckman's studies of Barotse law are perhaps the best known and fullest example (Gluckman 1967, 1972, cf. also ed. Bloch 1975). The Lozi have an extensive vocabulary of terms for describing various types of excellence – or failing – in argument. These relate to such matters as relevance (not straying from the point), astuteness in questioning, the ability to make the correct distinctions, being decisive in judgement and so on. In many ways the law-obsessed Lozi are strongly reminiscent of the highly litigious Greeks (Athenians especially) of the classical period. But while the Lozi have an operational notion of proof beyond reasonable doubt, that notion is still not made explicit, let alone made the subject of self-conscious analysis (Gluckman 1967, pp. 107ff, 137).

When we turn to the evidence on these matters from ancient Greece, we should begin, as usual, with a caution: our information on certain points is not as full as one should like and there are some particular gaps in the record and tricky problems of interpretation to which I shall be drawing attention in due course. But some points are sufficiently clear.

So far as our extant evidence goes (and here there is no need to suspect that we lack anything important) the first explicit analysis of proof in the strict sense comes (as I said) in Aristotle's formal logic. Aristotle also gives a full account of what counts as proof in rhetorical and dialectical contexts, where it is a matter not of incontrovertibility, but of what will persuade an audience, and there he is certainly drawing on earlier discussions, many by writers whom he cites by name. Plato especially had had much to say on persuasion, which indeed he often contrasted with proof though without giving a formal analysis of the latter (e.g. *Phaedo* 92d, *Theaetetus* 162e). Earlier still, we hear from both Aristotle and Plato of a series of writers who composed treatises on rhetoric called *Arts*, beginning with Corax and Tisias in the mid-fifth century B.C., and at *Phaedrus* 266e ff., 273a., Plato indicates that Tisias, Theodorus and Evenus dealt with aspects of proof and refutation, though we know nothing of the details.

But while in the study of rhetoric Aristotle was far from being the first Greek in the field, we have no reason to contradict his own claim, in *On Sophistical Refutations* (183a37ff., b34ff.), to have given the first formal analysis of deductive argument. He defines demonstration (*apodeixis*) as deductive, specifically syllogistic, in form, and as proceeding from premisses that must be true, primary, indemonstrable, immediate and indeed explanatory of the conclusions (*Posterior Analytics* 71b19ff.): for the knowledge or understanding that demonstration yields is, strictly, not of the mere facts, but of their explanations or causes. Thus Aristotle is clear on two fundamental points: (1) deductive argument is wider than demonstration, for deductive arguments may be valid or invalid, and valid deductions can be drawn from premisses irrespective of whether those premisses are true or false. (2) Not all true propositions can be demonstrated: for the primary premisses from which demonstrated conclusions follow must themselves be indemonstrable – to avoid an infinite regress. For what premisses could they be demonstrated from?

Aristotle's position is, on the whole, clear and well known. But when we try to trace the background and context of his work in this area, the problems are severe. How did it come about that the ancient Greeks developed this notion? Allowing always for Aristotle's own originality, the explicit concept of rigorous proof did not exactly spring fully armed, like some Athena, from his head. As possibly relevant antecedent factors, four different topics are worth following up, where again we shall need our distinction between informal, and strict, proof. The first of these is arguments in the legal and political domain, the second those in early Greek cosmology and medicine, the third mathematics in the pre-Aristotelian period, and the fourth deductive argument in philosophy. The first two of these relate, primarily, to informal, the second pair to rigorous, proof, and we shall pay particular attention to what these two concepts owed to each other.

The litigious Greeks had – like the Lozi – a rich vocabulary for use in the context of evaluating evidence, examining witnesses, arriving at an impartial judgement and so on. But (unlike the Lozi) they also refer explicitly to proving their case, using especially a variety of nouns and verbs, such as *epideixis, apodeixis, deiknumi* and its compounds, where the meaning of the main root is 'show'. We cannot date precisely when they were introduced, but we have ample evidence of their use from as soon as we begin to have extant original oratorical texts. These start in the middle of the fifth century B.C. with Antiphon, closely followed by Lysias, Andocides, Isocrates, Isaeus (late fifth, early fourth century) on down to

Aeschines and Demosthenes, and this evidence can be supplemented from that in other prose writers, the historians especially (cf my 1966, p. 424ff. for a summary account). 'Proof', we should note, can be attempted either with respect to the facts of a case (what was done or who did it) or with regard to their interpretation (the motives of the agents, for example) and especially concerning the guilt or innocence of the parties involved – a particularly prominent theme in Antiphon's *Tetralogies*. What counts as a proof is what the speakers believe will establish their point beyond reasonable doubt, though they are aware that their own claims to have proved their case will often be rejected by the other side – to whose objections they will in turn object (if they have the chance to do so) as being quite *un*reasonable.

The essence of the situation in the law-courts was *ad hominem* argument. Indeed this was so in two separate respects. First you had to defeat your opponent (prosecutor or defendant as the case may be) and meet his points with your own refutation of them. Then, secondly, the whole debate was directed, by both sides, at convincing the court – the dicasts who acted both as jury and judges – for it was after all their votes and their votes alone that counted.

The same vocabulary, not just of evidence, examination, judgement, but also proof, appears also outside the specifically legal or political domain, notably in a variety of contexts in early Greek speculative thought. Both cosmology and medicine provide examples, and some extended passages from the Hippocratic Corpus merit particular attention. As I have already noted in chapter 2, many medical theorists claim to have *shown* the doctrines they advance even on such difficult and obscure topics as the fundamental constituents of the human body, and some go even further and suggest that they have shown the *necessity* of their conclusions. The treatise *On the Nature of Man* provides some particularly striking instances of claims both to have proved certain theories positively and to have refuted rival doctrines.

In ch. 2 (170 3ff) the writer states: 'I for my part shall show [*apodeixō*] that the substances that I believe compose the human body are [. . .] always the same and unchanging: in youth and in old age, in cold weather as in warm. I shall produce proofs [*anagkas*] through which each thing is increased and decreased in the body.' His theory is that the body is made up of the four humours, blood, phlegm, yellow bile and black bile, and he mounts some telling arguments to demolish the position of those who had claimed that the body is composed of just *one* of these. 'In my opinion these views are incorrect, even though the majority declare that this, or something very like it, is the case. But I say that, if man were one thing, he would never feel pain, since if he were one, there would be nothing to

78

cause hurt. Moreover even if he should feel pain, the remedy too necessarily would have to be one. But in fact there are many remedies: for there are many things in the body which when they are abnormally heated or cooled or dried or moistened by one another cause diseases. Consequently there are many forms of diseases and many cures' (ch. 2, 168 2ff.).

The heart of the physician's argument is that experience shows that there is more than one essential constituent of the body. The argument is structurally an informal version of *reductio ad absurdum*, or at least can be represented as such. Suppose that human bodies were of only one substance, *then* certain conclusions would follow. But those conclusions contradict aspects of everyday experience, that bodies can feel pain, that there are different diseases with different causes and different cures. This contradiction of what we know shows that the initial assumption, that bodies consist of one substance, must be wrong.

But while the Hippocratic writer produces some good arguments to refute a rival view, when it comes to clinching the case for his own theory he is, as I have already remarked, much weaker. The main evidence he cites for his own element theory is that the four humours are all found in the excreta (chh. 5ff., 176 10ff, 180 2ff, 182 12ff, cf. above p. 49). Moreover a similar criticism can be made of many other theories claimed to have been proved by other early Greek medical and cosmological writers. Judged from the standpoint of formal demonstration, or even just of deductive argument, their performance often looks pretty feeble: the evidence cited is often well short of substantiating their claims, and the inferences are shaky, even if the premises are conceded (cf my 1987a, ch. 3 for further examples). But then it may be that that is not the right standpoint from which to evaluate such texts. It might be suggested that the more appropriate comparison is with those orators I have just mentioned, who claim that the witnesses on their side are the reliable ones and who end their perorations with the suggestion that all doubt on the issue has now been removed when they know very well that it has not. But if that is the comparison that is adopted, it shows how vulnerable those sections of early Greek speculative thought were to the criticisms of those who were, eventually, to demand rigorous demonstration in philosophy and science.

Alongside these and other contexts that illustrate merely informal (though self-conscious) notions of proof, there is good evidence for the development of formal techniques of demonstration in other areas, especially mathematics and philosophy. So far as Greek mathematics goes, our first really solid information relates to the work of Hippocrates of Chios some time around 430 B.C. (he is not to be confused with his namesake, the physician, Hippocrates of Cos). It is true that some of our later sources, such as Proclus (fifth century A.D.) ascribe a number of theorems and their proofs to much earlier figures, to Thales (c. 585 B.C.) and Pythagoras himself (who lived later in the sixth century B.C.). Yet it is right to be sceptical about these reports, both insofar as they concern knowledge of the theorems and *a fortiori* as regards their proofs. There are well known tendencies in the late Greek commentators to make overoptimistic attributions of sophisticated ideas to the heroic founders of Greek philosophy, and these seem to be cases in point. At least if Aristotle is anything to go by (who is of course much closer in time to those concerned), he always expresses himself in very guarded terms about Thales – who indeed probably left no writings. And as regards Pythagoras too, Aristotle ascribes no concrete mathematical doctrines to him, but contents himself with a report on the general views of the Pythagorean school, where he is thinking primarily of figures at work in the middle of the fifth century, or in the case of Philolaus even later (cf Burkert 1972). So it becomes very difficult to credit Proclus, some nine centuries after Aristotle, even when Proclus claims to be drawing on the history of mathematics composed by Aristotle's pupil Eudemus. At least it would appear that the evidence available about Thales, even in the fourth century B.C., was in most cases mere hearsay, and the situation as regards Pythagoras is complicated by the difficulty of distinguishing between his work and that of those who passed, or represented themselves, as his followers.

The evidence concerning Hippocrates of Chios is of an altogether different quality. This is not a matter merely of general reports of his work, for example that he was the first to compile a collection of 'elements', that is that he was the first to attempt the systematic presentation of a body of geometrical theorems.[2] Simplicius, our chief source, devotes some fourteen pages in his commentary on Aristotle's *Physics* (55 25–69 34) to a detailed description and criticisms of Hippocrates' work on the quadrature of lunes. Now it is true that the chief source Simplicius says he is drawing on is – once again – Eudemus (60 22ff.) and there has been a protracted scholarly dispute on such questions as where precisely Simplicius is quoting Eudemus verbatim (as he says he will) and where he is not, as also on where Eudemus' account (when it *is* his) faithfully records what Hippocrates himself wrote (see Heath 1921, 1, pp. 183ff. with references to earlier literature and cf. Mueller 1982, Knorr 1986, Lloyd 1987b). Yet even though in the convoluted process of transmission some of the terminology has undoubtedly been modified, and maybe some of the arguments too, we can and should still accept that the substance of the four proofs given represents the work of Hippocrates himself. These four proofs give the quadratures of lunes with an outer circumference equal to, greater than, and less than, a semi-circle and that of a lune together with a circle.

These proofs are impressive not just for the extent of the mathematical knowledge shown, but also for the general rigour of the demonstrations. For instance Hippocrates does not just construct lunes with outer circumferences greater, and less, than a semi-circle but in both cases provides proofs of these inequalities. But if the quality of the proofs is high, the lack of technical vocabulary to describe his procedures is remarkable. Thus later mathematicians were generally careful to specify the nature of the indemonstrable primary premisses or starting-points (e.g. definitions, postulates and axioms or common opinions) on which their demonstrations were based. When we are told by Simplicius (61 5ff) that Hippocrates took as the starting-point (*archē*: the word may mean simply beginning) for his quadratures the proposition that similar segments of circles are to one another as the squares on their bases, this was clearly in no sense an axiom. It was indeed a proposition that (we are told) Hippocrates *showed* by *showing* that circles are to one another as the squares on their diameters.

It looks then as if Hippocrates was not at all concerned, at this point, to draw a firm, in principle, distinction between indemonstrable primary premisses and what can be derived from them, even though we cannot rule out that he had some such distinction when he set out the body of geometrical theorems which later writers refer to as that collection of 'elements'. In the concrete examples of proof for which we have detailed direct evidence he seems to have used 'starting-point' (or some equivalent term) in a quite general and loose way that ignored that distinction.

The first sustained deductive argument in philosophy (the first such extant in European literature) antedates Hippocrates by some decades. This is in Parmenides' philosophical poem, usually thought to date to around 480 B.C.. What he calls the *Way of Truth* takes as its starting-point the proposition that 'it is'. One way to understand this is to take it that he is claiming that for any inquiry to get anywhere it must be an inquiry into something: it must have a subject-matter. However, Parmenides then proceeds to show a whole series of highly counter-intuitive conclusions, for example that coming-to-be and change are both impossible. Coming-to-be has to be ruled out because the only thing 'it' could come to be from is what is not, and nothing can come to be from the totally non-existent. Apply this to the world in general, and we can see the force of the point: it is hard to understand what it would mean to say that it came from nothing. Moreover Parmenides drives the point home by asking why it should do so at any one time, rather than at any other: and that too is a good question for Big Bang or any other theory of cosmological creation.

But Parmenides is not just interested in, as it were, unqualified coming-to-be, but in any kind: for he goes on to refute change too, precisely on the grounds that it involves a coming-to-be (that is to say of the new situation created by the supposed change) and coming-to-be had just been ruled out (Parmenides, Fragment 8, Owen 1986, pp. 3ff., Mourelatos 1970, Kirk, Raven and Schofield 1983).

Many aspects of the interpretation of Parmenides' philosophy are controversial, but it is not the content of his argument, but its form, that concerns us here, and that is not in serious doubt. Evidently he is attempting to arrive at a set of incontrovertible conclusions by deductive arguments from a starting-point that has to be accepted. Even so – a point similar to the one I have made about Hippocrates of Chios – the terminology in which he himself describes what he is doing is a very limited one. This is not just a matter of his not having any terms to describe the various argument schemata, such as *reductio* or Modus Tollens, that he uses. He has no word for deduction, nor for premiss. What is usually called the 'premiss' of the Way of Truth, that statement that 'it is', is simply the 'way' that Parmenides says he will follow. True, he offers what he calls a 'much-contested *elenchos*' (Fragment 7 5f., see most recently Lesher 1984), and this has sometimes been taken to be translatable as 'proof'. However it seems more likely that the primary sense here is that of refutation – as in the Socratic *elenchus* where he exposes the inconsistencies in his interlocutors' beliefs in Plato's dialogues. As for the sequence of conclusions set out in the sequel of the Way of Truth, they are simply introduced with the remark that there are many sign-posts or marks, *sēmata*, on this way that, for instance, it is ungenerated, indestructible and so on.

Both mathematics and philosophy thus provide excellent examples of rigorous demonstrations from the fifth century B.C., though in neither field is there, at that stage, any formal analysis of the concept and indeed the vocabulary available for describing the elements and procedures of a proof is very limited. One question that has been much discussed but that need not detain us long is whether it was the philosophers or the mathematicians who first invented such rigorous arguments and who then influenced whom, where Szabo advocates an origin in philosophy and subsequent influence from philosophy on mathematics, while Knorr claims independence for the mathematical developments (Szabo 1964–6, 1978, Knorr 1975, 1981, 1982).

The first point that is worth emphasising is a general one about what philosophy and mathematics themselves stood for in the period before Aristotle. Though there were professional mathematicians in the sense of people like Hippocrates of Chios who were expert in mathematics, they were not professionals in any other sense. In particular they did not make their living by mathematics (and even later in antiquity the chief if not quite the only aspect of the work of those called 'mathematicians' by which they earned money was astrology). Again those whom *we* conveniently label the Presocratic philosophers differed much more in interests, style and approach than that label warns us to expect. Thus although both Empedocles and Anaxagoras knew Parmenides' work and reacted against his ideas, especially his denial of change and his monism, they were otherwise very different characters indeed. Anaxagoras was a hard-bitten debunker of the supernatural: but Empedocles was a religious leader who refers in one passage to the transmigrations of his soul ('I have been boy and girl and bush and bird and a dumb fish of the sea', Fr. 117) and in another speaks of himself as coming to the people of Acragas as 'an immortal god, no longer mortal' (Fr. 112). Among those who engaged in *mathematical* investigations of one type or another before Aristotle, we find people who *also* had extensive interests in epistemology and ontology and who thereby rate the title of philosopher (Democritus, for instance, the evidence for whose mathematics is set out by Guthrie 1965, pp. 483ff.), and others who besides being interested in philosophy as well as mathematics were also prominent medical theorists, such as the Pythagorean Philolaus (Guthrie 1962, pp. 329ff, Lloyd 1963).

In those circumstances what it was for 'mathematics' to influence or be influenced by 'philosophy' was a very different matter from the situation that obtained once these two became more clearly demarcated specialisations. So far as the *solid extant* evidence on the question of priority goes, that is easily answered: Parmenides' Way of Truth antedates Hippocrates' quadratures, we said, by several decades. But two fundamental reservations must be added. First Hippocrates' work clearly presupposes some, and we may believe fairly considerable, mathematical inquiries before him. So far as proofs and not just theorems go, it would be most surprising if he were *totally* original, even though (as I said) we may doubt the reports that trace particular theorems back to the likes of Thales and Pythagoras (both of whom, we may note incidentally, are usually labelled 'philosophers' of some kind). But *just how* extensive the mathematical inquiries of Parmenides' contemporaries were we are in no position to determine.

Moreover secondly, so far as influences go, it seems clear that some of the developments that took place in mathematics are quite independent of those we can trace in philosophy (for example in ontology and epistemology). It is true, and not at all surprising, that at a very general level, the same deductive argument forms appear in both: *reductio*, or indirect proof, is as common in mathematics as it is in philosophy. Yet there are several quite distinctive mathematical procedures that have no parallels in philosophy. One (used already by Hippocrates) is the construction known as *neusis*, verging: another is anthyphairesis, the reciprocal subtraction algorithm (Fowler 1987): a third (in the fourth century) is what was to become the mathematical proof procedure *par excellence*, the so-called method of exhaustion, attributed to Eudoxus (Knorr 1975, 1986).

For our concerns, the more important question relates to the primary motivations and preoccupations of the search for demonstration in the two fields. There are both similarities and differences between mathematics and philosophy here that should be carefully assessed. Let us begin with some of the differences. In Parmenides himself, we said, the strategic aim was incontrovertible conclusions from a starting-point that itself had to be accepted – for how could anyone deny that 'it is', taken, for example, in the sense that for there to be any inquiry at all it must be into something. This would yield not just certainty, where before – in cosmology, for instance – there had been just arbitrary speculation: this was the *whole* truth. The formal demonstrations in early mathematics, on the one hand, include some that are anything but all-embracing in scope, even within the field of mathematics.

It is true that one mathematical discovery has been thought to have had very wide repercussions indeed. There has been much talk of a foundation crisis, a *Grundlagenkrisis*, at some stage in Greek mathematics, a reaction (so it was claimed) to the discovery of the incommensurability of the side and the diagonal of the square. Both the date of that discovery and the original method of proving it are much disputed, though a date early in the fifth, let alone in the sixth, century now seems most unlikely (Knorr 1975, chh. 2 and 6). But it is essential to be clear on what that discovery did, and what it did not, threaten. The threat, if there was one, was to a philosophical or ontological position, namely the view ascribed by Aristotle to certain Pythagoreans (though usually as an *inference* from the positions they were committed to, rather than as a report of one of those positions themselves), the view, namely, that all things are in some sense numbers (*Metaphysics* 985b27ff., 1080b16ff., 1083b11ff.: cf Guthrie 1962, pp. 229ff., Burkert 1972, ch. 6, pp. 401ff.).

Incommensurability, as the statement that the ratio between the side and the diagonal cannot be expressed as one between integers, certainly provides one sure-fire exception to the principle that all things are expressible numerically (let alone are constituted in some sense by numbers). Yet while any Pythagorean who actually held that view mentioned by Aristotle would have a problem, incommensurability did not threaten anyone engaged in mathematical investigations as such. On the contrary: although we cannot say for sure which of several possible ways of demonstrating the result was the original one (cf. Knorr 1975, chh.

2 and 6), the *discovery* of incommensurability *is* the discovery of its *proof*. The very fact that this is such a good example of a demonstrable – and demonstrated – result would give every encouragement to practising mathematicians to keep up the good work. And in fact that was clearly what happened. Not only is there no evidence of any sudden suspension or break in mathematical inquiry from the time of Hippocrates on: but we know from a text in Plato's *Theaetetus* (147d) that by about 400 B.C. incommensurability was even turned into something of a research programme by those in Theodorus' circle who set about investigating the proofs of all cases up to that of $\sqrt{17}$. So far from undermining confidence in the activity of mathematicians, it confirmed it. As Aristotle was later to say, while the uninitiated are, to begin with, surprised that there is no common measure, for the mathematicians the surprise would be if there were.

Demonstrative procedures were the pride of Greek mathematics from some time in the middle of the fifth century and work on the elements – that is the primary propositions from which the rest of mathematics can be derived – was a major preoccupation of mathematicians from Hippocrates to Euclid, as we know from the lists of those who contributed to this field. Proclus, in his Commentary on Euclid's *Elements* (66 14ff.), mentions no fewer than fourteen mathematicians, between those two, who worked in this area, the most notable being Archytas, Theaetetus and Eudoxus. The nature and status of the indemonstrables were progressively clarified and the systematicity of the proofs improved. Yet if the goal of writers of *Elements* was undoubtedly to be comprehensive *within mathematics*, it was not as if that was held to comprehend, in Parmenidean style, the *whole truth*.

So one major *difference* between ontology and mathematics that might be suggested relates to the all-embracing ambitions of the Way of Truth and of philosophical systems constructed in its manner. However, the *similarities* or *common aims* may be even more important, especially when we compare and contrast the two fields in which formal demonstration was attempted with those areas of informal proof we considered earlier.

In part, the ambition to make arguments rigorous, and to analyse what makes them so, in philosophy and mathematics, no doubt stems from factors internal to those disciplines. But in part the bid to achieve incontrovertibility may be related to dissatisfaction not just with informal techniques of showing points, but with rhetoric. It was all too obvious that what persuaded people in the law-courts and the political assemblies might or might not be true. In some contexts in speculative thought (as we saw in medical theory) informal notions of proof appear mainly directed to persuasion: and given the ancient physician's constant preoccupation with *winning over* his clients and his patients, that is readily understandable. But for some purposes and in other contexts that clearly would not do, and the merely persuasive came to be strongly contrasted with the incontrovertibly true.

The development of demonstration may, in this, be unlike other aspects of the development of formal logic. When Aristotle first formulated the principles of non-contradiction and of excluded middle, he evidently aimed to make *explicit* rules that are *implicit* in all human communication, the rules, indeed, that state the *conditions* of intelligible communication. But whatever we may think of the success of that Aristotelian enterprise,[3] it differs from the development of the concept of demonstration in Greek philosophy and mathematics. The latter clearly represented a departure from, or a revision of, the standards and practices recognised in ordinary informal discourse, and did not merely set out to make those practices explicit.

Once again, however, we are dealing with no merely neutral piece of logical analysis. The opposition between persuasion and demonstration could be, and was, extensively used, by philosophers (if not by mathematicians) as a way of contrasting their rivals' work with their own and of course of claiming superiority for the latter. Plato develops the theme in one dialogue after another in his recurrent polemic with those he calls sophists (*Gorgias* 452e ff., 458e ff., *Phaedrus* 259e ff., 272d ff., *Philebus* 58a ff.: cf Lloyd 1979, pp. 100ff.). Aristotle too, while allowing rhetoric its place, is careful to contrast rhetorical and dialectical arguments with demonstrative ones (*Prior Analytics* 68b9ff., *Topics* 100a25ff.), and he leaves us in no doubt that the aim of the philosopher as philosopher is demonstration.

Moreover in a number of contexts, and not just on abstract points, Aristotle delivers on his promise to demonstrate his conclusions. One notable case in his natural philosophy is the proof of the sphericity of the earth (a theory that was, however, not original to Aristotle, since it is proposed already by Plato in the *Phaedo* 108c ff., cf. *Timaeus* 62c ff). Admittedly in that instance some of Aristotle's arguments depend on specifically Aristotelian doctrines – for example that all heavy objects fall 'downwards', 'downwards' being defined as towards the centre of the earth – and so would be considered by opponents to be quite inconclusive. However among the more powerful points he adduces in *On the Heavens* 297b23ff. are (1) the changes in the visibility of the circumpolar stars at different latitudes, and (2) the shape of the earth's shadow in lunar eclipses. To be sure, the latter point too is inconclusive until one adds that the shadow is the same shape wherever on the ecliptic an eclipse occurs (for a disk-shaped earth could account for one such circular shadow), and to be convinced, one needed first to know that the cause of a lunar eclipse was the earth's intervention. However, given that addition and such basic knowledge, the demonstration went through.

The impressive feature of such essays was that they showed conclusively that common assumptions – here, that the earth is flat – stand in need of correction. With some such *proofs* of *unexpected* conclusions to its credit, the new natural science – in the wake of the new mathematics, in many cases – could lay powerful claim to be able to reveal the hidden causes of obscure natural phenomena that had earlier just been found perplexing or frightening – not that in fact that natural science, in Greek antiquity, always or even very often provided satisfactory explanations of such phenomena, let alone demonstrated them.

Thus far I have attempted to sketch the background to the first explicit analysis of formal proof in Aristotle. But the subsequent history of the application of this concept in Greek thought raises important questions. While Aristotle was the first to formulate the ideal of rigorous demonstration, the person who above all exhibited what the comprehensive presentation of a body of knowledge set out in rigorous deductive form looked like in practice was Euclid in the *Elements*. Just how far Euclid was directly influenced by Aristotle – and how far he was following and elaborating the model provided by those earlier mathematicians who had worked on the elements – is unclear. We do not know, for example, how much Euclid's triadic classification of indemonstrables (namely definitions, postulates and common opinions) may owe to Aristotle's, the only earlier such classification that is extant: Aristotle's triad of definitions, hypotheses and axioms (*Posterior Analytics* 72a14ff.) is not exactly the same as Euclid's (Mueller 1969, 1974) even though it so happens that one of Aristotle's axioms corresponds to Euclid's third common opinion ('if equals be subtracted from equals, the remainders are equal').

But those are subsidiary points. What is both uncontroversial and of first rate importance for the subsequent development of Greek science is the role that Euclid's *Elements* itself had as providing *the* model for the systematic demonstration of a body of knowledge. Thereafter proof *more geometrico* became all the rage, and not just in geometry, but also for example in optics, in parts of music theory, in statics and hydrostatics, in parts of theoretical astronomy, and not just in the would-be exact sciences, but in some of the life sciences as well. Many of these developments, in the exact sciences especially, are accounted among the most notable achievements of Greek science, and certainly they are, as I observed, among the most easily recognisable ancient ancestors of later scientific investigations. At the same time – a point that is less often attended to – focussing on these success stories should not be allowed to distract us from noticing some of the more negative features of the same demand, even at points an obsession, for proof *more geometrico*. Three such features need to be noticed, one to do with the life sciences, a second relating to mathematics itself, and the third and most far-reaching a problem to do with the exact sciences themselves. Let me summarise as briefly as possible the chief points in each case.

My first observation concerns the bid for demonstration in the geometrical manner in fields or contexts where it is fairly clearly *in*appropriate. One instance is provided by the ambition to turn aspects of such studies as medicine and physiology into exact sciences, an enterprise dear to the heart of Galen in the second century A.D. (Barnes forthcoming, Hankinson forthcoming). Now Galen is no mean logician. He made several important original contributions to formal logic, and we might have been able to say he made many more if his great fifteen-book work *On Demonstration* had survived. When he argues that 'the best doctor is also a philosopher', one of his points is that the doctor should be trained in scientific method, especially in demonstration. It is wholly admirable, no doubt, that doctors too should be able to tell a valid from an invalid inference. But Galen wants far more: that the doctor should be able to present scientific demonstrations of theoretical points throughout his work. That may sound laudable too – except that we must bear in mind the state of the 'science' of medicine at that time.

The problem here is one that goes back as far as Aristotle. It was always difficult to see how the schema of the *Posterior Analytics* was to be applied in, for instance, zoology, although that was indubitably part of Aristotle's original aim and intention. What were going to count as the indemonstrable primary premisses in the study of living things?[4] The general axioms, such as the laws of non-contradiction and excluded middle, apply everywhere, of course, but nothing *follows* from them: they are, in his view, the principles that regulate all communication, but they do not figure in specific scientific demonstrations. There are no obvious candidates for the role of special axioms in zoology on a par with the equality axiom in mathematics that we mentioned above (take equals from equals and equals remain, e.g. *Posterior Analytics* 76a41, 77a30f.). Of course there will be plenty of definitions and as in Aristotle's view these contain the essences, their contents will figure in demonstrations, even though definitions themselves are indemonstrable.

That may look rather promising, but two fundamental difficulties remain. First when it comes to his zoological works the *actual* definitions of particular natural kinds he appears to envisage are far more complex than the neat formulae that are easily deployed in syllogistic arguments – formulae of the type 'man is a rational two-legged animal'. Worse still (though this point is more controversial) the requirement that terms be univocal that is essential to his whole formal logic and is presupposed in his concept of demonstration is under very considerable pressure, in practice, from the results of his zoological inquiries. It turns out, for example, that such a term as 'biped' is 'said in many ways', the bipedality of birds is not the same as that of humans, and so too 'blooded' 'concoction' and many other key biological terms fail the test of univocity (cf my 1987a, ch. 4). If demonstration still remained an ideal in zoology, as in mathematics, it was an ideal that had to recede the more Aristotle's zoological researches progressed.

Similar points also apply, *mutatis mutandis*, to Galen. It may be that we can say that the principles that nature does nothing in vain, and – for a doctor – that opposites are cures for opposites, act as some kind of regulative principles or axioms, and one can see plenty of scope for definitions too. But in fact neither medical science nor physiology could be said to have secure primary premisses that are *both* indemonstrable *and* true, from which to derive incontrovertible conclusions. In that situation, while valid inference is always a virtue, the attempt to give formal demonstration is often an irrelevance.

My second observation concerns mathematics itself. Although the incontrovertibility of its arguments was its pride, the insistence on rigorous demonstration could and did have certain inhibiting effects. The best known and most obvious illustration of this comes from Archimedes' *Method*. Quite exceptionally, for Greek mathematical texts, that work discusses discovery as well as demonstration and presents a method which, Archimedes says, is heuristic without being demonstrative. The method is called a *mechanical* method and it depends on two interrelated assumptions, first that a plane figure can be thought of as composed of the parallel lines that it contains, and secondly that it can be thought of as balanced against some other area or set of lines at a certain distance (the distance being imagined as a balance from which the plane figures are suspended). Now it is not clear from what Archimedes says, and it is disputed in modern scholarship, whether his reason for refusing to think this method a demonstrative one was the use of the mechanical assumption or that of indivisibles – which were evidently in breach of the assumption of the geometrical continuum (Knorr 1981, 1982, Sato 1986, 1987). But that point need not concern us here: the point that does is that Archimedes allows informal methods no more than a heuristic role and he insists that the results thereby obtained must thereafter all be proved strictly using *reductio* and the method of exhaustion.

The inhibition that Greek mathematicians generally, and not just Archimedes, felt about presenting results other than in strict demonstrative form must have acted as a break on investigation. Archimedes' heuristic method remained unexploited by later Greek mathematicians (indeed all but ignored) and if that was partly because the treatise that describes it was not generally known, that is not the whole story, since some of the theorems in his *On the Quadrature of the Parabola* implicitly depend on a similar method. The problem was the more general one of that reluctance to rely on informal methods. It is in this respect especially that the contrast between ancient Greek mathematics and the mathematics of Cavalieri and others in the seventeenth century is so marked. Once that reluctance was overcome, the effect was a dramatic liberation: they went all out for results, leaving their formal demonstration to be worked out later.

My third and final observation takes us into the heart of difficult and controversial matters concerning the role, in Greek science, of idealisations and/or simplifications of the problems dealt with (cf. my 1987a ch. 6). The bid for demonstration *more geometrico* in such exact sciences as optics, harmonics, statics and astronomy produced, we said, some outstanding work. But in each case, for the inquiry to be mathematised, for example geometrised, certain of the physical aspects of the phenomena had to be discounted. This raises the problem, first, of the relationship between the physics of the physical phenomena that constitute the *explananda* and the mathematics used in their *explanation* – and then that of the relationship between physics and mathematics more generally

In many cases what is discounted is, no doubt, unproblematic. In harmonics, for instance, when the investigator is studying pitch on the monochord, such factors as the thickness of the string, its material constitution and its tension are all irrelevant (though he knows, of course, that if these are altered, so too will be the pitch of the note): the only data he is concerned with are the lengths that correspond to certain notes. Again in his statics Archimedes evidently discounted for the purposes of his investigation of the lever, such factors as the possible variation in the material composition of an actual metal bar, and more importantly, that the movement of a bar about a fulcrum will be accompanied by friction, just as in his hydrostatics he stipulated explicitly in his first postulate that the fluid be perfectly homogeneous and totally inelastic. Here too the types of idealisations involved are uncontroversial: they are indeed essential for the success of the inquiry, for without them the underlying relationships will not be revealed. It is, however, the case that the more that is discounted – and the greater the idealisations – the more the investigation will cease to be a contribution to *physics* and will become (just) geometry. We can see this already in Archimedes' statics and hydrostatics, where in the second book of both *On the Equilibrium of Planes* and *On Floating Bodies* his studies become increasingly straightforwardly *geometrical* investigations. These relate, for example, to such questions as the centres of gravity of plane figures and of paraboloids of revolution of various kinds.

A recurrent problem that can be illustrated in most of the ancient Greek exact sciences is that exactness may be obtained only at the cost of applicability. One tradition of writers on harmonics indeed reduced that study to number theory, although that move was resisted by others who insisted that harmonics was more than the purely mathematical investigation of which numbers are 'concordant' with one another since the essential subject-matter was audible phenomena. We can trace a similar divergence of approaches also in astronomy. Some studies were purely mathematical in character. One such is the work of Autolycus of Pitane (fourth century B.C.), *On the Moving Sphere*, which deals chiefly with questions to do with intersecting great circles on a rotating sphere. That is *relevant* to astronomy, for sure (for the astronomer is concerned with the speeds at which sections of the ecliptic rise and set) but it is not applied directly to any problems in astronomical model-building.

But there is another tradition, represented by the most distinguished Greek astronomer whose major treatises have survived, Ptolemy, in which the aim was more than just the development of mathematical models. The prediction of positions was not his sole preoccupation. In one treatise, the *Planetary Hypotheses*, he attempts a detailed physical account of the spheres on which the heavenly bodies move and he even tries to answer the dynamical question of *why* they move, namely, he suggests, because they are alive. Within his primarily mathematical discussion in the *Syntaxis*, too, he recognises constraints on his account that come from purely physical considerations, notably from the assumption that the earth is at rest in the centre of the universe. Here too while mathematisation was allowed and indeed required, this was not to be at the cost of abandoning the further requirement that the account correspond to the physical realities.[5]

This takes us, then, to more general problems to do with the relationship between physics and mathematics. The mathematisation of physics has often been regarded as one of the major constituent elements in the changes associated with the development of science from the seventeenth century onwards. Unlike the development of an axiomatic deductive system which, as we have seen, was the subject of explicit analysis, the ancient Greeks rarely provide clear-cut expressions of anything that could be described as a general *programme* of the mathematisation of physics. It is true that the doctrine that in some sense 'all things are numbers' is, as we have noted, ascribed to the Pythagoreans, and some later writers in that tradition advocate attacking mathematically natural phenomena as a whole.

The clearest statement to that effect is to be found in Iamblichus, *On the Common Mathematical Science* (ch. 32), in the fourth century A.D. Yet that does not inspire confidence since he seems prepared to cite almost any example of the application of numbers to support his overall thesis. These include not just astronomy but also astrology;[6] he has, too, obscure and evidently speculative remarks to make about investigating the four elements by using 'geometry or arithmetic or harmonics',[7] and his claims for mathematics are not *limited* to natural phenomema, for he also cites the 'symbolic' study of the pentad and argues that mathematics is useful also for ethics and politics, for example for the inquiry into the good (chh. 6, 15, 18).

So when we come to inspect what might seem promising statements of the idea of applying mathematics to natural science, we find some fanciful, not to say fantastic, notions given free rein. On the other hand, even without convincing explicit statements of what the programme of the mathematisation of physics would comprise, we cannot deny that many ancient Greek scientists applied mathematics, in practice, to a number of fields of inquiry and did so with considerable success.

It could be argued that such studies constitute one of the most profound changes in scientific practice in antiquity: that they represent not just a new methodology, but a quite new appreciation of the possibilities of arriving at an understanding of natural phenomena. Here, if anywhere, therefore, one might be tempted to describe the changes that occurred, in Greek scientific development, as a veritable transformation of mentalities – a temptation that has certainly proved seductive to some students of science in the Renaissance and subsequently, where Vickers, for example, we may recall, explicitly contrasted scientific and occult mentalities (Vickers 1984).

However, so far as the Greco-Roman world at least is concerned, any such hypothesis of a new mentality encounters three main objections. First we have to pay due attention to the point already mentioned, namely that the occasions when we find any statement in an ancient author that can be taken as *explicitly advocating* some such idea as the application of mathematical notions to the understanding of physical phenomena in general are rare and unconvincing. To talk, therefore, of that as a *programme* of ancient science is rather *our*, observers', interpretation, not a report of *their*, actors', view, and we have seen the attendant dangers of such a procedure on other occasions.

But to that the answer might be that (as we pointed out in the introduction) mentalities have often been held to correspond to unconscious or merely implicit assumptions or attitudes, rather than or in addition to explicit ones. But then the second more serious difficulty is that the examples that *we* might cite in support of some such generalisation are highly *diverse*. We have noted that Archimedes, for example, presents an idealised, mathematical, statics and hydrostatics. There the movement of thought is not so much one of attempting to apply mathematics to physical phenomena, as one of so idealising the physical phenomena under consideration that they can be handled mathematically.

But when we turn to Iamblichus, by contrast, who provides as we said our most *general* ancient statement of the idea of attacking natural phenomena as a whole mathematically, *his* conception of what that means is a long way from any we could associate with Archimedes in his *On the Equilibrium of Planes* and *On Floating Bodies*, notably in Iamblichus' indiscriminate inclusion of ethics and politics, and purely symbolic studies, as examples to illustrate the importance of the applications of mathematics.

If the contrast between Archimedes and Iamblichus is extreme, we have further reason to be cautious about generalising about ancient attitudes if we consider the underlying philosophies of mathematics. It is true that both the main positive positions on that important topic – that is, very broadly, the Platonist and the Aristotelian ones – are both in some sense realist. Yet the way in which that realism is to be understood differs profoundly in the two cases. I shall come back to elaborate that point shortly.

The third major objection to the application of the notion of a mentality in this regard to the ideas of ancient scientists is simply this. It is far from being the case that the attitudes stemming from the postulated mentality run through *all* the work of the same individual scientist, even within a single field. Ptolemy, for example notably combines the sophisticated use of mathematical models in his theoretical astronomy (in the *Syntaxis*) with attempts, in his astrological treatise, the *Tetrabiblos*, to use traditional symbolic relationships to suggest correlations between human characters and events on earth on the one hand, and planetary configurations on the other. Nor is this true just of his work in that area, for in his harmonics too and in the very same treatise (the *Harmonics*), we find juxtaposed (1) the mathematical analysis of musical scales and concords, and (2) the speculative exploration of the way in which the faculties of the human soul, and their virtues, illustrate harmonic relationships. In *Harmonics* III ch. 5 he cites not just one but two tripartite theories of the soul and associates its three parts with the three principal concords, octave, fifth and fourth. He even goes on to compare the *numbers* of the virtues of each part of the soul (three of the appetitive, four of the spirited, and seven of the reasoning

93

part on the Platonic model of tripartition) with the three, four and seven species of the principal concords which he had identified and discussed in the previous book (II chh. 3ff).[8]

In neither of these two fields of investigation does it seem at all possible to describe Ptolemy's work as throughout guided and controlled by a single vision, corresponding to some distinctive mental attitudes. In such a case (and many others like it, and not just from the ancient Greek world) the spectre of a hybrid, even schizophrenic, mentality would loom. We would do better to see his work as reflecting not a combination of traditional and new mentalities,[9] but as a highly complex reaction in which Ptolemy attempts a synthesis of a number of competing and overlapping views on the proper subject-matter, methods and aims of the inquiries in question. That there are tensions in his work – as indeed again in that of many other ancient scientists and philosophers – is undeniable: but we should see these as the outcome of his ambition to be synoptic, not as corresponding to some feature or features of his own or his predecessors' mentalities.

Let me return now to the very considerable differences in the underlying philosophical positions that underpinned the studies we have been considering. Both Platonists and Aristotelians recognised the usefulness of mathematics to certain inquiries, but they did so in quite different ways, reflecting radical differences in their views on the status of mathematics itself. For Platonism, for a study to be science, it has to be confined to the intelligible realities, the transcendent Forms, ontologically divorced from the perceptible particulars. Mathematics, while inferior to dialectic, has a claim to yield knowledge since it deals with the intelligible world. Some account of physics is possible – Plato gives one in the *Timaeus*: but he calls that only a 'likely story' or indeed 'likely *muthos*' and it is in any case, in its element theory, mathematical in character. But the Platonist is a realist in science because proper science deals with the intelligible realities.

But the Aristotelian is a realist too, though that has to be cashed out in a very different way. For the Aristotelian, *physics* is realist because it deals with substances (studying especially of course the immanent forms or essences). Moreover mathematics does not study separate intelligible entities (as it does for Plato) but rather the mathematical properties of *physical* objects (taken in abstraction from the other properties that make them the physical objects they are). Mathematics, thanks to that process of abstraction, can be, and is, exact, but it does not float free from the underlying physical constraints. In principle (though he sometimes found this hard in practice) Aristotle's own mathematical idealisations should all be translatable back into physical terms.

As those last remarks indicate, whether we are dealing with varying

94

interpretations of the applicability of mathematics to physics, or with the more explicit development of the notion of an axiomatic deductive system, due attention must, of course, be paid to the complex set of philosophical positions as a whole within which the varying ideas in question were advanced. However, at an admittedly very general level the ambition that unites certain mathematical, philosophical and scientific investigations was, we said, to secure incontrovertible conclusions by valid deduction from premises that had to be accepted. Whatever the differences in the actual elaboration and implementation of that idea in, say, Euclid's *Elements*, in Aristotle's philosophy of science and in Galen's biology, that ambition may be said to be common to them all.

But once again there is no call to ascribe that ambition to some new or distinctive mentality – any more than there was in the case of the 'programme' of the 'mathematisation of physics'. On the contrary it is clear that the individuals in question recognized very well that the possibility of the fulfilment of the goal *varied in different fields and contexts*. Indeed Aristotle explicitly insisted that the degree of exactness to be expected in different subjects varied, and that grave mistakes arise from ignoring that fact (e.g. *Nicomachean Ethics* 1094b23ff., *Posterior Analytics* 87a31ff., *Metaphysics* 995a6ff.). Nor when it comes to a much later scientist such as Galen can it be said that, keen as he was on demonstration, that keenness led him totally to ignore the question of whether it is possible or appropriate in any given context. To give just a single example, he is careful in his *On the Opinions of Hippocrates and Plato* to distinguish the strength of the claims he makes for the evidence and argument localising the three vital faculties in the liver, heart and brain respectively: he is clear that he can *prove* some of his conclusions, where the evidence from dissection is conclusive, but not others.

It is not the case that there is a *uniformity* in the work of any of these individuals – let alone in *all* of them – that suggests an underlying distinctive and pervasive set of mental attitudes. We can say that the development, in Greece, of the demand for *certainty* sprang in part from a dissatisfaction shared by a variety of individuals with the merely persuasive. But it is also clear that the ways in which the concept of proof was *actually* deployed correspond to those individual's responses to *specific* problems as they arose in connection with the various philosophical and scientific issues they investigated. But the important factors *we* need to study – and that constitute *our* problem in attempting to understand these developments – are, in the latter case, the *specificities* of those responses, and in the former, the polemic in which, as a means of outbidding the opposition, the claim to certainty was preeminent: it could be denied, but it could not be surpassed.

So we must return in conclusion to that polemic. We have related other intellectual developments that took place in early Greek thought, and other changes in styles of reasoning or the conduct of interpersonal exchanges, to the political and social background, for example the extensive experience that many Greeks had of evaluating arguments in the law courts and assemblies. The study of the concept and practice of proof is particularly interesting in this regard, since it can be suggested that the influence of that background is twofold, both direct and indirect, corresponding to the informal and the formal notions that we have distinguished.

First the political and legal fields are important not just for the deployment of informal notions of proof but also for the development of the corresponding vocabulary. To be sure our extant evidence from the texts of the orators does not antedate the other uses we have described. Yet we can hardly doubt that the political and legal domains provided and continued to provide the primary sphere of application of those notions. It is from those domains, principally, that the terminology of evidence, witnessing, scrutiny and proof beyond reasonable doubt comes, and the similarities in the techniques of argument and persuasion, in these respects, between the orators and the medical writers, for instance, are a sign of the growth or spread of rhetoric outwards from that primary sphere of application in the practice of political and legal debates.

But that political and legal experience may also be relevant indirectly to the development of formal or rigorous proof as well. It is true that we have no direct evidence bearing on the motivations or concerns of either Parmenides or Hippocrates of Chios, both of whom, in any case, we said, have procedures of rigorous proof that are more highly developed than the terminology in which to describe them. But certainly by the time we come to Plato, the contrast between the merely persuasive and proof is drawn in the sharpest terms and the latter used as one powerful way to mark off Plato's own conception of philosophy from the work of the sophists in particular and from rhetoric in general. But philosophy, on his view, was no mere academic discipline, nor did it turn its back on and ignore sophistry and rhetoric. On the contrary, the claim was that it achieved, what they failed to do, namely to secure the truth and give a rational account of it.

On that basis we should conclude that here too, as in our other studies, the political and legal background plays a role at least at the beginning of what might otherwise seem a merely intellectual development. However the qualification to the thesis that must be entered is that, in this instance, that role was not as a source of positive, but rather of negative, models. If the sophists claimed that they could teach you how to win your arguments in the courts and in general,[10] Plato's counter was to require that kings be philosophers – indeed to be trained in his style of philosophy.

Once again the competitiveness characteristic of so much Greek intellectual life and culture is in evidence, and the nature of the claims to superiority advanced by the philosophers is particularly striking. On the one hand, Plato, and Aristotle though to a lesser extent, left no one in any doubt about their sense of the inadequacies, even the possible deceptiveness, of the merely persuasive (though both were not above exploiting it for their own purposes). On the other, they may be said to share – even while they reinterpret – one recurrent preoccupation of much Greek political and legal debate, namely the demand for the *justification* of a point of view – except that now, in the highest style of philosophical inquiry, this was redefined as no mere matter of what was subjectively convincing, but on the contrary one of objective certainty, an incontrovertibility secured by rigorous demonstration.

As with metaphor, magic and myth, so too demonstration in this strict sense provided a potent means of criticising and undermining rivals. Indeed appeal to this criterion was often a way of dismissing or downgrading not merely the practitioners of rhetoric, but rhetoric as a whole, since its arguments were defined by contrast with those of demonstrative philosophy. For their part, the practitioners of political argument might accept with some equanimity that their proofs were not conducted in the geometrical manner – except that if they wanted to counter, and not just to ignore, the potential criticisms of a Plato or an Aristotle, they had better be in a position to give *some* account of the criteria by which those proofs of theirs were to be evaluated. Here, too, as in our other studies, once the step of drawing the distinction – between informal and rigorous proof – had been made and those concepts made explicit, the character of the debate changed and the stakes were higher: what passed as traditional ways of argument became in principle liable to a new style of challenge.

Supplementary note: *geometry and 'proof' in Vedic ritual*

As the question of whether Vedic ritual presupposes an explicit notion of proof is both complex and important, I have thought it necessary to devote a separate note to the issues. I accordingly deal here, in (I), with sources and dating, and in (II) with the geometrical knowledge and interests displayed in the key texts, the *Śulbasūtras*. In (I) I give grounds first for resisting a common line of argument that has it that where geometry is put to ritual use in Vedic texts, that justifies the assumption that the geometrical knowledge in question goes back to the origins of the ritual concerned, and secondly, that so far as the *Śulbasūtras* themselves go, they cannot be dated more precisely than to some time in the period between c. 500 and c. 100 b.c.. In (II) I consider the geometry used in the *Śulbasūtras* and conclude that while the authors evidently knew, for example, the relationship we refer to as Pythagoras' theorem, there are grounds for doubting that they had a rigorous notion of proof or that they were interested in geometrical rigour and exactness for its own sake at all.

I am particularly grateful to my colleague Peter Khoroche for help with the interpretation of the Sanskrit texts.

(I)

The Vedic texts we are concerned with include, besides the *Ṛg Veda* itself, the *Taittirīya Saṃhitā*, the *Śatapatha Brāhmaṇa*, and most important of all, the *Śulbasūtras*, the *Baudhāyana Śulbasūtra* and the *Āpastamba Śulbasūtra* in particular. (For a first orientation, see, for example, Keith 1925, 1928, Winternitz 1927, Ruben 1954, 1971, Gonda 1975, 1977.)

Geometrical knowledge is used in several texts in connection with the account of the construction of ritual altars. However the degree of detail into which the authors enter varies greatly, and while the conservative tendencies of Vedic religion are well known, to assume that it was totally *unchanging* is, as we shall see, quite unjustified. Rather, each class of text has to be evaluated separately, even though the difficulties of interpretation are formidable.

In the *Ṛg Veda* itself, references to altar construction are generally very vague. There is, for example, a passage at I 67 5 which Seidenberg 1960–2, p. 509, translates: 'skillful men measure out the seat of the agni' (i.e. the fire altar). This is quite indeterminate, and it is, moreover, open to doubt, at least if one compares the translation offered by Renou, 1964, p. 14, of the whole paragraph: 'Il porte toujours la terre comme (l'être) non-né. Il étaie-toujours la Terre (et) le Ciel à l'aide de Formules-sacrales réelles. /Veille (ô Agni) sur les traces aimées du bétail! (Pour) toute la durée-de-vie (des hommes), ô Agni, tu vas de (lieu) secret en (lieu) secret.' Although the divergences in these attempted renderings of this text in the *Ṛg Veda* appear very great, they are not at all exceptional. Again at X 90 we have: 'Purusha was 1000 headed, 1000 eyed, 1000 footed', where Seidenberg 1960–2, p. 509, commented: 'This means either that [...] there already existed the thousand-brick altar; or, possibly, that the altar was [...] conceived as thousandfold.' Earlier translators have, however, taken Purusha in the ordinary sense 'man' and the references to one thousand to stand in for any very large number.

More definite references to altars of various shapes are to be found in some later, though still very ancient, texts, the *Taittirīya Saṃhitā* (for example V 4 11) and the *Śatapatha Brāhmaṇa* (for example III 5 1) – both of which antedate 600 B.C. (see Gonda 1975, pp. 339ff., 360). However, in the latter, lengths are obtained by pacing (obviously an inexact method) and both texts justify some of the numbers in play by reference to their symbolic associations. Thus in *Śatapatha Brāhmaṇa* III 5 1 7ff. the reason given for the numbers of the steps that give the lengths is that these are the numbers of syllables in certain verse metres.

Compared with all the earlier Vedic literature, the *Śulbasūtra*s themselves are exceptional in the detailed geometrical knowledge displayed or presupposed (see below, II), and the first question is how far back does that knowledge go? As for the *texts*, Seidenberg remarked in his 1974–5, p. 287, that their dating is vital. Yet in his 1960–2, pp. 500f., he had claimed: 'The date of the manuscript or text is, however, irrelevant. If we went out some fine day and caught a fish of a kind never before seen, would we try to fix its position in the evolutionary scale by the date on which it was caught?' Following Thibault, whose translations of the *Śulbasūtra*s he uses, Seidenberg there supposed that whatever the date of the texts we have, the accounts of altar construction they contain can be used as evidence of practices that go back to the period of the Veda itself. Thus at 1960–2, pp. 514f., he claimed that the rituals he is interested in may be dated well before 1700 B.C., and at p. 523 that 'by 2000 B.C.' the ritual 'was already old'.

The situation is complicated by the undeniable fact that in other areas of inquiry, such as astronomy, the Indian texts (eventually) show clear signs of having been influenced, directly or indirectly, by Greek ideas (see, for example, Pingree 1981). Thibault himself was concerned to evaluate the originality of Indian science and argued (1875, p. 228) that 'whatever is closely connected with the ancient Indian religion must be considered as having sprung up among the Indians themselves, unless positive evidence of the strongest kind point to a contrary conclusion'.

But even if we have possible evidence for a concern for correct altar construction in the earliest Vedic literature, any further claim to the effect that *uniform* geometrical knowledge underlies the entire corpus of Vedic writings from the earliest to the last is quite unjustifiable. We can see this from a comparison between the *Śulbasūtras* and the commentaries on them. This brings to light certain differences that point to a gradually increasing mastery and sophistication in the handling of geometrical materials. Thus at one point the commentator Kapardisvāmin evidently knows that a procedure described for obtaining a circle equal to a square yields only an approximate result and he adjusts his reading of the original text to accord with that fact (see further below, II, pp. 102f.). But if, where we can control the comparison, there are divergences that reflect increasing geometrical knowledge, it is clearly unwarranted to suppose that the *Śulbasūtras* themselves contain knowledge that existed in precisely that form in the second millennium B.C.

So the date of the key texts in the *Śulbasūtras* does become, as Seidenberg's later view put it, 'vital', although precision on that question is quite unattainable. Thus Keith 1928, p. 517, remarked that the works belong to the late Sūtra period, 'possibly of c. 200 B.C., though this is mere guesswork'; Gonda 1977, p. 476, cited one authority as wisely not attempting greater precision than, for example, 'from any time between the 6th or 7th century B.C. to about the second century'; Michaels 1978, pp. 53ff., cited archaeological evidence from Kauśambi to arrive at a terminus ante quem of 225–185 B.C. for the sacred geometry the *Śulbasūtras* contain; and Pingree 1981, p. 4, concluded that the earliest of the *Śulbasūtras* was 'perhaps written before 500 B.C., and the remainder presumably antedate the Christian era.' Seidenberg himself, 1960–2, pp. 505ff., expresses agnosticism on the date of the texts, but remarks, p. 514, 'we have had to struggle to get them back of 0 A.D.'

We have to recognise, then, that neither the upper nor the lower limit can be fixed more definitely than to some time around 500 and some time around 100 B.C. respectively. While on the lower dates quoted by these scholars Greek influence could not be ruled out on purely chronological grounds, there is nothing that positively suggests such influence and indeed nothing to cast any doubt on the supposition that this geometry is entirely indigenous in origin. Moreover one final complication is that, so far as both the *Baudhāyana Śulbasūtra* and the *Āpastamba Śulbasūtra* go, the possibility that the texts we have have been subject to revision after they were first composed is a distinct one (see Gonda 1977, p. 476, and cf. Seidenberg 1960–2, p. 517, who himself suggested possible interpolation of the material on the squaring of the circle).

(II)

Thibault, who first drew attention to the geometry in the *Śulbasūtras*, remarked that the authors evidently knew and used such relationships as those we express with what we call Pythagoras' theorem. He went on to add (Thibault 1875, p. 232): 'They express it [Pythagoras' theorem], it is true, in words very different from those familiar to us; but we must remember that they were interested in geometrical truths only as far as they were of practical use, and that they accordingly gave to them the most practical expression [...] The result is, that we have two propositions instead of one, and that these propositions speak of squares and oblongs instead of the rectangular triangle.'

A number of results are clearly set out and there can be no doubt that the authors' confident handling of problems to do with the areas of squares, rectangles, trapezia and right-angled triangles is based on considerable geometrical knowledge. One example to illustrate this is *Āpastamba Śulbasūtra* V 1–7 where the area of an isosceles trapezium with height 36 units and parallel sides of 24 and 30 units is found as 972 square units (see Seidenberg 1960–2, p. 519, 1974–5, pp. 289f., 1977–8, pp. 322f., and van der Waerden 1980, p. 42, cf. also Michaels 1978, pp. 132ff.). Yet the notion that the authors in question had a clear and explicit *concept* of proof is subject first to the general doubt I express in my text – that to obtain results is one thing, to have that concept as an explicit one is another. Until such time as the concept is *made* explicit, we cannot be sure what conditions were thought to have to be fulfilled for a result to count as having been *proved*.

It also falls foul of one further fundamental difficulty. This is that no clear distinction is drawn in these texts between the rules that are expressed to arrive at what *we* should call *approximations* and those that are employed to yield what *we* should call *exact* results.

Two examples of the former may be given, the formula to measure the diagonal of a square (Thibault 1875, p. 239, cf Michaels 1978, pp. 142ff.,

Pingree 1981, p. 5) and those for converting a square into a circle or vice versa (Thibault 1875, pp. 251ff., cf Michaels 1978, pp. 153f., Pingree 1981, p. 5). Thibault in his own comments on the former is chiefly concerned to point out how good an approximation to the value of what we should call $\sqrt{2}$ is used. The latter cases are discussed by Seidenberg 1960–2, pp. 515ff., though he concentrates, in his remarks, on the differences between arithmetical and geometrical approaches and, as noted, suspects that the passage regarding the squaring of the circle may be an interpolation.

But the very fact that *no* clear differentiation is made between the rules stated in these two types of case – viz., between those that give exact results and those that yield mere approximations – seriously undermines any claim that the authors *had* a *concept* of proof or were concerned with *proving* their results. There is a particularly revealing divergence, in this regard, between the text of the *Āpastamba Śulbasūtra* and the interpretation put upon it by one of the later commentators, namely Kapardisvāmin (who himself cannot be dated, though since he is himself referred to by other writers from about the 11th century onwards he must have lived before then). In his discussion of the conversion of a square into a circle Āpastamba put it that the line found 'regularly' (*nityā*) gives the circle: sā nityā maṇḍalaṃ, *Āpastamba Śulbasūtra* III 2. And he went on to: 'for as much as there is cut off from the square [. . .] quite as much is added to it'.

Thibault took *nityā* in the stronger sense of 'exactly' and proceeded: 'I must remark that Kapardisvāmin, Āpastamba's commentator, combines the two words "sā nityā" into sānityā (= sā anityā), and explains: this line gives a circle, which is not exactly equal to the square. But I am afraid we should not be justified in giving to Āpastamba the benefit of this explanation. The words 'yāvad dhīyate, &' seem to indicate that he was perfectly satisfied with the accuracy of his method and not superior, in this point, to so many circle-squarers of later times. The commentator who, with the mathematical knowledge of his time, knew that the rule was an imperfect one, preferred very naturally the interpretation which was more creditable to his author' (Thibault 1875, pp. 252f.). According to Thibault, then, Āpastamba committed an elementary blunder, claiming exactness for his square-circle conversion, and if that line of interpretation is accepted, then one can only assert that Āpastamba had an explicit notion of proof at the price of attributing to him gross mistakes in its application.

However one counter to Thibault resuscitates Kapardisvāmin's view while still staying with Thibault's own rendering of nityā/anityā as exact/inexact (see for example Chakravarti 1934, cf. Michaels 1978, pp. 153f.). Accordingly to this view sā nityā should indeed be read as sānityā, i.e. sā anityā, and Āpastamba himself should be seen as pointing out that the rule in this case is *in*exact. But to this there are two objections. The first is that, as Thibault already pointed out, Āpastamba went on with the words 'for as much as there is cut off [. . .] quite as much is added [. . .]' *If* Āpastamba had wished deliberately to point to the *in*exactness of the result, it is extraordinary that he should proceed with a statement that clearly implies a claim for the *correctness* of the procedure concerned.

Secondly the very same expression, sā nityā, occurs in another collocation later in *Āpastamba Śulbasūtra*, namely at XII 5, where there is no question of the procedure being inexact: a square is constructed double the area of a given triangle. I shall return to this point later.

Āpastamba's evident satisfaction with his square to circle conversion from the point of view of *his own* concerns takes us to the central question of what those concerns were and with whether nityā has the strong sense 'exact' that is common to the interpretations both of Thibault and of some of his opponents. The root meaning is rather one of regularity, as C. Müller 1930, pp. 180ff., intimated and as was suggested to me independently by my colleague P. Khoroche. Āpastamba is satisfied with his conversion procedure not because he believes it to be exact, but simply because that was the regular way the circle was obtained. The continuation in Āpastamba shows that he has confidence that his procedure will do, but that is because it yields satisfactory results from a practical point of view – that is from the point of view of anyone faced with the practical task of constructing a circular altar equivalent in area to a square.

Kapardisvāmin's gloss amounts to a comment that the procedure is irregular, and no doubt *his* reasons for considering it such may well include his realisation that the result is only approximately correct. Yet Kapardisvāmin's interpretation cannot be accepted as a faithful reflection of the original meaning, where Āpastamba's expression implies that the method *will* regularly yield the circle.

Thus so far as Āpastamba himself is concerned, the outcome is clear. Either – on Thibault's interpretation – he thought all his rules are exact: in which case he made some egregious blunders. Or – far more probably – Āpastamba was not concerned with exactness at all, but rather with practical results. For that purpose he formulated rules of different kinds without distinguishing between them. As we have seen, he was happy enough to describe as 'regular' some procedures that we should consider *are* exact (as in XII 5) and others that *are not*.

On either view it becomes extremely difficult to credit the authors of the *Śulbasūtra*s with an explicit notion of geometric proof or with any interest in the question of the conditions under which a claim to have proved a result could be maintained. As Thibault already suggested, their concerns are practical ones, with the procedures to be followed in constructing altars with given areas, and in that context where approximations are inevitable, they are tolerated without any qualms and without any indication that the difference between exact and approximate results was of any concern to them. As Thibault 1875, p. 263, commented on one construction of a wheel-shaped altar the area of which had to be equal to that of a square: 'of course, we have to make the necessary allowance for the inevitable error introduced by the square having to be turned into a circle'.

Moreover the contemporary, modern tradition that stems from the *Śulbasūtras* also, it seems, allows approximate procedures, at least to judge from the evidence that Seidenberg 1977–8, p. 336 n. 53, quotes from Professor Staal's inquiry about how a cord is nowadays divided into five equal parts. 'According to the answer, one makes the cord overlap itself five times approximately and then makes a couple or so of adjustments.' We noted in (I) that already in the *Śatapatha Brāhmaṇa* inexact procedures are used to get certain lengths: it would appear that before, in, and after the *Śulbasūtras*, right down to the modern representatives of that tradition, we are dealing with men who tolerate, on occasion, rough and ready techniques. They are in fact interested in practical results and show no direct concern with proof procedures as such at all.

4

A test case: China and Greece, comparisons and contrasts

Thus far this study has attempted an analysis of some of the phenomena associated with the idea of divergent mentalities, and the thrust of my argument has been to suggest that much of the talk of mentalities does nothing to advance and may in certain respects positively impede understanding. Such talk often merely identifies what has to be explained, but without itself providing any adequate explanation: and it may even point away from any hope of one by invoking unverifiable psychological states or processes. In relation to some of the problems that provided part of the original stimulus for the invocation of divergent mentalities, our first step should be to pay due attention to the contexts of communication and in particular to the availability or otherwise of explicit concepts of linguistic categories. The Greek experience is particularly suggestive since we can there study how some such concepts came to be made explicit and the role they played in the development and legitimation of new styles of theorising. In connection, notably, with the Greek contributions to the development of natural scientific inquiry, we have no need to postulate some revolution in mentality, for the key moves consisted, rather, in the development of such new styles of theorising, based on, among other things, a self-conscious use of explicit categories. To understand those developments in turn a variety of factors may be appealed to, but among them the distinctive social and political circumstances of the sixth to fourth centuries B.C. are, it may be argued, of primary importance.

Hard-edged explanations of complex intellectual phenomena are no doubt not to be expected and I have acknowledged the elements of uncertainty and of sheer speculation in the arguments I have advanced. Nevertheless we should make the best use we can of the opportunities that present themselves for testing those arguments by a judicious and critical application of the comparative method. I have already made some comparisons and contrasts between ancient Greece and the far older near Eastern civilisations of Egypt and Babylonia. Further afield both India and

105

China present further considerable opportunities. Of these two the data for China appear especially promising, for the reasons we have mentioned before. Chief among these are first that there is, comparatively speaking, a substantial body of primary material that is datable at least within broad limits (in India, by contrast, as already appeared in our brief discussion of the evidence for early mathematics, claims concerning the provenance of ideas from remote antiquity are often merely speculative). Secondly the level of scholarship is such that important results can now be taken to be reasonably secure. In the West it is the work of Joseph Needham especially that has led to a greater interest in and appreciation of Chinese contributions in many areas of science and technology – work that has stimulated in turn many further important studies both in China and in the West, including research on a wealth of newly accessible data from archaeology.

The particular natures of ancient Greek and ancient Chinese civilisation may make it peculiarly tempting to appeal to the notion of distinct mentalities in description, if not also in attempts at explanation. In trying to clarify this issue in this chapter the crucial question is whether the same *types* of factors as we have invoked in our discussions of Greek thought are applicable also to China. Do we need more than reference to the contexts of communication and the deployment of certain self-conscious categories to characterise the Chinese experience, bearing in mind that in some respects it parallels, while in others it diverges from, the Greek? How far, in turn, do the distinctive characteristics of that Chinese experience reflect, and how far can they be said to be explicable in terms of, their socio-political circumstances?

One immediate and very obvious point is of substantial importance. Just as I have insisted that it is not just hazardous but often downright misleading to generalise about Greek thought, culture and politics, ignoring the immense diversity within the philosophies proposed, the scientific work undertaken, the political systems developed in theory and in practice, at different periods, so too it is clearly impossible to advance generalisations valid for the whole of Chinese history or for the totality of the many diverse traditions of thought exemplified in Chinese culture. That immediately offers one important conclusion on the issue of mentalities, namely that the locus of the problem is not and cannot be the characterisation of a supposed Chinese mentality, or a supposed Greek one, as such, as if the whole of the vastly manifold and heterogeneous phenomena that we need to take into account in each case could each be treated as reducible to or derivable from some set of basic features. The most that could conceivably be offered (with what legitimacy we shall eventually try to determine) is a characterisation of one or more dominant strands in those two complex sets of traditions. But just as when dealing with Greek science, philosophy, politics, we must acknowledge diversity, recognising, for instance, that what is true of Greek medicine may not hold in Greek astronomy, or again that what applies at one period does not at another, so too the same is evidently true of the Chinese experience. Indeed there the point has all the greater force in that we are dealing not just with several centuries in antiquity – the Greek episode, as one might say, in the development of European culture – but with a history that stretches right down to the present day.

With those cautions in mind we may, nevertheless, turn first to certain broad parallelisms in both the political situation and the intellectual and technological outputs of ancient China and Greece that appear, at least at first glance, to offer fruitful and interesting bases for comparison. It should be emphasised that we are dealing, at this stage, with very broad characterisations indeed and that the picture will need substantial modification in due course. But let us first summarise certain salient points in respect of two periods, (1) roughly from the sixth to the third centuries B.C. and (2) again roughly from the third century B.C. to the second century A.D. The first of these two periods (1) spans the end of what is called the Spring and Autumn period (usually dated 722 to 480 B.C.) together with that of the Warring States (480 or 475 to 221 B.C.). The second of the two periods we are interested in, (2), comprises the Qin and Han dynasties, and the key event that marks the division between this and the earlier period is the unification of China under the first Emperor, Qin Shi Huang Di, in 221 B.C.

At approximately the same period as the first philosophical and scientific inquiries began to be undertaken in ancient Greece there was an upsurge of philosophical interest in China too in political circumstances that bear a certain resemblance to those that obtained in Greece. The customary classification of some five or more distinct philosophical 'schools' in the pre-Han period is largely a product of later commentators (and sometimes even of modern scholarship) and must be viewed with caution, since the term school may imply more of an institutional framework and greater doctrinal coherence than we have reason to believe was the case. The Chinese themselves eventually spoke of *Jia*, families or lineages, whose main role was to hand on a group of texts. However it is clear that there was very considerable philosophical activity and speculation in the late Spring and Autumn, and more especially in the Warring States, periods, and some diverging tendencies and positions can be identified.

Confucianism was to undergo many shifts in fortune and to take many different forms: but its founder, Confucius, Kong Fu Zi, is generally thought to have lived from about 551 to 479 B.C., and some at least of the writings that pass under his name belong to the Spring and Autumn period. The supposed founder of the *Dao*, Lao Zi, is a legendary figure whose claims to historicity are tenuous (Lau 1982, pp. 121ff.), but two of the early Daoist classics, the compilations known as the *Dao De Jing* and the *Zhuang Zi*, contain material that goes back to the fourth century B.C. Again the Mohists, and the philosophers later known as the Legalists and the Logicians,[1] all began in either the fifth or the fourth century B.C.

Much of the important philosophical vocabulary was developed from straightforward concrete applications and was not the sole preserve of any one philosophical group. This is true notably of the *Dao*, the Way or Road, itself, a term used in a variety of senses in early Confucian texts as well as in the Daoist classics. Again *yin* and *yang* were originally applied to the shady and the sunny side – of a hill for instance – and the terms themselves have even been traced already in the Anyang oracle bones dating from the second millennium B.C. However in the form of the two fundamental opposing universal forces their use eventually comes to be widespread as also does the related theory of the five elements or rather five phases (Wood, Fire, Earth, Metal, Water). The latter had various applications including to moral qualities, before it became an elaborate cosmological theory that explained the cyclical changes in physical phenomena and at the same time provided a macrocosmic justification for the imperial political order seen as reflecting the order of nature (Sivin 1987, pp. 71f.). This theoretical development should again be seen as a long-drawn-out process initiated in the Warring States period and culminating in the more or less definitive versions of the *Huang Di Nei Jing* (the *Inner Canon of the Yellow Emperor*) and the *Tai Xuan Jing* (*Canon of Supreme Mystery*) of the first century B.C. (Nylan and Sivin 1987).

Negatively the political situation of the Warring States period is characterised by the lack of a central government. The processes of state consolidation which had begun already in the Spring and Autumn period continued (Walker 1953) and many of the very large number of smaller states were swallowed up in larger units. Yet as already mentioned, the first grand unification, under effective central control, of the major areas of what is now China was achieved by the first Qin Emperor and marks the beginning of the second of the two main periods I identified above (p. 107). The Warring States themselves were of varying sizes and populations and the principal ones all operated over areas much larger than those governed by any Greek city-state (I shall return to this point later). However they were autonomous, movement between them was, within certain limits, possible, and they were controlled by independent rulers (often compared, by no means entirely accurately,[2] with feudal princes). Many of these rulers held courts to which they attracted artists and scholars in a fashion that is not too dissimilar – once one makes due allowances for scale – from that of some Greek tyrants.

Both in the China of the Warring States and in Greece in the classical period the importance of a pluralist political situation for scholars and intellectuals of many different kinds is clear. The existence of a number of autonomous states offered a variety of alternative sources of patronage or support – or more simply just places to live and work. Individuals who fell out of favour in one state or with one ruler might move to another state or court. In Greece many prominent so-called sophists of the fifth and fourth centuries B.C. travelled extensively from city-state to city-state giving lectures and attracting pupils as they went – though we should be careful not to imagine them to be themselves state-less, for it is clear that many were much honoured by their home states and indeed some acted as ambassadors for them (Lloyd 1987a, pp. 92f.). Again many Greek doctors in the classical period and later regularly moved from state to state in their medical practice.

In a broadly analogous way in China at the end of the Spring and Autumn period when Confucius was exiled from his home state of Lu (modern Shandong province) he spent a number of years wandering from one state to another followed by a group of disciples and on the look-out for a sympathetic ruler who would give him the chance to put his ideas into practice – though that chance never came. Among later Confucians, the most famous, Mencius (Meng Zi), acted as adviser to the rulers of Liang and Qi in the fourth century B.C.

In that century and the next, the two most prominent Logicians, Hui Shi and Gongsun Long, also acted in a similar capacity, and the Mohists especially were much concerned with the relationship between rulers and philosophers, offering practical advice to the latter about how to please the former, and indeed themselves cultivating practical skills in part with that end in view. Alongside their more abstract or theoretical interests, in logic, for instance, they gained well-deserved reputations as skilled engineers and architects, specialising in the design and construction of defensive fortifications (Graham 1978, pp. 3ff.).

Positive interest on the part of the rulers themselves in fostering the work of philosophers can be illustrated by the case of the prince Xuan who in 318 B.C. founded the important Ji Xia academy outside one of the gates of his capital city of Qi. Here clearly, from the point of view of its foundation at least, the Museum set up by the Ptolemies at Alexandria in the early third century B.C. would be a closer analogue than the schools of philosophy at Athens – Plato's Academy, Aristotle's Lyceum, the Porch of the Stoics and the Garden of Epicurus – where in each case the foundation was the outcome of the philosophers' own initiatives. However, the evidence for the early Chinese academies offers no direct parallel to that other Ptolemaic foundation, the Alexandrian Library.

The changes in the political situation between the Warring States period and the two dynasties that followed were dramatic. The dynasty founded by the great unifier, the first Qin Emperor, did not survive the weak reign of his own son, but the dynasty that followed, that of the Han, lasted, with some interruptions, from 202 B.C. to 220 A.D. Again a broad comparison is possible, between China thus brought under central rule, and the period when most of the lands around the Mediterranean were dominated, if not also directly controlled, by Rome. Hardly surprisingly, in both Han China and in Imperial Rome, the control of vast areas brought with it, since it largely depended upon, the development of administrative and bureaucratic skills. In China this involved the institution of a professional civil service access to which was via examination. Moreover the chief basis of those examinations was provided by the teachings of Confucius, who came to be revered, in Han times, not just as one among many important philosophers, but rather as a semi-divine authority. Confucianism became, indeed, at that period, something of an official cult, and even more importantly it came to be used as an intellectual support for imperial rule.

There is no question of any slackening in the pace of technological advance, in the periods of the Qin and Han dynasties. On the contrary the list of technological innovations is enormously impressive, in metallurgy (with the invention of the double-action piston bellows), in textiles, in architecture and ship-construction, not to mention the invention of paper (Needham 1956– , Du Shiran ed. 1983, pp. 383ff., 392ff., 479ff.). However the proliferation of new philosophical systems, which had been such a feature of the period of the Warring States, certainly slowed or ceased. The first Qin Emperor himself is alleged to have suppressed and to have attempted to burn all the books he could lay hands on with the exception of certain technical treatises he considered useful.[3] Neither the Mohists nor the Logicians survived as viable philosophical groups beyond the Warring States period. It is true that new religious ideas and practices were promulgated. Buddhism entered China from India in the first century A.D. and Daoism comes to form the basis of an organised religious movement in the following century.

However while philosophical innovation certainly did not die out, the framework within which it mostly occurred altered. Most of the original thinkers who made important contributions in Han times later came to be labelled Daoists or more often Confucians (that even includes the sceptic

Wang Chong of the first century A.D., to whom we shall be returning). But the use of those categories can be highly misleading (Sivin 1978, 1988, pp. 53f.). Even where there is some evidence of a thinker representing himself as in some sense following Confucius, it would manifestly be a gross error to treat that as a sign of adherence to a single standard orthodoxy, any more than those who at different periods in the West considered themselves to be Platonists or Aristotelians agreed about what it meant to be such. It follows that it is easy to underestimate, in both cases, East and West, the originality of the work done in the guise of following a tradition: we have already noted, for example, the elaboration of the five-phase theory during the early Han period. But as with the period of the major commentators from the second to the sixth centuries A.D. in the West, so too in Han China with the beginnings of the long dominance of 'Confucianism' there is a broad shift in emphasis in one respect, in the move away from the initiation of new philosophical systems, to a concentration of effort on the preservation, interpretation and, it is true, creative reinterpretation of earlier wisdom. With the Confucians themselves especially innovation took place within, and was set against the framework of, a received body of teaching, rather than in conscious opposition to it or in a bid to outdo it.

Thus at an admittedly very high level of generality it seems possible to make a case for some broad comparisons both between the political situations and between certain aspects of the intellectual life in China and in the West during these two, very approximately contemporary, periods.[4] However a note of caution is necessary before we proceed to a more detailed examination of the similarities and differences in question. Certainly if we pursue the subsequent histories of those political and cultural developments, the distinctiveness of the experience in China on the one hand, in the West on the other, is generally far more striking than anything they may appear to have in common. To see the period following the Han as some kind of Chinese Middle Ages provides a typical example of the artificialities that arise from imposing ideas derived from the Western experience (cf. Gernet 1982, p. 172). The great political alternations, of unification and partition, that punctuate Chinese history have no real parallel, however remote, in Europe where, after the decline of the Roman Empire, total political control was never achieved by any one power. Conversely the overwhelming influence of the Christian Church both as a political factor and in religious and cosmological thought, has no Chinese analogue.

Again, although China was repeatedly subject to foreign invasion and influence, Tartar, Tibetan, Mongol, Manchu, the continuity of Chinese culture was secured mainly by the continuity of Chinese language and literature. While Latin might be thought to play a similar role as the lingua franca of educated Europe, the disanalogies are more striking. Latin was not the language in which most of the important early philosophical and scientific works had been written, nor was it the language in which they were then transmitted by Islam, and the relationships between classical Chinese and other dialects is generally closer than that of Latin to most of the vernacular languages of Europe. To this must be added a further fundamental point for which there is no analogue in the West, namely the widespread intelligibility of the Chinese ideographic script as *written*, however it may be *pronounced*. This has been one potent factor among others contributing to cultural and sometimes political unification and it has, in turn, made China very much a culture mediated by the written, more than by the spoken, word. This too is a topic to which we shall return.

The later periods of heightened activity in philosophy and science in the West and in China also follow divergent patterns, and even where they appear to coincide the chief factors at work are often manifestly different. Thus it so happens that the rise of the school of Paris took place at approximately the same time (the mid-thirteenth century) as the Yuan dynasty, notable for the brilliance of its mathematicians and astronomers. But a major factor in that European episode for which no Chinese analogue exists was the recovery of the writings of Aristotle: the Chinese had no such deep discontinuity and so no such recovery.[5]

Above all it is as one approaches the sixteenth and seventeenth centuries, and the developments often considered to be decisive in what is conventionally dubbed 'the' scientific revolution, that the lack of parallelism between the experience of China and the West appears most striking. This is not the place to embark on an analysis of those changes in Europe, of what they owed to earlier periods as well as of what was new. But however they are to be described and explained, they were specific to Europe (cf. Needham 1969, Elvin 1973, Graham 1973, Sivin 1984, Hall 1985) and it is from Europe that the eventual end-products of those developments have been diffused.

With these reminders of the subsequent diversities in the histories of these complex civilisations we may turn back to reconsider the two earlier periods we spoke of, where, as we said, the notion of certain resemblances in broad patterns of development appears at first sight to have a certain plausibility. So far as intellectual activity is concerned, the point can be elaborated both in respect of the types or fields of subject studied, and perhaps more remarkably in some of the ways in which they were

112

investigated, the styles of investigation. The philosophers of the Warring States period engaged in as wide a range of inquiry as did their Greek counterparts. These inquiries included especially ethics, cosmology or natural philosophy, medicine, astronomy (in China, as in Greece, often associated with astrology) and mathematics. Moreover logic, at least an interest in modes of argument, is represented, in China, by the Mohists and the Logicians especially, and reflection on certain epistemological questions (as we should call them), such as the reliability of sense-perception or the role of reason or the intellect, can also be illustrated readily enough in philosophers of the Warring States and Han periods.

For the Mohists, for example, there were three sources of knowledge, report, explanation and observation (Graham 1978, pp. 30ff.). They argued that what eye-witnesses reported they had seen or heard should, in general, be accepted, and used that, indeed, as one basis for their acceptance of the existence of ghosts and spirits, though they had two further arguments for this, namely first that even if the witness of humble people is denied, one cannot deny the evidence of the ancient sage-kings, and secondly that people behave better if they know that the spirits are watching them (Graham 1978, p. 15). Thus ch. 31 of the *Mo Zi* puts it (trans. Needham 1956, p. 169): 'The way to find out whether anything exists or not is to depend upon the testimony of the eyes and ears of the multitude. If some have heard it or some have seen it then we have to say it exists. If no one has heard it and no one has seen it then we have to say it does not exist. So why not go to some villages or districts and inquire? If from antiquity to the present, and since the beginning of man, there are men who have seen the bodies of ghosts and spirits, and have heard their voices, how can we say that they do not exist?'

However the Mohists were criticised not just for this conclusion but also for the criteria they used to get to it by the first century A.D. sceptic Wang Chong. Ch. 67 of his *Lun Heng* attacks them rather tendentiously, not to say unfairly, first because there is no question of the Mohists themselves excluding reason and secondly in that Wang Chong ignores the ethical aspects of the Mohist argument. However he writes (trans. Needham 1956, p. 170): 'The fact is that truth and falsehood do not depend (only) on the ear and eye, but require the exercise of the intellect. The Mohists, in making judgements, did not use their minds to get back to the origins of things, but indiscriminately believed what they heard and saw. Consequently, although their proofs were clear, they failed to reach the truth.'

That text also serves to illustrate the point that as in classical Greece, so also in China, philosophers sometimes proceeded not just positively by stating and defending their own position, but also negatively by criticising those of other groups or individuals. Again just as we find in many Greek philosophers and scientists a more or less marked streak of egotism, when they claim propriety for their own ideas and assert their own originality (Lloyd 1987a ch. 2), so similar traits can be found, if usually expressed less aggressively, in Chinese writers.

Again Wang Chong may be cited to exemplify the point. In the *Lun Heng* (chh. 83f. especially) he often introduces objections to his own position which he then rebuts in replies that state his own point of view marked as such, namely as his own. Moreover he explicitly justifies what he acknowledges to be a novel type of writing that puts forward novel ideas. When he does so, the model he still has in mind remains, clearly, that of the great Classics – but Wang Chong argues that when *they* first appeared they must have seemed new and uses this to defend his own work (ch. 84).

While, as many texts illustrate, support for a position is often, naturally, sought from what is represented as earlier wisdom or tradition – and Confucius especially saw himself as a transmitter of the wisdom of ancient sages rather than as an innovator – that clearly in no sense precluded new ideas and interpretations, and not just tacit innovation but also, on occasion, explicit claims to originality. In mathematics, for instance, we sometimes find later theorists not just citing earlier work but positively exulting in the fact that they can solve problems that had defeated everyone who had worked on them before. A classic example is the solution to the volume of the sphere, where Zu Geng (fifth century A.D.) improves on the work of Liu Hui (third century A.D.) and Zhang Heng (first century A.D.). Where Liu Hui, unable to give an exact result, had written a little poem to express 'the mathematician's frustration', Zu Geng completes his exposition with a poem to mark 'the mathematician's triumph' where he contrasts his own success with his predecessors' failures (Wagner 1978b, p. 209).

Most strikingly, perhaps, there are general expressions of doubt, a conscious withholding of judgement, an awareness of the limits of what is knowable. Chinese scepticism comes in different forms (Sivin 1986). First there are some notable occasions on which certain writers explicitly reject popular beliefs in ghosts, demons, ogres and the like, as well as certain traditional practices such as particular techniques of divination. Both Xun Zi in the third century B.C. and especially Wang Chong in the first century A.D. attacked a variety of such beliefs, Xun Zi offering a rationalisation of the origin of some of them (*Xun Zi* ch. 21, trans. Needham 1956, pp. 26f.): 'Whoever says that there are demons and spirits, must have made that judgment when they were suddenly startled, or at a time when they were not sure, or confused. This is thinking that something exists when it does not [...] Thus when a person, having got rheumatism from dampness, beats a drum and boils a sucking-pig (as an offering to the spirits to obtain a cure), then there will necessarily be the waste resulting from a worn-out drum and a lost pig, but he will not have the happiness of recovering from his sickness.' Wang Chong in turn produces a battery of arguments to show, among other things, the inconsistencies in many common beliefs about the nature and power of spirits (Needham 1956, pp. 368ff.).

A further recurrent theme in writers of different philosophical persuasions is the rejection of what was represented as useless speculation about what was beyond the limits of human knowledge. Doubt about the possibility of a genuine understanding of nature can be exemplified in different forms both in Daoist thought (Graham 1981, p. 58 on *Zhuang Zi* ch. 2) and in a certain strand of humanist Confucianism, although there the point was sometimes used rather to downgrade the study of nature as a whole in favour of a concentration on what were represented as the all-important social arts (cf. below, p. 122). Elsewhere the thrust of the argument was directed chiefly at *others'* pretensions to superior knowledge. Thus although the Mohists do not name their opponents, they mounted withering dialectical attacks on other philosophers' claims to wisdom and in particular on any pretence at certainty (Needham 1956, pp. 172ff., Graham 1978, p. 61). We should recognise, therefore, that in expressions of the idea of the ultimate inscrutability of nature, the addition of the term *ultimate* could be where the emphasis lay. That view could be combined with a determination to pursue investigations as far as they could be taken, though on the other hand it might also go with a reluctance even to try.

At this juncture the substantial similarities that can be suggested in both the contents and the styles of Chinese and of Greek philosophical inquiry might lead one to the conviction that the two were indeed basically parallel in their internal patterns of development at least in their early stages. So far as the contents of inquiries go, many of the same fields can be exemplified in both cases (including some of the same second-order inquiries, such as in the theory of knowledge), and as to the manner of their investigation, the investigators were in neither case inhibited from expressing their criticisms of traditional beliefs and of their rivals' positions. Moreover in both cases some developments of the second-order inquiries can be associated with the rivalry that existed between the various philosophical groups or individuals. It might even look as if one could go further and say that these similarities reflect a broadly similar socio-political situation: that is to say, the claim might be that a degree of political pluralism was in both cases one factor contributing to the proliferation of those rival philosophical groups. However, such conclusions both as to effects and as to causes would be premature.

A closer look at several key areas of inquiry reveals important differences underlying the broad similarities we have identified. We may take first some to do with four fields in turn, cosmology or natural philosophy, epistemology, logic and mathematics before we consider the problems insofar as they relate to ethics and politics. In the last case we have to deal not just with moral and political philosophical *speculation*, but also with the *actual* political situations, where we must examine more closely the arguments we presented in chapter 2 concerning the interaction of political experience and intellectual life in ancient Greece. So far as the leading characteristics of certain scientific and philosophical investigations go, a crucial difference will emerge between ancient Greece and China: this relates to how far theoretical speculation is geared to, or remains unconstrained by, practical ends and the extent of the preoccupation with the foundational justification of theoretical positions. As for the question of actual political experience, we shall see that the nature of the pluralism that obtained differed profoundly in the two societies – with far-reaching consequences for the type and intensity of political involvement in each.

We may turn, then, first to natural philosophy. As already noted, the dominant theory that was developed in classical Chinese philosophy was based on the five phases, Wood, Fire, Earth, Metal, Water, and the doctrine of the opposing forces of *Yin* and *Yang*. These ideas were often combined with a conception of the unitary nature of the universe and with a view of the perpetual cycle of birth, death and rebirth, to the point where the only thing that is permanent is the existence of change. The five phases were linked by relations of mutual production (in the sequence Wood, Fire, Earth, Metal, Water) and of mutual conquest (in the sequence Wood, Metal, Fire, Water, Earth, where Wood overcomes Earth, Metal overcomes Wood, Fire Metal, Water Fire and Earth Water). This whole set of principles provided an extraordinarily comprehensive and flexible framework within which almost any physical phenomena, objects or events could be described and in some sense explained.

Obviously certain similarities can be detected, both in the structure of the theories and more especially in the comprehensive way in which they were applied, between this ancient Chinese doctrine and what was for long the predominant ancient Greek physical theory, namely that based on the four simple bodies, earth, water, air and fire, often (as in Aristotle) associated with four primary qualities, hot, cold, wet and dry. Yet the fundamental differences should not be overlooked. First each of the five

116

phases is not so much a physical element as a manifestation or modality of *Qi* (breath: often compared with, even translated as, *pneuma*) (Sivin 1987, pp. 46ff.). This means that in some sense *Qi* underlies in the way matter does – while the principle of organisation is *Li*, the immanent order of things. But if in that respect the Chinese concept seems like the Greek form/matter dichotomy, one immediate contrast with most Greek ideas is that for the Chinese, matter, *Qi*, is itself vital, not inert. Again if *yin* and *yang* have often been compared to Greek theories deploying opposites, we have to bear in mind that the latter took very diverse forms, and that the correlativity, interdependence and mutual cyclical exchanges of *yin* and *yang* comprise a set of distinctive features the combination of which has no Greek parallel. Moreover once we begin to take note of other aspects of Greek speculation on change and coming-to-be, further divergences emerge, both in the great variety of theories proposed in Greek natural philosophy and more especially in that some of the positions there entertained were extreme.

Thus already in the fifth century B.C. Parmenides was led to deny change altogether, on the basis of the famous or notorious argument which we have considered in chapter 3. This starts from the bald statement that 'it is', proceeds via the denial of the possibility of anything coming to be (on the grounds that it cannot come to be from what is not, understood here, it seems, as the totally non-existent) and concludes that change too must be ruled out, since it presupposes a coming-to-be (to wit of the new state of affairs produced by the postulated change) and coming-to-be had just been ruled out. I am not concerned here to go back over the details of Parmenides' argument, but rather with his conclusion, with his evident preparedness to express a view that flies in the face of all physical experience.

The converse extreme theory, according to which change is constant, was also put forward at about the same time by Heraclitus, and this might look more like – it has often been compared with – those Chinese ideas concerning the permanence of change. However if, as seems probable, Heraclitus' view is correctly interpreted not in the weak sense – that things are subject to change from time to time – but in the stronger one, that *every* physical object is constantly undergoing change at *every* moment of time, it is again *extreme* in its implications, in its denial of common assumptions of ordinary experience. The appearance of stability of the physical objects we can seemingly so readily reidentify was held to be a mere appearance.

To be sure many specific Chinese physical theories involved a redescription and reinterpretation of what was normally taken for granted, and many common assumptions were, in the process, supplanted by highly theory-laden explanations. Moreover there can be no doubting the massive theoretical elaborations of the *Yin–Yang* doctrine, of the analysis of objects and events in terms of the five phases, of ideas to do with their transformations and with the symbolic correlations set up between items associated with them (Needham 1956, pp. 253ff., Graham 1986, Sivin 1987, pp. 59ff., 70ff.). Yet positions as extravagantly counter-intuitive as some Greek views were not normally entertained. Certainly the flat denial of change and plurality that we find in Parmenides and his Eleatic followers has no Chinese analogue.

No doubt it would be much too simple just to say that Chinese pragmatism and concentration on the practical ruled out such wild speculation. At the same time the general resistance to – or rather ignoring of – abstract theorising *just* for theory's sake is a feature of Chinese natural philosophy and is one that recurs, as we shall see, in other domains as well. Moreover in natural philosophy as in other fields a Greek concern with the question of the ultimate justification of a position is apparent. If the clear evidence of the senses conflicts with what reason suggests or can justify, then – so some Greeks were prepared to argue – so much the worse for the senses. We have found considerable evidence of Chinese interest in a variety of epistemological questions, such as, indeed, precisely, the reliability of perception and the role of reason. Yet that interest appears not to have extended as far as countenancing the absolutely uncompromising extreme view that would have it that sense-perception is of *no* value whatever and that it yields *no* reliable basis for understanding at all.

This has already taken us into our second field and to some further consideration of epistemology, the topic of the foundations of knowledge. We have noted the variety of forms that Chinese scepticism takes, many of which have close analogues in ancient Greek thought. There appears, however, to be no exact Chinese equivalent to the radical version of scepticism associated with Pyrrho of Elis (third century B.C.) as reported, for example, by Sextus Empiricus in the second century A.D. Pyrrhonism undermined *all* claims to knowledge, all attempts to establish a criterion of truth, whether in sense-perception or in reason. The Pyrrhonist was, however, careful not to assert positively that nothing can be known – for to have done so would have been as dogmatic as the claims of those who asserted that it could – the position known as negative dogmatism. Rather the Pyrrhonist suspended judgement on the issue. This was a scepticism not merely with respect to knowledge, but also to belief. The Pyrrhonist neither knew nor believed that the honey he tasted *is* sweet: he withheld judgement on all questions to do with the underlying realities and limited himself to saying merely that the honey *appeared* sweet to him.

Certainly the theme of the contrast between reality and appearance can be exemplified in several forms in Chinese thought, notably in versions of Buddhism developed from around the second century A.D. onwards. So too the topic of the relativity of judgements found expression frequently enough, in the *Zhuang Zi* and among the Mohists and the Logicians (Needham 1956, pp. 185ff., Graham 1978, pp. 338ff., 365ff., 1981, pp. 52ff.). But while there is, as we have seen, a good deal of evidence to indicate Chinese interest in aspects of the question of the foundations of knowledge, none of it suggests that they were as prepared as some Greek philosophers were to adopt extreme solutions on the basis of abstract argument, neither the total rejection of sense-perception advocated by Parmenides and his followers, nor the radical scepticism of Pyrrho.

In the third field, that of logic, too, there are significant differences within the broad similarities already suggested. Those similarities include a general interest in argument forms found in both China and Greece. Certainly the ancient Chinese, like the Greeks, were interested in techniques of persuasion: there is a section (12) devoted to this in the *Han Fei Zi* (third century B.C.), for example, although this does not proceed in the style of Aristotle's *Rhetoric* to treat the topic as capable of systematic analysis. However the Chinese were often not just skilled dialecticians, but self-conscious analysts who reflected with acuteness on aspects of the nature of dialectic, as for example on the legitimacy of certain techniques of argument. Mohists and Logicians use paradox to surprise or impress on many occasions, and even fallacious reasoning too in order to outwit an opponent (Needham 1956, pp. 189ff., Graham 1978, pp. 19ff.).

Now the strategic interests of those Chinese thinkers who discussed logical subjects were very various. Graham, for instance, has suggested (1978, pp. 31ff.) that the primary motivation of Mohist concern with disputation was an interest in the problem of the relation between knowledge and temporal change. On other occasions, the eventual aim was rather the more straightforwardly pragmatic one, of insuring success in argument, of persuading the person you sought to persuade – often, as in *Han Fei Zi* ch. 12, the ruler whose policies you hoped to influence. But the Chinese interest stopped short of the purely abstract analysis of argument schemata, involving, for instance, the use of symbols for terms or propositions, as in Aristotle's syllogistic or in Stoic logic. Stated in the most summary fashion, the Chinese interest was in dialectic, not in formal logic.

To do justice to the similarities and differences between Greek and Chinese mathematics – our fourth subject area – would require a full length study to itself. It has been said, for example, that where the Greeks' forte was in geometry, Chinese mathematics was, rather, algebraic and arithmetical in character, though that is no more than a very broad generalisation that needs substantial qualification. First the Chinese were skilled geometers, eventually developing, for instance, sophisticated methods for determining segment areas used in particular to arrive at approximations for the value of *pi* (He Shaogeng 1983). Secondly and conversely, Greek work in algebra is easy to underestimate as our sources are particularly poor: Diophantus has survived, but much of the tradition on which he evidently drew has not.

Yet one point that is of particular interest to our inquiry here, as it relates to topics we have discussed in chapter 3, concerns the proof techniques used in Chinese mathematics. First it is clear that Chinese mathematicians gave proofs and not just in one or other of the informal senses (of what convinces an audience, or of checking a result) that we spoke of before.[6] We have, rather, general demonstrations using procedures that were self-consciously deployed. Even though, as we shall see, those procedures, and the underlying preoccupations, differ in certain respects from those of Greek mathematics, we have a set of concepts in Chinese work that are the subject of explicit reflection.

One good example is that of the *Gou Gu* theorem (known in the West as Pythagoras' theorem) which is enunciated in the first-century B.C. text *Zhou Bi Suan Jing* (*Arithmetic Classic of the Gnomon and Circular Paths*) as also in the *Jiu Zhang Suan Shu* (*Nine Chapters on the Mathematical Art*). For evidence concerning the proofs of the theorem, however, we have to turn to the later commentators, notably Zhao Shuang and Liu Hui, both of the third century A.D. (Wu Wenchun 1983, Lam and Shen 1984). There is some disagreement in recent scholarship on the reconstruction of those proofs, which are at points quite inexplicit though some of the diagrams have survived and provide the chief clue as to their nature. On one interpretation the proof presupposed certain theorems concerning similar triangles but proceeded directly to show that the square on the hypotenuse is equal in area to the squares on the other two sides by means of what is called the out–in complementary principle: this governs the manipulation of equal areas and constitutes the main technique on which the proof is based (Wu Wenchun pp. 71ff.). Although the other main detailed modern analysis (Lam and Shen) differs at certain points, the authors agree in their conclusion that what we have is deductive geometry which produced proofs of an entirely general kind.

Neither here nor elsewhere did Chinese mathematicians attempt a systematic presentation of *the whole* of elementary geometry, as was done in Euclid's *Elements*, although the *Gou Gu* theorem studies are not the only early examples of sets of propositions treated in deductive sequence. Moreover the axioms employed were not stated explicitly, but left implicit

120

– with which we may compare the modern notion of leaving appropriate primitives in a system to be defined implicitly by the geometry constructed on their basis. Again no justification was attempted for the out–in complementary principle itself and much besides the axioms was also taken for granted or left implicit (cf. Wagner 1979, p. 182). Nevertheless the ancient Chinese undeniably produced conclusive general demonstrations of their results. As Lam and Shen suggest in relation to the third-century commentators (p. 110), their proofs of the numerous relations connecting the sides of a right-angled triangle effectively explode the myth that ancient Chinese mathematicians had no deductive geometry.

Once again we have an interesting combination of similarities and differences. On the one hand both traditions of mathematics practised proof and both deploy concepts to describe their procedures that are the subject of explicit reflection and comment. On the other hand three major differences emerge. The first relates to the nature of those explicit reflections I have just mentioned. Chinese mathematicians do not embark on Aristotelian-style definitions of strict demonstration as such. Comments are certainly made to the effect that such and such a formula, such and such an algorithm, is the correct one to use, but the further abstract justification of those algorithms is not attempted (cf. Libbrecht 1972, especially pp. 396f.). The principles are confidently deployed, but without the type of self-conscious analysis of *them* that an ancient Greek might have required.

Secondly and relatedly the Greek concern with ultimate foundations, with the classification of different types of indemonstrable primary premisses, axioms, postulates and definitions, and with making those used explicit at the outset of a sequence of demonstrations, has no analogue in ancient China.

Then the third and most fundamental point is this. Where the Greeks repeatedly demanded, as we said, rigorous demonstration – a preoccupation that had, as we saw, both negative and positive effects in their science as well as in their mathematics – the Chinese were evidently less concerned with giving proofs. That is not to say that they were *simply and solely* interested in results – though concern for the usefulness, including the practical applicability, of their work can be exemplified readily enough.[7] However proof is not *their* preoccupation: their style of mathematical reasoning has more to do with exploring analogies and common structures (in groups of problems, procedures, formulae) than with demonstration as such – a style that itself remains close to that favoured in other genres, including poetry, also remarkable for its interest in correlations, complementarities, parallelisms.[8] The contrast, here, with the Greek *opposition* of proof and persuasion – fuelled by the quest for incontrovertibility – could hardly be more striking.

We may now turn back to what is, from the point of view of our present concerns, the most important cluster of questions of all, those to do with the nature of ethical and political inquiry, with the practice of politics, and with the relations between those two, in each of the two ancient civilisations. Many Chinese philosophers manifest a deep-seated concern with moral questions, and in a certain strand of Confucianism the arts of social life were the primary preoccupation (though cf. Nylan and Sivin 1987 for other sides to Han Confucianism). By the time the *Yan Tie Lun* (*Discourses on Salt and Iron*) was written by Huan Kuan in the first century B.C. questions to do with the relations between natural philosophy and morality were controversial but Huan Kuan uses the latter to downgrade the former. In ch. 53 there is an imaginary debate between officials and Confucian scholars in which the latter quote Confucius himself as saying: 'People who do not know how to manage human affairs, how should they know about the affairs of the gods and spirits?' The folly of attempting to investigate the 'Great Ying Ocean' when you do not know what is near at hand is spelt out and the conclusion drawn that one 'should have nothing to do with things which are of no practical use. What is not concerned with government matters he should not investigate' (trans. Needham 1956, pp. 251f., cf. Loewe 1974 on the background). Already during the Warring States period, as also later, there were extensive discussions of political issues, with the Legalists, especially, concerned to advocate the importance of positive law (*fa*) over and above the mere customs and conventions of society (*li*).[9] We may note in passing the careful distinction thus drawn between two concepts of law that could be kept apart, but that were in fact more often run together – as *nomos* – in Greek political discussions.

Yet all of the Chinese debate presupposed the existing framework of monarchic government (Sivin 1988, p. 53): indeed the ideals remained those of a government with total control and of a single political orthodoxy. There might well be important differences, at different periods, in the actual power and influence exercised by different groups, the nobility, the civil servants and administrators, the merchants, and so too the positions and prosperity of the peasants and craftsmen themselves fluctuated. But the basic system of rule, with ultimate power concentrated in the hands of the prince or ruler, remained a constant even while administrative arrangements varied and were the subject of considerable discussion. It is true that it is possible to trace an evolution in Chinese political thought about sovereignty from the second century B.C. to the second century A.D. in that there is a shift from the idea that sovereignty depends on might to the idea that it requires the authority of Heaven. Yet both ideas take *sovereignty* as a given and the whole framework of the debate remained one of accepted monarchic despotism. Constitutional experimentation in *that* regard was not attempted in practice – nor in any real sense in theory. Constitutional variations proposed by different philosophical groups were variants of that basic form, and discussion focussed primarily on the failure of existing regimes to implement certain ideals or on their errors of commission.

Thus the *Dao De Jing* (sec. 57ff.) and the *Zhuang Zi* both express critical comments on the topic of government and sometimes suggest quietist ideals and withdrawal from public life, at least in certain circumstances (for example *Zhuang Zi* ch. 28). Yet both generally take the existing institutions as given even while they criticise the ways of rulers and offer advice about good government. Again Mo Zi is said to have advocated universal love. Yet even more than the Daoists, the Mohists worked within the existing political framework. Graham comments (1978, p. 10): 'Certainly the Mohists themselves are not a revolutionary league, at any rate in the fourth and third centuries; if there were anything seditious about them their enemies would be sure to say so. Like the Confucians, they seek audiences with princes and hope to be appointed to high office.' The disorders of the world were attributed to the want of a ruler: the Mohist aim was to improve the existing institutions, not fundamental constitutional reform.

Of course Greek political debate was often of no more than merely theoretical interest, with no practical consequences for the actual conduct of politics. This is true most strikingly of the debate reported by Aristotle on the question of whether the institution of slavery is natural or artificial – a debate that had no practical effects whatsoever in the shape of any move to abolish slavery or even to improve the lot of those enslaved (Aristotle, *Politics* 1253b14ff., cf. Finley 1980). However on the other side the Greek inquiry into constitutional forms both reflected, and was itself reflected in, the plurality of actual constitutions, ranging from monarchy to extreme democracy. The possibility of implementing new political ideas existed when new colonies were established, some of which, we know, were founded on the basis of constitutions drawn up specifically for the occasion. Thus the pluralism we have spoken of in the actual political situation in the China of the Warring States period, and in classical Greece, took different forms, for in China it was a question of a plurality of monarchical states, but in Greece one also of a variety of *types* of political constitution.

This suggests a profoundly different orientation of interest in Chinese, and in Greek, political debate. We have noted before the Greek preoccupation with foundational questions in other areas of inquiry. In ethics this took the form of a concern with the ultimate nature of right and wrong. In political philosophy questions were raised similarly concerning the underlying principles that serve as the basis for constitutions of different types, concerning the possible permutations of those principles, and the abstract classification as well as the evaluation of constitutions. By contrast the recurrent Chinese preoccupation, in theory as well as in practice, was with the orderly and efficient running of the state under its ruler: the aim was to maximise the state's resources and power for the benefit whether of the state as a whole or of its ruler, and the proper relations between ruler and ruled were considered with respect to the goal of achieving those ends. Little interest was shown in the theoretical question of possible alternative expressions of political power, or rather the possibility of such alternatives was viewed with abhorrence. The character of Chinese political philosophy in the fourth and third centuries B.C. is thus well summed up by Gernet (1982, pp. 89f.): 'The essentially practical aim of these schools of teaching and their close links with the political, social, and economic preoccupations of their time explain the eclectic character of most of them and the facility with which reciprocal influences made themselves felt. We are not dealing here with systems, with disinterested philosophical constructs, but with currents of thought between which it is sometimes difficult to establish clear lines of demarcation. However, this practical bias does not impair the value and the intrinsically philosophical interest of the questions which Chinese thinkers of this age put to themselves; the abstract, logical way of philosophizing is not the only one.'

We may now take stock of some of the suggestive correlations that have emerged both between political inquiries and political practice, and between political inquiries and other kinds of inquiry, in ancient China and Greece. Our examination of a number of fields of investigation, both first-order ones such as natural philosophy and second-order ones such as logic, reveals a recurrent contrast, at least in terms of general bias. On the one hand there is a Greek preoccupation with foundational questions and a readiness to countenance extreme or radical solutions to theoretical issues. On the other the Chinese manifest well-developed pragmatic tendencies, with a focus on practicalities, on what works or can be put to use: while often engaging in sophisticated theorising, the idea of pursuing abstract speculation for its own sake is alien to them.

We argued in chapter 2 that Greek science and philosophy reflect Greek political experience in two related ways especially: first the radical revisability tolerated in the latter – in practice as well as in theory – may have helped to release inhibitions on that score in other areas of thought;

secondly the style and even the vocabulary of the debates developed in philosophy and science may presuppose an audience trained, or at least experienced, in the evaluation of evidence and argument in the political field. Now speaking once again in the most summary fashion, the fundamental contrast between the actual political situation in ancient China and in classical Greece may be said to relate primarily to the absence, in the former, of anything that corresponds to the Greek city-state, let alone to the *polis* in its democratic forms. It is true that the suggestion has been made that some of the archaic states of the Spring and Autumn period bear some resemblance to Greek city-states. In particular Rubin (1965–6) has considered that possibility in a study of the state of Zheng under Zi Chan in the late sixth century B.C. (cf. also Graham 1978, p. 8). However his account brings to light as many differences as it does similarities: among the latter are the codification of the laws and a certain 'need to take the people's opinions and sentiments' into account in the power struggles between ruler and nobles. Among the differences are the absence of a citizen assembly and of law-courts manned by, and in the control of, the citizen body. Moreover as Rubin himself acknowledges, the situation at that time in that state is exceptional in Chinese history (cf. Walker 1953, pp. 66ff.) and he observes in conclusion that the importance of Zi Chan in the political history of ancient China is not very great (Rubin p. 34).

But having investigated the possible direct and indirect influences, on Greek speculative thought, of the framework provided by the *polis*, and specifically the democratic ideology, in chapter 2, we may ask similar questions of China here. How far can we delineate the contexts and manner in which Chinese philosophers and scientists developed and presented their ideas? Whom were they hoping to persuade and how was their typical or model audience constituted?

No doubt the answers to those questions are extremely complex. Exchanges of ideas, whether mediated by the spoken or the written word, certainly took many diverse forms. But one dominant model may be significant – that of the submission of advice to the ruler or prince (cf. Nakayama 1984, p. 37). As we have seen, that may take place in competitive circumstances, where several advisers are rivals for the attention of the ruler, and in some real or imagined debates there is no ruler present, even if one may sometimes still be the ultimate target. Again we should not underestimate the diversity of interests of princes whether they too were real or imagined. Yet clearly insofar as the ideas a philosopher produced were directed at a ruler whom he was hoping to influence, and insofar as the ruler himself was the final arbiter of the value of those ideas, those factors may well have imposed certain constraints on the ideas considered worth putting forward, constraints that may be thought to have inhibited, if not excluded, the development both of radical solutions to problems and of theoretical, abstract, impractical ones.

Conversely there are no direct analogues, in China, for the highly open-ended situation that, in the classical period at least, many Greek intellectuals faced, where their goal, when not to reach the abstract truth itself, was to persuade an undifferentiated general audience, even if one imagined to be no tyros in the matter of the evaluation of evidence and argument. In practice, no doubt, the actual audiences who attended the lectures, discussions or debates, or who read the books, in China and in Greece, were in both cases highly heterogeneous. Yet a difference in emphasis may still be remarked. In the political arena, especially, much important Chinese writing takes as its target the persuasion of the prince, while at the limit, in Greece, the undifferentiated audience was the citizen body gathered in assembly. This is not just a matter, then, of the broad contrast that stems from the *relative* predominance of the written to the spoken register in Chinese culture (above, p. 112) and of the *relative* importance of the oral mode of Greece (p. 37): the *particular* type of spoken exchange that exerts a far-reaching influence on Greek thought was, we suggested, the public debate adjudicated by a lay audience.

We have one further major topic to consider that once again permits a complex comparison and contrast to be made between the ancient Chinese and ancient Greek data. I refer to the availability and use of certain explicit linguistic categories – an issue that has generally received less attention than the analysis of such central primary concepts as *physis* in Greek thought, the *dao* or *yin–yang* or *li* (immanent order)[10] in Chinese, significant as those topics also undeniably are. In chapter 1 I suggested that it is of particular importance, in assessing apparently paradoxical or counterintuitive statements or beliefs, not to introduce category-distinctions alien to the actors themselves, and in particular to consider the availability or otherwise of a contrast corresponding to the one we – following the ancient Greeks – draw between the literal and the metaphorical. Once that distinction is available, a particular type of challenge, as to the meaning of a statement or the commitment to a belief, may be put more forcefully, and that factor may be important in two ways, first in *our* avoiding overinterpretation of those actors' statements and beliefs (with the premature diagnosis of divergent mentalities, or even of irrationality) and secondly in the assessment of the character of interpersonal exchanges in a society, in a group or in particular contexts (where indeed there may be significant differences in style).

So we may ask: did the ancient Chinese too, like the Greeks, draw a contrast between the literal and the metaphorical; and if so how did they deploy it? One part of the answer is clear. The primary context in which some such notion as that of the metaphorical is developed appears to be that of literary analysis. Already in a discussion of the three main types of poetry Confucius is supposed to have identified one that depends on metaphor or comparison, the likening of one thing to another.[11] The fact that not all poetry was held to fall into that category indicates, however, that what is in question is rather a matter of particular – and particularly effective – uses of comparison, not a fundamental feature of all poetic discourse. Nor is there any suggestion, in the Confucian theory or elsewhere, that poetry in general, or particular types of poetry, should be deemed inferior – because dependent on metaphor or comparison – to other modes of discourse free from such a dependence.

The Chinese, like the Greeks, certainly drew contrasts not just between different styles and types of poetry, and between poetry and prose, but also between different genres of prose writing, including philosophy itself along with history (the writing of Annals), novels, treatises on mathematics, medicine and other technical subjects, and much else besides. Again there was sometimes rivalry between different authors at least within the same genre: we have seen that the criticism of one philosophical group by members of another is common. But while we have, in Confucian theory, the notion of the metaphorical as a virtue of a certain style of poetry, neither there nor elsewhere in Chinese thought do we find the Aristotelian notion according to which the opposition between the metaphorical and the literal is one between the deviant and the norm, where, when judged as a vehicle for expressing the truth, metaphor is a vice, and where poetry is deliberately downgraded with respect to philosophy from just that point of view. Indeed in Confucian thought poetry was considered a powerful instrument of moral injunction and in that as valuable as philosophy itself.

In prose as well as poetry Chinese writers are often critical of *particular* comparisons or analogies (for a striking example from Wang Chong, see Day 1972, pp. 26ff.). But it is not as if every kind of metaphor or every type of comparison was thought of as mistaken or inadequate – as being obscure, for example, as Aristotle called all metaphorical expressions (above, p. 21). Rather the Chinese concern is with making the *right* comparisons, in using the *correct* analogy, a concern that certainly does not deny, but clearly presupposes, the legitimacy of analogy and comparison when so used.

The available concepts of linguistic categories and the way they were used, are, in the Chinese case too, pointers to the styles of reasoning, argument and confrontation to be found. What is common, here, between the Chinese and the Greek experience is a certain self-conscious explicitness with regard to such categories: both Chinese and Greeks have a rich vocabulary in which to discuss aspects of the nature of language, the forms or genres of discourse, meaning, the relations between words and things (the last being particularly important, in China, as we shall see, under the heading of the rectification of names). But while the notion of metaphor as the, or a, use of likeness is found in China, the treatment of it as deviant is not. Nor accordingly do we find, among the many manifestations of rivalry exemplified in Chinese culture, that distinct – Aristotelian – form that represented philosophy, or rather one particular style of philosophising, as the sole repository of the truth in opposition to all comers. But that is rather to say that just as there is a certain extremism in many specific Greek theories (as we found in physics and in epistemology for instance) so too there are certain well-known extremist tendencies in the extent to which Greek competitiveness – the agonistic spirit – was developed. Caution needs, no doubt, to be exercised in interpreting recurrent Chinese statements of the overriding importance of harmony and of reconciling opposite views: appeals to an ideal of harmony certainly did not prevent criticism, even hostility, from finding open expression often enough in a variety of contexts. Nevertheless differences remain.

As we said with proof, the literal–metaphorical dichotomy is not *their* preoccupation. By contrast one recurrent second-order concept that does play a prominent role, in Chinese thought, is what they called the rectification of names (*Zheng Ming* see especially *Xun Zi* sec. 22, Watson 1963, cf. Needham 1956, pp. 9f., 28f.). It may be significant that unlike the Greek contrast between literal and metaphorical, the rectification of names is an idea that tends rather to unite than to divide fields of inquiry. In particular it is striking that – where metaphor was deemed by Aristotle to be especially 'poetic' – the *Xun Zi* treats the rectification of names as covering *both* the correct *practical* function of simple names in the clear communication of meaning *and* the pleasing or *aesthetic* function when used in combinations (Watson p. 147). The idea encompasses far more than the merely logical or linguistic concern with correct definition that the conventional English translation might suggest. The emphasis was more often not on getting names to correspond to (given) realities so much as on getting the (social) realities to correspond to given, established, orthodox names. Matters to do with the determination of statuses and social conditions, indeed with good order generally and the avoidance of moral confusion, are implicated (cf. Gernet 1982, pp. 96f.).[12] As the *Xun Zi* diagnoses the problem (trans. Watson, p. 141) it is when 'strange words come into use, names and realities become confused, and the distinction between right and wrong has become unclear'. Indeed according to this text it is only thanks to the existing confusion, and to the contentiousness that this generates, that persuasive speaking must be used, for, previously, the enlightened ruler had no need of such (Watson, p. 146). The rectification of names is here considered as an antidote or remedy for argumentativeness: once again this suggests a poignant contrast with the agonistic Greeks for whom argument was not a symptom of a failure to have reached the truth, but the means whereby to attain it.

The lessons to be learnt from our comparisons and contrasts here are twofold. We have insisted from the outset that many different cultures and periods have their contribution to make to the emergence of proto-science. We may now suggest that the nature of the proto-science that was developed in ancient China on the one hand, in ancient Greece on other, reflects among other things not just the fact that certain explicit concepts of linguistic categories were available but also and more particularly the particular concepts that were given prominence in either case. The very existence of certain such concepts is significant in China too, as in Greece, for the types of question that can be raised. Some of those we considered from ancient Greece we found to be crucial for the definition of the inquiries themselves. But proto-science did not just take its Greek form, and the Chinese contrast illustrates an alternative line of development, corresponding, in part, to different emphases in the deployment of these second-order concepts. In view of the great influence that the Greek dichotomy between the literal and the metaphorical has exercised on later Western thought, it may be especially significant that the absence, in China, of such a sharp dichotomy correlates – negatively – with less antagonism between competing approaches to the truth and with less exclusivity in the claims made on the part of one particular style of inquiry. The converse, positive, correlation is with a greater shared confidence that an orthodoxy can and should be achieved.

Our excursus into Chinese thought has necessarily been highly selective and we must emphasise, once again, the complexities of the material under discussion. This evidently makes generalisation about the totality of Chinese thought absurd. But where does this admittedly restricted survey leave us with regard to the problems of mentalities that are our strategic concern?

First the problems presented by those very complexities in Chinese thought for any hypothesis of a global mentality have already been pointed out. There can be no question of diagnosing a single such mentality, even at a single period. Moreover the interactions and cross-influences of Chinese philosophical lineages make it only slightly less transparently difficult to postulate specific mentalities in any particular such lineage, as it might be Confucian, Daoist, Buddhist and so on.

However it does seem possible – and relevant – to talk of varieties of styles of inquiry, of reasoning and argument, of interpersonal exchange, both within China and between ancient China and ancient Greece. It was in those respects especially that both the similarities and the differences we attempted to specify seemed particularly suggestive. On the one hand the intellectual products of both ancient civilisations are, in certain respects at least, strikingly similar. In both there is a proliferation of philosophical systems in the fifth and fourth centuries B.C.: both manifest sustained concern with questions of moral philosophy, both have advanced mathematics and complex natural-philosophical theories, both show an interest in aspects of epistemology and logic.

On the other hand certain differences have also to be taken into account. First the practical orientation of much Chinese philosophical and scientific theorising – one of its undoubted strengths – may be held to contrast with a recurrent taste for abstract theorising for its own sake in much Greek thought – in political philosophy and in formal logic, for instance. Again in both these fields of inquiry and in others such as mathematics and natural philosophy and as they said physics, the Greek pursuit of foundational questions, and a concern with ultimate justification, seem exceptional. While the Chinese appealed to reason often enough, and in connection with some sophisticated theories, they were less inclined to demand ultimate foundations. Conversely what, for many ancient Greeks, counted *as* a justification was what satisfied abstract reason alone and they accordingly referred less readily to the criterion of the pragmatic test, that the theory worked, that it delivered results, whether in the form of mathematical theorems or, in physics, of ideas that had some practical applicability.

Again while there are important broad similarities in the *manner* in which various inquiries were pursued – including a certain self-consciousness, explicit claims to originality, explicit criticisms of others' views, and varieties of scepticism not just about popular beliefs but also about the limits of human knowledge – these features are often present in different degrees or otherwise exhibit certain divergences. Though tradition was by no means followed slavishly in China, its importance was often expressly emphasised, in contrast to what is generally true of Greece in the classical period (even though appeals to what is sanctioned by tradition play a more prominent role in the Hellenistic period: I shall come back to this). Above all, competitive, agonistic traits are displayed, at least in certain contexts, in Greece to a quite unprecedented and unparalleled degree – with the negative as well as the positive consequences we have pointed out. We are not, let me repeat once again, attempting to characterise whole civilisations or their 'thought' in their entirety. But in piecemeal comparisons a checklist of points with varying degrees of relevance can be accumulated each of which has a contribution to make to the complex pictures we wish to present of aspects of the intellectual activity of each.

If, in these complex pictures, these are the similarities and differences that we should focus on, namely in styles of reasoning and interpersonal exchange, then to *describe* these in terms of mentalities appears cumbrous and at best redundant, while to attempt to *explain* them in such terms more obviously runs the risk of being merely circular. That leaves an obligation, for sure, to say what types of explanatory factor might be invoked – while still not expecting, as I said, that hard-edged explanations of complex intellectual phenomena can be given. This question too has enormous ramifications and only some salient suggestions can be canvassed here.

Thus reference to economic conditions in China and Greece, and in particular to the specific types of economy that flourished, has been thought to be helpful, and no doubt a certain level of economic development is necessary for the maintenance of groups who could devote time to such luxury pursuits as speculative philosophical inquiry. In ancient China as in ancient Greece this prosperity was based in part on slavery or at least on unfree labour, though comparative evaluation here is difficult because of the different modalities that took in East and West.[13] At the same time a general economic argument will not take us far, for we have to bear in mind that some economically prosperous civilisations produced nothing like the self-conscious philosophical investigations we find in both China and Greece (cf. Lloyd 1979, ch. 4).

Again it has been remarked that China's wealth always depended primarily on agriculture, and certain features of Chinese thought have been related to the preoccupations of farmers as opposed to herdsmen (Gernet 1982, pp. 13ff., 26ff., Needham 1956, pp. 576ff.). Here too, however, it would seem rash to suppose that all basically agricultural societies emphasise harmony both in human social relations and in man's relations to nature, any more than all pastoral societies share aggressive and competitive traits that reflect the experience of the need to control the animals they herd. Certainly the data for the great variety of political systems developed in Africa that Fortes and Evans-Pritchard assembled in their classic collective study strongly suggest – as they themselves noted (Fortes and Evans-Pritchard 1940, p. 8) – that those systems are not straightforwardly determined by the modes of livelihood (for example as agriculturalists, or pastoralists) of the societies in question. Moreover the representation of all agricultural societies as consensual fails to discriminate between those that did, and those that did not, engage in the systematic investigation of nature.

Caution also needs to be exercised in considering how far features to do with the technology of communication will serve as explanatory hypotheses for the explananda we are concerned with. True, the structure of the Chinese language and the character of Chinese writing are undeniably of pervasive importance in a number of respects. I have noted that the common language, represented in a script that can be read by speakers of quite different dialects all over China, contributed to the cultural and political unification of the country (cf. Gernet 1982, pp. 29ff), and that the written register was, from certain points of view, the privileged one. The possible influence of the Chinese language on the interests that were developed in logic is a theme that has been fruitfully developed by a number of scholars (Needham 1956, pp. 198ff., Graham 1964, 1978, Reding 1986 and forthcoming). Yet again there are limitations to this argument: at least the distinctive features of much Chinese work in such fields as astronomy or medicine or natural philosophy do not appear to stem directly from the character of the language.

So far as the West is concerned, much has been made of the argument that the advent of an alphabetic system of writing – and the spread of literacy that followed – brought about major, even fundamental developments and were largely responsible for the differences between Greek and ancient near Eastern intellectual inquiries in particular (Goody 1977). But it is abundantly clear that the lack of an alphabetic system of writing in China did not prevent the growth of a range of philosophical and scientific investigations which are, at least from some points of view, as we have seen, closely analogous to those of the ancient Greeks. In China the spread of literacy depended more straightforwardly on education (Rawski 1979, pp. 1ff.). Moreover the early introduction of printing in China carried with it certain undoubted advantages but brought about less dramatic changes than have been seen to stem from the analogous technological development later in Europe (Eisenstein 1979). Whatever the history of the development of *European* thought may owe to factors relating to increasing literacy, appeal to such factors appears to be of only limited usefulness in explaining the specific characteristics of *Chinese* intellectual inquiries that we have identified, whether where they resemble, or where they differ from, those of the West, or in explaining the historical developments they underwent. This much may, however, be said, that proto-science, whether in its Chinese or in its Greek form, evidently presupposes *some* degree of literacy, that is the existence of *some*

132

fully literate individuals – for certainly complex mathematical reasoning, for instance, depends on the written register.

But how far can the type of socio-political hypotheses we developed for ancient Greece be applied also to the Chinese data? At least here we can suggest correlations not just for some of the similarities, but also for some differences, between the two civilisations. First so far as the broad similarities go, we said that the courts of the Warring States period provided support and refuge for intellectuals of various kinds and thus offered the opportunity of alternative bases for their activities: and similar alternative bases, if not much positive support, were available in the Greek city-states of the classical period. Though it would be rash to see the development of independent critical philosophising in the crucial early stages in both China and Greece as directly produced by the measure of freedom of manoeuvre that the political situation in each case secured, a weaker argument, to the effect that that freedom of manoeuvre at least aided that development, seems plausible enough. Conversely when that freedom declined, in China, with the Empires of the Qin and Han dynasties, the growth of specifically new philosophical systems did too, even though by no means all creative philosophical activity did. Similarly in the Greco-Roman world the period of greatest philosophical innovativeness may be thought to correspond to that of the greatest political strength of the autonomous city-states, even though creative work continued, in the Greek case too, in the early Hellenistic period (Lloyd 1987a, ch. 2).

But then so far as the major differences go, the chief contrasts in the actual political situations in Greece and China in the period from the sixth to the fourth century relate, we said, first to the variety of existing constitutional types in the former and to the extent of the direct political experience that the democracies, especially, there afforded. But the Greek *theoretical* inquiry into the classification of constitutions seems clearly linked to the *actual* experience of that variety of constitutional types, even though two reservations must be made. First the theoretical inquiry evidently outran the actual experience, in that theoretical solutions to political questions were explored that were never implemented in practice. Secondly the relationship between theory and practice is one rather of mutual interaction, not a causal link in one direction only. Conversely it is not surprising that Chinese speculation, in this area, generally took the existing monarchical political framework as a given: both in theory and in practice that remained unchallenged.

But this in turn may suggest a more general observation concerning the differences we noted in the attitudes towards tradition and the degree to which it provided the framework of inquiry. Over and above such factors as the relative importance of agriculture and of the influence of attitudes associated with it, it may be that that contrasting political experience is relevant also here. At least the possibility of *radical* innovation and of radical revisability that existed in the political domain – though only in the sixth to fourth centuries B.C. – in Greece may (I suggested) have released inhibitions concerning radical innovation in other areas of experience, including in a variety of fields of theoretical inquiry. Moreover the shift towards tradition and away from radical innovation that may be detected in many areas of theoretical inquiry in Greece after the fourth century B.C. again seems to mirror the changing political situation we have noted and the circumscription of possibilities there.

Finally there are those other features that in kind or in degree appear to be distinctive of much Greek theoretical inquiry, and not just in political philosophy, but also in physics, in epistemology, in formal logic and even in mathematics, first the concern, at points the obsession, with foundational questions and with ultimate justification, and secondly the aggressiveness of much intellectual debate. Once again these differences too may be held to correspond to differences in political experience: what appears to have no parallel in China at any period is the extensive first-hand experience that a substantial proportion of Greek citizens had of adversarial advocacy in debates in the law-courts and assemblies, and of a recurrent concern, in those contexts, with, precisely, justification and accountability.

There is no doubt much that eludes this line of explanation on its own and indeed when taken in conjunction with the other suggestions I have mentioned. Certainly not every feature of the intellectual activities of the many individual geniuses that China and Greece produced can be reduced to, or even remotely connected with, one or more of the explanatory factors that we have considered. But while we should never lose sight of the difficulty of any attempt to identify the influences at work, the hypothesis of the importance of political factors – both as necessary conditions and as positive stimuli – is not weakened by, and indeed appears to derive some positive support from, an examination not just of where the experience of ancient China resembles, but also of where it diverges from, that of ancient Greece. Moreover whatever may be thought about the viability of available explanations, that examination tends at least to confirm that the *explananda* are best described not in terms of divergent mentalities, so much as in terms of the specificities of styles of inquiry and of interpersonal exchange.

Conclusion: mentalities demystified

The starting-point of our inquiry was the question of the validity and usefulness of the notion of mentalities and we may now attempt, in conclusion, to reassess that general issue in the light of the findings of our case-studies. As we saw at the outset, the notion of mentalities has been invoked in a variety of contexts, notably in social anthropology, in philosophy, in history and in psychology. The strength of the claims made in connection with the use of this notion has varied considerably. In some writers talk of a mentality seems to amount to little more than talk of certain recurrent attitudes, views or interests. At the same time some other appeals to the notion appear to have very sweeping implications indeed. This is true particularly when it is assumed that a whole culture, or a society at a particular period of time, or again each of a number of stages in universal human cognitive development, exhibits certain distinctive mental characteristics.

Evidently not all uses of mentalities are equivalent, and in particular it is not always clear just how far there is a commitment to those potentially sweeping implications. Again the ramifications of the appeal to mentalities in the methodological debates of historians, or in those of cognitive psychology, stretch well beyond the particular problems we have tackled here – as also do many other related issues to do with meaning and culture that have been aired in debates in linguistics, in philosophy and in social anthropology. The question for us now is how far in the cases we have considered the notion of mentalities, when pressed, withstands scrutiny, and how useful it is as the basis of a solution to those problems.

The fundamental issue that underlies much of the debate on mentalities is the question of the nature of the uniformities, and the grounds of diversity, of human thought. No one doubts that the *contents* of human thought – the ideas or beliefs themselves – vary enormously and that so too do their means of expression. But the notion of mentalities raises and suggests a positive answer to the further question of whether certain differences in content should be held to reflect differences in the under-lying characteristics of the mind – whether these are described in terms of structures, processes, operations, habits, capacities or predispositions. The associations of these and other terms used to describe the character-istics in question differ, but all serve to treat those characteristics as mental ones. That is they serve to relate differences in the contents of thoughts to differences in the minds that do the thinking, where there is more to this suggestion than the merely tautological point that *any* thought has to be that of some thinker.

Two other approaches to aspects of the question of the uniformities and diversities of thought may help to throw light on distinctive features of the analysis in terms of mentalities. First there are well known arguments originally propounded by Sapir and Whorf concerning the influence of language upon thought (Sapir 1949, Whorf 1956). Few would nowadays accept the strongest version of the thesis, according to which language totally *determines* thought, if only because of the unacceptability of the apparent implications for the impossibility of expressing certain thoughts in certain languages. Communication across languages, even if no doubt imperfect, poses obvious difficulties for the idea that thought is entirely constrained by one language. However it may more readily be agreed that language at least *influences* thought in the sense that different languages may favour or impede the expression of certain types of ideas, for example of certain category distinctions. Indeed the Sapir–Whorf hypothesis has sometimes been formulated to imply no more than this weaker position (compare for example Hoijer 1954, Hockett 1954 and Benveniste 1971, and cf. the critical assessment of Lukes 1982, pp. 267f.).

But the diversity of human languages is a fact of language and leaves untouched the major issues to which the notion of mentalities has been applied. However much preferred expressions peculiar to a particular language or group of languages may be associated with specific nexuses of ideas, it has never been argued that any given mentality varies solely and directly with the language in which it finds expression. Even if it is true and important that certain key terms undergo shifts in their meaning at certain historical junctures, notably in the course of scientific revolutions, that does not – and cannot – apply to languages in their entirety. No more are transformations in whole languages envisaged by those who have spoken of mentalities in connection with stages of cognitive development.

Conversely a second, diametrically opposed, approach would proceed by an analysis of the claims to universality that might be made on behalf of logic. Thus it has been argued – though the claim has, to be sure, been disputed – that there are, as Aristotle held, logical universals in the sense of principles of intelligibility presupposed by all human communication –

though it would be a further step to accept Aristotle's own specific suggestions (the laws of non-contradiction and of excluded middle, see above, p. 86 and n. 3) as to what those principles are.

Now that argument, if accepted, would have the consequence of ruling out, *a priori*, the extreme version of a mentality that is pre-logical or non-logical. There could be no such mentality, if all communication presupposes logic in the minimal sense of principles of intelligibility. However, as with the converse argument from the diversity of languages, that does not dissolve the issues to do with mentalities in general. The development of Lévy-Bruhl's own thinking on the subject illustrates that there is more to the notion of mentality than the specific suggestions he made concerning pre-logicality: for, as we saw (above, pp. 1ff.), he came to abandon the latter entirely, while still maintaining a modified role for the general notion.

Unlike entirely general arguments from the relativity of thought to language or from postulated universal principles of logic, the notion of mentalities is, of course, invoked to deal with particular problems in characterising particular sets of beliefs or assumptions, sometimes held by individuals but more often by collectivities. The defence that might be offered against the line of argument from logical universals would be that *if* there are such (though many of the proponents of mentalities would deny that) then clearly these are shared by *all* mentalities. But that – on the view of those proponents – would not do away with the need to discriminate *between* mentalities. Again to the line of argument from the relativity of thought to language the answer would be to deny that mentalities vary directly with any given natural language.

In other words the claim would be that appeal to a *specific* mentality is always a response to the need to make sense of particular circumstances – the ideas, beliefs, assumptions of a society, a group or a period, where those ideas, beliefs and assumptions exhibit certain distinctive and recurrent characteristics that serve to mark out the underlying mentality. No single such characteristic need be unique, but their conjunction has clearly to be sufficient to yield a definition, or at least a determinate description, of the underlying mentality.

If indeed there is to be more to the use of the term than just a vague gesturing towards certain differences in attitudes or views, then it requires some such justification and argument. The nub of the matter is whether the particular circumstances in response to which appeal to a mentality is made are *ever* such as to require that notion or even to legitimate it as the most appropriate or economical response. Are the particular apparently irrational beliefs or assumptions of society X or group Y such as to tell in favour of an underlying mentality? Are the world-views, preoccupations, patterns of behaviour, of particular historical periods or of cultures as a whole sufficiently determinate and distinctive to do so? The limited case-studies we have investigated here certainly suggest specific difficulties of a variety of kinds for any such view.

Two of the most important objections may be summarised briefly. First we said that to make any tolerable sense – certainly to justify a claim to provide an economical account of the phenomena – the mentality postulated should indeed be recurrent and pervasive, and should inform, or be reflected in, a substantial part of the ideas, beliefs and assumptions of the individual or group concerned. Yet in our study of magic ancient and modern we found that magicians *combine*, readily enough, beliefs and behaviour patterns that are considered deviant, with others that the dominant ideology deems normal. Similarly it is not as if the *whole* of the mental activity of modern scientific research workers conforms to a single pattern which could be said to incorporate the scientific method and so be held to reflect a supposed scientific mentality.

The recurrent objection here lies in the apparent difficulty of attributing a plurality of mentalities to a single individual or indeed to a collectivity as such, a plurality that corresponds to the diversity of their observed activities and beliefs including the diversity in the procedures the agents or actors themselves deem to be appropriate to verify or justify those activities and beliefs. In many societies it would, no doubt, be hard to find exact parallels for the case of the scientist who may behave in an apparently quite unscientific fashion in certain contexts outside the laboratory. But there is no reason to doubt similarly striking contrasts between the exceptional, and the ordinary, beliefs and behaviour both of ancient magicians, wonder-workers and shamans and of their modern counterparts. On the contrary there is every reason to insist on that possibility – against the implications of the strong notion of mentality which suggests that ideas and beliefs reflect and conform to determinate and distinctive structures, processes or predispositions.

If so, in some of the very cases that have been taken to favour the notion of mentalities – namely in dealing with apparently irrational beliefs or patterns of behaviour – it would appear that due attention to the full range of the ideas and activities of the individuals concerned points rather to the *in*appropriateness of ascribing to them a *single determinate* mentality. Lévy-Bruhl himself recognised on several occasions that in their technical and practical performances the members of primitive societies do not differ significantly from those of his contemporaries in France (Lévy-Bruhl 1975, pp. 38, 55, 62). Yet he did not recognise the difficulty that that surely presents for the idea of a mentality characteristic of, or dominant among, 'primitive peoples' as such: for surely that technical and practical behaviour reflects *thought* and so constitutes one part – and no merely subsidiary part – of their mental lives just as much as religious beliefs, for example, do another (cf. Jahoda 1982, pp. 229f., and already Evans-Pritchard 1934, p. 10).

The second principal objection develops a converse point: while the first difficulty focusses on the problem of individuals who must be supposed to possess a plurality of mentalities, the second raises the problem of how a mentality, once acquired, can ever be modified (cf. Chartier 1982, pp. 25 and 31, Burke 1986, p. 443). If the notion of a mentality is to have any force, it must correspond to certain recurrent and pervasive patterns of ideas, beliefs or behaviour. But the more pervasive and stable these are thought to be, the more difficult it becomes to see how shifts in mentalities can occur, whether in individuals' mentalities in the short term, or in those of groups or whole societies in the long. The supposed stability of the underlying structures or processes is, in part, what justifies talk of a *mentality* – as opposed to reference merely to the contents of beliefs. But then how those structures change over time becomes problematic.

That has been raised as a difficulty for those who represent the cognitive development of the child in terms of a sequence of clearly demarcated stages. But analogous problems arise on a larger scale when the notion of mentality is applied to the broad contrasts between historical periods. While the notion of mentalities may facilitate generalisations concerning the *contrasts* between one period and another, that notion comes under pressure when questions to do with the *transition* from one period to the next are raised. Mentalities are not to be imagined as changing totally overnight. But to speak of the erosion or replacement of *part* of a mentality – by another – risks incoherence or appears to dissolve the stronger notion of mentality into the weaker, looser one where no more than some particular views or attitudes are in question. The particular transition we have discussed in some detail – that represented by the emergence of certain new styles of inquiry in ancient Greece in the fifth and fourth centuries B.C. – offers, as we saw, no justification, indeed no purchase, for the suggestion that one *mentality superseded* another, either in the individuals concerned or in particular determinate groups of them.

But in default of appeal to some such notion as that of mentalities how can the phenomena that that notion addressed be described, let alone then explained? We have emphasised that, in the face of the immense variety of apparently highly counterintuitive, puzzling or paradoxical statements that can be collected from any given society, let alone worldwide, generalisation is out of the question. Each such statement or reported belief poses its own individual problems of interpretation, many of them, no doubt, severe and with no guarantee of even partial success in understanding. However in the cases we have considered there is no call whatsoever to invoke some mentality purportedly indifferent to contradiction or tolerant of incompatibility.

To make some headway in our understanding of such statements we need first to pay due attention to two interrelated factors especially, namely the contexts of communication and the availability of explicit concepts of linguistic and other categories. So far as the latter goes, in some cases the speaker clearly cannot anticipate the types of question that we as observers might feel tempted to press, for example as to whether a particular statement is intended literally or metaphorically. This is not to make any claim that somehow in the absence of certain explicit linguistic categories the interpretation of puzzling statements is transparent to the speakers and their audiences themselves. True, some such statements that appear puzzling to *observers* only do so because they lack the contexts in which they are to be understood. To pick up one of my earlier examples, Plato's remark that the Form of the Good is 'beyond being', quoted without context, can hardly fail to generate considerable bafflement in any reader ancient or modern (and some of that feeling may well remain, in that case, even when the context is supplied).

However on other occasions the strangeness may be no mere artefact of the distance between the observers' and the actors' points of view. In two types of situations it is easy to see that puzzlement may be genuine enough. First there may be contexts when an individual may be driven to adopt admittedly strange or paradoxical solutions to recalcitrant problems. This can be exemplified not just from religious beliefs, but also from scientific theories: we have mentioned wave–particle duality in the theory of light before. Secondly there is the *deliberate* exploitation of the puzzling – for that is clearly not confined to societies that can avail themselves of a particularly rich set of conceptual tools in the form of complex linguistic and logical categories. Obfuscation and mystification may be used to claim, or demonstrate, superior, esoteric, knowledge, or as devices to maintain secrecy, and no doubt for many other linguistic and extra-linguistic purposes.

It is not as if such comments as these are meant to exhaust the contexts in which linguistic extravagance of one kind or another may be displayed, let alone extravagance of belief or in behaviour. Rather they serve as a reminder of the variety of resources available both to insiders and to outsiders as a means of reaching some provisional interpretation of any such extravagance – while we should not deny that there may still be plenty of occasions when, intentionally or otherwise, a speaker's statements do indeed *resist* attempts at interpretation. The baffling cannot always be unmasked to reveal the clear: indeed in some domains of discourse, not just in the expression of religious beliefs or speculation about the obscure but also in the most modern science, the ultimately baffling may be finally inescapable.

To revert once again to an example from the religion that many have held to be compatible with the most advanced scientific knowledge, when a Christian accepts that God is three and God is one we may understand at least this much, that that indicates commitment to a particular religious belief and belonging to a particular faith. But quite what *proposition* is being accepted is not at all clear and indeed the subject of intense theological debate. But then again the analysis of religious meaning in *strict propositional* terms will always be likely to have to leave a good deal out of account and that applies not just to the analysis of religious meaning. It is striking that in his discussions of the assumptions 'we' make concerning the laws of nature Lévy-Bruhl several times qualified his statements concerning their universality to allow for 'the exceptional case of the miracle'.[1] Whether or not there are traces of irony in his so doing,[2] he evidently acknowledged that there are, after all, instances of religious belief in European thought that defeat any claim to the effect that the regularities of natural cause and effect are assumed by 'us' to be of universal, exceptionless applicability.

As a reaction to the apparently irrational in beliefs and practices the appeal to a distinct mentality itself appears excessive and it diverts attention away from what seem more promising avenues of investigation. The importance of the contexts of communication and of the presence or absence of explicit concepts of linguistic categories emerges again with particular force in situations such as those that obtained in ancient Greece when a variety of traditional beliefs came to be subject to challenge and new styles of inquiry began to be undertaken. Those changes often relate directly to the development of concepts that could be, and were, used to press home radical challenges to justify theories or beliefs, whether new or old. Although, as we noted, even without such explicit concepts as that of the metaphorical, or myth, or magic, the beliefs in question are not totally immune to challenge of any kind, the modes of challenge and the likelihood of it in part reflect the availability of such concepts.

That new Greek preoccupation with the justification of theories and beliefs in general parallels and is, we argued, influenced by a similar preoccupation in the contemporary political and legal experience of Greek citizens. Moreover the association of those features of Greek speculative thought with those aspects of Greek political life, when tested against the evidence from ancient China, seems to withstand the test and thereby gain some, indirect, confirmation. At least, despite the many important similarities between the intellectual and political developments that took place in *both* Greece and China, neither the characteristic Greek preoccupation with foundational questions and ultimate justification (and the corresponding readiness to countenance radical innovation) nor again the corresponding marked adversarial qualities, in both practical politics and speculative thought, can be closely paralleled in either domain in ancient China. It is not just that there is a general sense in which Greek philosophy reflects the circumstances of Greek political experience: rather the latter is at least one important formative influence on the styles of debate that are typical of the former.

To a Lévy-Bruhlian it might now appear that to talk, as I have done, of certain of the distinctive characteristics of Greek – or of Chinese – speculative thought and political life, and to speak of certain preoccupations, even obsessions, in either domain, is, after all, tantamount to the description of the underlying mentality. However, the difference in approach, between one where attention is directed to the supposed mentalities as such, and what is advocated here, where the focus is on the contexts of communication, on styles of reasoning and eventually on their political background, remains fundamental. This is not just a matter of a general objection – that talk of mentalities is bound to remain speculative and unverifiable, when indeed it is not straightforwardly circular, that is where the only evidence of the mentality postulated is the very data that that postulate is supposed to help us to understand. One point at which the talk of mentalities does not just fail to provide an accurate description, but positively misleads, relates to the *diversities* that exist between interpersonal exchanges of different types within the same culture at the same period.

What helped to generate new styles of inquiry in ancient Greece, for example, was, we argued, a type of debate marked by its strongly adversarial qualities. Yet the characteristics displayed by speakers and audiences in those contexts (the demand for justification, the competitive manipulation of the resources of persuasion) were not necessarily in evidence elsewhere. Those who participated in the political assemblies and law-courts, and who attended the debates of the sophists, did not, we may be sure, *always* behave in that marked adversarial fashion: they did not *always* bring to bear the keen critical acumen in the evaluation of evidence and arguments that they *often* did in *those* contexts. If rationality in the sense of the demand for an account to be given – *logon didonai* – was often the watchword of the new-style inquiries, as of much political debate, that certainly did not mean an end to irrationality, and the very same groups who deployed the watchword were capable of ignoring it or of suspending the criteria it implied, and not just in politics but in science as well. The new inquiries did not drive out the old: they certainly did not do so in ancient Greece – nor have they done so today, even though, as we said, there have been important changes, amounting almost to an inversion, in the relationship between 'magic' and 'science' in our own society.

The audiences that emerging Greek proto-science presupposes were experienced in competitive debate, and that factor is crucial, we suggested, for understanding the appeal of that proto-science there in the early stages of its development. While Chinese proto-science is far less adversarial than Greek, it too seeks to persuade and we found that certain characteristic concepts and certain dominant contexts of communication are important, here too, to our understanding. At least we saw reason to believe that when the real or imagined target is the ruler, that had repercussions both on the style of presentation and on the content of what was presented.

But whatever the differences between early science in its Greek and Chinese forms, in both it is certainly both highly heterogeneous and of merely limited impact – though neither point should surprise us since both remain true to some extent even of science as we know it today. Tradition coexisted with innovation in both these ancient civilisations. Even when innovation and justification were all the rage among certain Greek intellectuals, their audiences certainly continued to engage in traditional activities, including religious and no doubt also magical practices, and they subscribed to some traditional beliefs without always – or rather, in many cases, without ever – demanding some kind of rational justification for *them*. There is no case for supposing that this involved some sudden switch in, or some strange combination of, mentalities: rather the contexts in which that type of justification was expected or thought appropriate were themselves socially circumscribed, even if that circumscription was far from precise or clear-cut.

Furthermore the same point can be confirmed not just in relation to targeted audiences, but with regard to some of the individuals who were active in the new styles of inquiries themselves – where again what is true of ancient Greece can be paralleled not just in China but also in later European science. Some famous early Greek philosophers combined their interest in those inquiries with roles as religious leaders or even as self-styled wonder-workers, as Empedocles did and as Pythagoras was sometimes represented to have done. While some of the individuals concerned loudly insisted that certain theories and ideas should be capable of withstanding scrutiny, there were limits not just to their actually applying such criteria, but also to their notions of the very applicability of such criteria – as Plato clearly illustrates. This is not just a matter of some prominent scientists and philosophers having other interests, as it might be in religion, in poetry or in mythology. The case of Ptolemy, whom we considered in chapter 3, is worth recalling, in that *within* what *he* thought of as his scientific activities – and even before we discuss such evidence as we have for his religious beliefs – he combines the most diverse styles, in his attempts to synthesise mathematical astronomy and traditional astrology, and again the mathematisation of acoustics with the symbolic exploration of the harmonies of the soul. Rather, the appropriate framework within which we have to tackle the problems of interpretation that such examples present is provided by the complex interactions and tensions between a variety of competing ideas and assumptions on the aims, methods and subject-matter of those investigations. It is those ideas and assumptions, together with the contexts of communication in which they are embedded, that define what I have been calling divergent styles of inquiry, and nothing is to be gained from resorting to an appeal to one or more supposed underlying mentalities.

In his early work Lévy-Bruhl specialised in the sweeping contrast between the primitive and the civilised. He never acknowledged that the uniformity of primitive thought is a mirage, the product of the distance from which it is viewed, and that such an idea could no longer be sustained as soon as any given society was studied in any detail or in any depth. This fact is all the more surprising in that the *social* influences on what he – like Durkheim – called the collective representations of particular societies were recognised, even if by him, maybe, not fully enough. However Lévy-Bruhl did come to see that the contrasts between the primitive and the civilised were less clear-cut than he originally supposed. 'There is', he wrote in the Notebooks (1975, p. 126), 'in the mentality of our societies a part (larger or smaller according to the general conditions, beliefs, institutions, social classes, etc. . .) which is common to it and to that of "primitive peoples".'

Yet the complication he thereby recognised he still diagnosed in terms of *mentality*. In those who have followed his lead, that term still facilitates the grand generalisation – about periods, groups, even whole societies – but does so at the price of still underestimating, in some cases drastically, the complexities of the phenomena to be explained. For we can only get to the mentality of an individual scientist, or of a magician, ancient or modern – let alone of a group – by resolutely denying or bracketing a great deal of their mental activity.

By the complexities of the phenomena I do not just mean the very diversity of what was referred to as 'primitive thought' – both diversities as between different societies and, just as important, diversity *within* any given society. There are also the complexities which cannot be ignored in the styles of reasoning, certainly in the styles of self-justification, in any of a number of major domains of discourse or inquiry or belief – including in science, as well as in myth, in magic and in religion. But given that the same individuals in our own society, in ancient Greece, in ancient China, among the Dorze, may exhibit *quite diverse* modes of reasoning in the process of expressing thought, belief, arguments, justifications, over *quite disparate* domains of discourse relating to theoretical or to practical affairs, it is rather those *modes of reasoning* that provide the locus of the investigation, not the reasoners themselves nor their supposed mentalities.

The synchronic question of the diversities and interrelations of those modes of reasoning in different domains of discourse pose, as we have emphasised, severe problems to be investigated case by case – and so too do diachronic questions as to how they may be subject to change, particularly how it is that challenge becomes possible where previously it had been beyond contemplation. But just as the analysis of individual utterances requires full account to be taken of the circumstances of delivery – the background information available to those concerned and the assumptions they make about the nature of the communication involved – so it may be argued more generally questions to do with systems of belief or modes of reasoning as a whole can only be answered if due attention is paid to *types* of social interaction and to the expectations participants may have concerning their nature and the manner of their conduct. To allow for the variety of contexts of interpersonal exchange, and for the availability and use of explicit second-order categories, is to take the first essential step towards providing a possible framework for those case by case investigations.

Notes

Introduction

1 The entries carry dates ranging from 20 January 1938 to 13 February 1939. Some were first published as 'Les *Carnets* de Lucien Lévy-Bruhl' in *Revue Philosophique* 137, 1947, pp. 257–81, and they are cited here according to the translation by P. Rivière, 1975, of the complete French edition of 1949: see pp. 7, 12, 37ff., 47ff., 99ff.

2 Some of Lévy-Bruhl's formulations refer to primitive mentality itself as if it were an item of past belief (e.g. 'what we used to call primitive mentality' 1975, p. 101). But when he writes, for example, that 'there is not a primitive mentality distinguishable from the other by *two* characteristics which are peculiar to it (mystical and prelogical)' (p. 101), what is being rejected is the *second* of those characteristics. In these and subsequent entries he continues to speak of the mystical orientation of the primitive mentality, even though he insists that what he *continues* to call the 'primitive mentality' is not confined to primitive peoples: see, for example, pp. 101, 126ff., 131ff., 137 etc. right down to the very last entry of all, p. 193.

3 Lévy-Bruhl 1975, p. 135: cf. p. 128 where after commenting that 'they do not derive from the use of their concepts what we derive from the use of ours', he continued: 'Not to exaggerate, however, their resemblance to us on this point. Doubtless they have concepts as we do and on a very large number of occasions the use to which they put them does not differ from ours. But in certain cases at least, the symbols which represent these concepts – words – differ from ours. For us the relation of words to the concepts which they express is arbitrary [. . .]. whereas, for the "primitive man" words, those symbols, participate, like other symbols, in what they represent.'

4 Already in 1912 Durkheim criticised the notion of a 'prelogical' mentality and represented the 'logic of religious thought' as differing from that of 'scientific thought' only in terms of the degree of restraint and sophistication exhibited: see Durkheim 1976, pp. 238f. Cf. also e.g. van der Leeuw 1928.

5 Since Quine (1953) 1961, cf. 1960, 1969, the literature on the philosophical issues has been immense: see for example Winch 1958, Skorupski 1976, Wittgenstein 1979, Putnam 1983, Davidson 1984 and the collections of articles ed. Wilson

1970, edd. Horton and Finnegan 1973, and edd. Hollis and Lukes 1982, which contain several studies that deal specifically with the issues to do with mentalities raised by Lévy-Bruhl, notably Gellner, Hollis, Horton and Lukes in ed. Wilson 1970, Colby and Cole, and Horton in edd. Horton and Finnegan 1973, and Lukes in edd. Hollis and Lukes 1982.

6 See especially Lévi-Strauss 1966, ch. 1 and 1981, pp. 657ff. In his 1966, ch. 9, p. 268, however, Lévi-Strauss explicitly criticised the opposition between a logical and a prelogical mentality as a false antimony.

7 See for example Cornford 1912, Harrison 1927, Schuhl 1949 pp. xiii f., Robin 1967, pp. 28ff., 44ff., Snell 1953, pp. 223ff. In Snell's case, for example, one further important influence was the work of Cassirer, especially 1953–7.

8 Criticism of Piaget on this score goes back to Vygotsky 1962, pp. 23f., and there has been extensive recent debate on the topic. See, for example, Dasen 1974, Cole and Scribner 1974, Brown and Desforges 1979, Jahoda 1980, pp. 108ff., Sternberg ed. 1982, pp. 663ff., Sternberg and Powell 1983, Gelman and Baillargeon 1983, B. Lloyd 1983.

9 Thus in Horton 1982 there is a reference to Finley's approval of Goody's work (p. 206 n. 3, cf. n. 71) and two further references to Greek thought (to evidence for despair and cognitive inaction in the first and second centuries B.C. p. 252, and to frontier communities of the sixth century B.C., p. 255), but in general a tendency to generalise about 'early European' or 'Western' thought, viz. up to 1200 A.D., as a whole, e.g. pp. 206, 237, 249ff.

10 The primary inspiration of this line of argument is J.-P. Vernant, e.g. (1962) 1982 and (1965) 1983. See further below, ch. 2, pp. 58ff., developing my earlier discussions of this topic in my 1979, ch. 4 and 1987a, ch. 2.

11 I ruefully observe that in my 1979, p. 8 n. 28, I wrote that such a study would require a full-length monograph and that by a specialist. That remains true but my hope is, nevertheless, that a brief foray by a non-specialist may serve to stimulate discussion.

12 Even though what we have is very impressive, nevertheless a great deal has been lost, especially from the pre-Han period.

13 Thus several classic texts of the Warring States period are compilations, evidently the end-products of the gradual accretion and incorporation of material in some cases over several centuries, and the problems of dating successive strata in these works are severe. For some Han, and later, texts, and for the *floruit* of some of the writers concerned, the situation improves and some fairly precise dates (within a decade or so) are possible.

1. Mentalities, metaphors and the foundations of science

1 We should not lose sight of the fact that normally canons of cooperation apply to acts of communication, even if not necessarily the precise 'cooperative principle' formulated by Grice (1975, 1978) in connection with his discussions of conversational implicature (cf. Sperber and Wilson 1986). While Grice's ideas relate primarily to ordinary conversations between adult members of the same society, they apply, *mutatis mutandis*, to the special cases of converse between members of different societies and of the more, or less, formal processes of instruction whereby members of a particular society or group come to learn to understand and accept certain beliefs, as for example among the Nuer that twins are birds. Cf. further below, n. 8, on charity in interpretation.

2 See Goody 1977, where he is concerned to deny radical discontinuities in the processes he is discussing. With qualifications, however, Goody still acknowledges differences in modes of thought, or rather (more often) in 'modes of thought' (in inverted commas): see Goody 1977, pp. 19, 81, 110f., Cf. Goody 1987.

3 It is true that in some cases the philosophers were being deliberately paradoxical and that in any event we are dealing with statements attributable to individuals or small groups, not with general beliefs commonly accepted in Greek society as a whole. However Greek religion, mythology and folklore provide examples enough of the latter that illustrate ideas that may well strike an outsider as extravagant, as can be documented even in works of high literature, such as Hesiod's *Theogony* (with its account of the births of the many grotesque divine or demonic creatures of Greek myth) and his *Works and Days* (with its catalogue of acts or behaviour to be avoided, 706ff.).

4 These appear as Fragments 53, 80, 64, 118, 98 and 52 in the Diels-Kranz edition, 1951–2.

5 The chief sources are Iamblichus *Protrepticus*, his, and Porphyry's, *Life of Pythagoras*, and Diogenes Laertius VIII 34f. They are collected in Diels-Kranz 1951–2, in the C section of DK 58, viz DK 58 C 3ff. See especially Delatte 1915, pp. 271ff., 285ff., Burkert 1972, pp. 166ff.

6 For these and other explanations, see, for example, Diogenes Laertius VIII 24, 34, Pliny, *Natural History*, XVIII 118 and cf. Guthrie 1962, p. 184.

7 A precisely analogous point has been made, taking a modern example ('Wittgenstein was a linguist and he was not a linguist') by Vennemann 1975, p. 327.

8 Davidson 1980, pp. 238f.: 'The basic strategy must be to assume that by and large a speaker we do not yet understand is consistent and correct in his beliefs – according to our standards, of course [...]. But we cannot make sense of error until we have established a base of agreement.' Cf. also Henderson 1987.

9 See Gellner 1970, p. 36, cf. Cooper 1975, p. 240. Gellner's point was originally directed at Evans-Pritchard's tacit hermeneutical principle of interpreting assertions in the light of *conduct*. Assertions, doctrines, Gellner commented, can easily be illogical: but the conduct of a society, a human group persisting over time, cannot easily be illogical.

10 For a more detailed account of Aristotle's distinction and of the background to it, with references to the extensive secondary literature, see my 1987a, ch. 4.

11 *homoiotētes, eikones, paradeigmata*: see for example *Phaedo* 92cd, *Phaedrus* 262a–c, *Theaetetus* 162e f., *Sophist* 231 ab, 236ab, 240a ff., *Politicus* 277 d ff.

12 Plato had already gone as far as banning the poets from his ideal state, for reasons partly to do with the moral content of their teaching, partly with the moral and psychological effects of the practice of imitation, *mimēsis*. The complexities of Plato's response to and criticism of poetry have now been well brought out by Ferrari (1989).

13 I owe this point to Dr Catherine Osborne, who has stressed the relevance, to this issue, of debates on such questions as the precise way of taking the notion of the 'Son of God' (see, for example, Athanasius, *Oratio I contra Arianos* 20ff., P. G. 26 53ff., *Epistola ad Monachos* 2, P. G. 25 693B, and Basil the Great, *Adversus Eunomium* I 14, P. G. 29 544). One may compare and contrast the much earlier traditions of allegorical interpretation (which in Greece go back to Homeric scholarship in the sixth century B.C.). This, too, often deploys a contrast between a literal and an allegorical reading, but often allows *both* to be valid, even while sometimes privileging the allegorical: see, for example, Mansfeld 1988, pp. 70ff., 83, on Philo of Alexandria.

14 Tertullian, *De Carne Christi* ch. 5. What Tertullian wrote was 'credibile est, quia ineptum' and 'certum est, quia impossibile', on which a group of variant expressions of this general type came to be modelled.

15 Yet Goody 1977, p. 64, has pointed out that these terms are often not indigenous actors' ones, but those of observers: 'I would claim that there is no such pair [of terms: viz 'nature' and 'culture'] in either of the two African languages known personally to me (LoDagaa and Gonja).'

16 As one example of a modern theologian wrestling with these problems, see Osborn 1981, pp. 54ff., 208.

17 See especially Holton 1973, 1978, cf. Feyerabend 1975, Kuhn 1977, Lakatos 1978a, Mulkay 1979, Hesse 1980, Brannigan 1981, Hacking ed. 1981.

18 I mention these as among the most readily agreed examples of Greek science not that they can be said to be typical of what any particular Greek theorist would have included under the rubric of the inquiry concerning nature, the scope of which was a subject of considerable controversy among the ancients themselves.

19 Pliny, for example, complained (*Natural History* XXVI 11) that in his day people were getting lazy and reluctant to 'go out into the wilds' to search for materia medica.

20 As in case 46 and case 24, respectively, from the Epidaurus inscriptions collected by Herzog 1931, pp. 26 and 16ff.

21 As for instance in case 48 from the Epidaurus inscriptions, Herzog 1931, p. 28. In the second century A.D. one of our main sources for later temple medicine, Aelius Aristides, frequently refers to the god overruling the diagnoses or therapies of ordinary doctors, e.g. XLVII 61–4, 67–8, XLIX 7–9.

22 The secondary literature on the topic is vast and includes such classic statements as those of Richards 1936 and Black 1962. For one recent particularly clear and forceful discussion, see Hesse 1982.

23 See my 1987, pp. 96ff., on the point as it applies to classical Greece, and on the theme in general, cf. Huizinga 1970.
24 One notable instance is Thucydides III 37ff., and cf. Plato, *Gorgias* 456bc *Politicus* 297e ff., and *Protagoras* 319b ff., on which see my 1979a, pp. 251 and 254. Cf. further below, ch. 2, pp. 58ff.

2. *Magic and science, ancient and modern*

1 For Lévy-Bruhl's interest in the problem of magic, see, for example, Lévy-Bruhl 1923, pp. 307ff., 442ff., 1926, pp. 227ff., and cf. also 1975, e.g. p. 109, and for evidence of the continued influence of his ideas, until recently, in analyses of witchcraft, see Fevret-Saada 1980, p. 255. Although Evans-Pritchard criticised Lévy-Bruhl's hypothesis of a pre-logical mentality, he too drew radical category distinctions between 'mystical', 'common-sense' and 'scientific' notions, defining the first as 'patterns of thought that attribute to phenomena supra-sensible qualities which, or part of which, are not derived from observation or cannot be logically inferred from it, and which they do not possess' (Evans-Pritchard 1937, p. 12).
2 Comte 1830–42, especially vols. 5 and 6. Comte's triad of stages differs, however, from Frazer's, in contrasting the religious, the metaphysical and the positive.
3 Hegel's theses on magic and religion are, indeed, discussed by Frazer in an appendix to the first volume of the *Golden Bough*, 1911–15, 1, pp. 423ff. Frazer notes these as a partial anticipation of his own views which, however, he says were developed independently.
4 I shall argue below that ancient Greek society provides a second example.
5 However, as the *Timaeus* shows, the same account can be described both as *logos* and as *muthos* interchangeably even without reference to the point of view of the different people who may or may not be disposed to believe it (e.g. *Timaeus* 59cd). The essential point, in that case, is that the cosmological account is qualified as (no more than) likely, viz. as an *eikōs logos*, when it is not called an *eikōs muthos*.
6 See, for example, Plato *Republic* 377b ff. and cf. above pp. 21ff. on the term 'poetic' use in certain contexts by Aristotle as a term of censure. It should, however, be noted that some of the early lyric poets themselves use the contrast between *muthos* and what is true in *their* criticisms of some traditional tales, as Pindar does when he objects to stories about the gods' immorality, *Olympian* 1 28ff., 52, *Nemean* 7 20ff., cf. also *Olympian* 9 35ff.
7 The arguments that have been used in attempts to identify the genuine works of Hippocrates have been evaluated critically by Edelstein 1967, pp. 133ff., Lloyd 1975b and cf. most recently Wesley Smith 1979.
8 On Hippocratic pharmacology and its relationship to earlier Greek and ancient near Eastern traditions, see, for example, Goltz 1974, Harig 1980. Some features of the innovativeness in Hippocratic medicine are discussed in my 1987a, ch. 2.
9 Thus *On Fractures* ch. 36, 540 9ff., recommends avoiding certain types of case 'if one has a respectable excuse', but *On Joints* ch. 58, 252 8ff., insists nevertheless that the study of incurable cases too belongs to the art of medicine.

10 As in case 46, Herzog 1931, p. 26, cf. above ch. 1 at n. 20. Other non-medical cases are case 24, Herzog 1931, pp. 16ff., and case 63, p. 32.

11 See, for instance, Tambiah 1973, pp. 220ff., for a qualified statement of a thesis that has been widely used, and cf. Tambiah 1990 on its origin and development.

12 The chief target of Hippocratic attacks, in this area, is the purifiers, but although temple medicine is not criticised directly, it was *indirectly* whenever the idea that the gods intervene in diseases was rejected. Apart from Hippocratic writers, others also had their criticisms to make of purifiers and others who claimed to be able to manipulate the gods, notably Plato at *Republic* 364b ff., and *Laws* 909a ff., 933a ff.

13 Cf. however below, ch. 4, on the Chinese evidence.

14 See most recently Todd forthcoming, and cf. Vernant (1962) 1982 and Humphreys 1985. Todd's conclusion, that in the law-courts witnesses were generally cited as support, and not as impartial observers whose primary duty was to tell the truth or establish the facts, may be said to find an echo in the way in which in philosophy and science tests were more often used in a corroborative role than to provide data to adjudicate between theories judged antecedently to be of equal standing (cf. e.g. Lloyd 1979, pp. 151, 224). By the middle of the fourth century, however, in the legal domain the Athenians were attempting to replace live witnessing by the written deposition of testimony.

15 Cf. my 1979, pp. 252ff. In the case of *basanizein*, however, the root, *basanos*, has as its primary meaning touchstone, from which the application of the noun and the verb both to torture and to other kinds of testing is derived.

16 According to Gagarin 1986, the formal procedures for settling disputes were well established already in Greece before the middle of the eighth century B.C. in the *pre-literate* period. On his view the most important use of the alphabet – in the next stage in the emergence of law – was in the public inscription of the rules that were to apply to judicial settlements, which itself, as he notes, requires an act of legislation. Though some details of Gagarin's discussion are open to question, it has the merit of drawing attention to the importance of law – both as *the* laws and as legal procedures – in Greek culture and to the value the Greeks themselves attached to it.

17 Thales' *floruit* is traditionally put at around 585 B.C., Anaximander's (on only very late evidence) to a generation later. Solon's reforms belong to 594, and Pisistratus' tyranny lasted (with interruptions) from 561 to 528.

18 It is true that the justification Solon himself offered did not proceed via any theoretical analysis but appealed to his moderation and to his holding the balance between the opposed factions of the rich and the people, see especially poems 3, 5, 23 and 24.

19 See Plato, *Republic* 555b ff., the account of democracy and the democratic man: the theme that philosophers must rule or rulers become philosophers is developed at *Republic* 473c ff.

20 At II 65 Thucydides remarks that, under Pericles, Athens, while still in name a democracy, was in fact coming to be under the rule of one man. In that passage Thucydides' criticisms of Pericles' successors are particularly forthright, but see

also his account of the assemblies at the time of the Mytilenian revolt and defeat, III 36ff. On Thucydides' own political views, see now Farrar 1988.

21 Hansen 1983 provides an authoritative account of the powers of the Athenian assembly in the fifth century and of how it operated in practice, as well as of the important changes that took place between the fifth and the fourth centuries, in particular the development of the distinction between *nomos* (law) and *psēphisma* (decree). These developments had the effect of limiting the sovereignty of the fourth-century assembly and of introducing a system of checks and balances into the Athenian constitution, which was increasingly formalised in a written code. Cf. also Murray 1987, p. 333, who observes that the restored democracy 'was also capable of continuous minor adjustments through the fourth century, demonstrating that the Athenian *demos* was consciously concerned with the continual renewal and perfection of the political system'.

22 The government of the 400 thereby set up was, however, short-lived, lasting, according to the *Constitution of Athens* (33.1), only four months (cf. Thucydides VIII 97).

23 *Philosophoumen aneu malakias*, Thucydides II 40. On the range of meanings of the term *sophia*, 'wisdom', see my 1987a, ch. 2, pp. 83ff., with references to earlier secondary literature.

24 Aristotle, *Politics* 1267b22ff., 1268b22ff., with the expressions of Aristotle's own reservations on the question of the advisability of innovation in the political field at 1269a13ff.: see especially the analysis of this text in Brunschwig 1980. The overriding importance of the political art among all disciplines is stressed by Aristotle at *Nicomachean Ethics* 1094a26ff.

25 Aristotle frequently cites arguments from Greek tragedy, along with those from the orators,in his own analysis of argument in the *Rhetoric*.

26 Admittedly we also find statements, as for example in Euripides *Suppliants* 349ff., 403ff., 429ff., of the principles that Athens stands for, the rule of law, the equal rights of rich and poor, free speech. Even in that case, however, it is Theseus the *king* who is responsible for the statements, even while he contrasts his own position with that of a *tyrant*.

27 *Parrēsia* was, however, sometimes given strongly pejorative undertones ('unbridled licence of tongue') especially in those who were opposed to democracy (see Isocrates VII 20, cf. Plato, *Republic* 557b, *Phaedrus* 240e, but contrast, for example, Euripides, *Hippolytus* 421ff., *Ion* 670ff.). According to Herodotus, V 78, it was Athenian *isēgoria* (equality in the right of speech) that was chiefly responsible for Athens' success, and even in Plato there is a recognition that there is more freedom of speech in Athens than elsewhere (see, for example, *Gorgias* 461e). On freedom of speech at Athens, see especially Finley 1973 and 1975, Momigliano 1973, and on *parrēsia*, Scarpat's monograph, 1964.

28 See pseudo-Xenophon, *Athenian Constitution*, 2.18f., and the scholium to Aristophanes, *Acharnians* 67.

29 Of the early philosophers both Xenophanes and Heraclitus especially attack aspects of conventional Greek religious beliefs and practices, notably,in Xenophanes' case, anthropomorphism: see Xenophanes Fragments 11, 12, 14–16,

Heraclitus Fragments 5, 14, 15. Democritus was later to rationalise belief in the gods as in part a mistaken inference from terrifying natural phenomena (according to Sextus Empiricus, *Against the Mathematicians* IX ch. 24) and further rationalisations of the origins of religious beliefs are attributed to Prodicus and Critias: see, for example, Lloyd 1979, pp. 11–15, with references to recent secondary literature.

3. The conception and practice of proof

1 Seidenberg 1960–2, 1974–5, 1977–8, cf. also van der Waerden 1980 (I discuss problems to do with the dating of the chief texts and the geometrical knowledge they contain in the Supplementary Note at the end of this chapter). For a quite different, though it must be said equally speculative, view, that denies that the Vedic priests themselves were responsible for the mathematics they use and argues that this was first developed – in the period of the first urbanisation – in response to the technical requirements of brick-making, see Chattopadhyaya 1986, pp. 112ff., 214.

2 The evidence comes from Proclus' *Commentary on the First Book of Euclid's Elements* (66 7ff.), where the term used is *sunegrapsen*. Doubts have recently been cast on whether this implies – what has often been held to be the case – that Hippocrates wrote a work with the title *Elements*, but he certainly began the systematisation of mathematical knowledge that culminated in Euclid's work of that name.

3 Apart from the problems that relate to the dispute over three-valued or non-standard logics, the range of application of the Aristotelian principles faces the difficulties we have identified in the Aristotelian conception of the literal. If these and other difficulties are pressed, then the principles will apply not to ordinary communication, but only (at best) to an idealised representation of it. However Aristotle's own intentions are clear. For him these were axioms of all discourse: his justification for them starts by getting anyone who disagreed to make *any* significant statement: cf Lear 1980, pp. 98ff.

4 With Gotthelf 1987 contrast Lloyd forthcoming.

5 See my 1978 and 1987a, pp. 293ff., on the scope and ambiguities of the ancient programme of 'saving the phenomena', and cf. Wasserstein 1962, Mittelstrass 1962, A. M. Smith 1981, 1982.

6 In ch. 23 of *On the Common Mathematical Science* Iamblichus, holding up the Pythagoreans as a model, cites first astronomy, then 'the whole of the predictive study of nature' (prognostic *physiologia*). But what he understands by that term includes not just the astronomical models of the likes of Hipparchus and Ptolemy, but also astrology (which Ptolemy himself had called 'prognostic', i.e. predictive, in his *Tetrabiblos* I ch. 1). Indeed Iamblichus justifies astrology partly on the basis of its mathematical methods in his *On the Mysteries* (sec. 9, ch. 4).

7 In the mention of harmonics Iamblichus goes beyond the type of geometrical atomism proposed by Plato in the *Timaeus* (though Plato had famously cut up the World Soul and arranged it in harmonic proportions to correspond to the circles of the heavenly bodies at *Timaeus* 34c ff.). The 'harmonic' attack on element theory in Iamblichus might suggest rather the association of the four

elements, simple geometrical solids and the harmonic relations of the heavenly spheres (as in Ptolemy's *Harmonics*).

8 In *Harmonics* III ch. 4 Ptolemy claims that the powers of harmony or attunement are best exemplified (1) in human beings and (2) in the heavenly bodies. He devotes ch. 8 to the end of the work (ch. 16, but the final chapters in our text are lacunose) to the latter, where he analyses the zodiac and the movements of the planets in terms of harmonic relationships. Chh. 5–7 explore various correspondences between the human soul, its parts and their various virtues, with the principal concords and their kinds. Just as the harmonious is a virtue or excellence in sounds, and the inharmonious a vice, so conversely, Ptolemy proclaims, in souls virtue is a harmoniousness, vice an inharmoniousness.

9 Indeed so far as dates go, the mathematical analysis of the musical scale had as much, or more, right to be dubbed 'traditional' in Greece as the type of symbolic associations developed in the psychological section of Ptolemy's *Harmonics*.

10 From Antiphon's *Tetralogies* onwards orators were expected to be able to support either side of a case (cf. also the anonymous *Double Arguments*), and some sources say that Protagoras claimed to teach this (Diogenes Laertius IX ch. 51, cf. Aristotle *Rhetoric* 1402a23ff.). But a common charge levelled against various representatives of the new learning was that they made the worse (or weaker) argument appear the better (stronger), a theme made much of in Aristophanes' *Clouds* which stages a mock contest between the just and unjust arguments (882ff.). According to Plato (e.g. *Apology* 18bc) this was a charge made against Socrates.

4. A test case: China and Greece, comparisons and contrasts

1 I use the term Logician conventionally to refer to the school of thought represented by Hui Shi and Gongsun Long (see pp. 109, 119). These were later known as the Family or Lineage of Names (*Ming Jia*) and they have sometimes been called Sophists. But on the distortions involved in speaking of a Chinese 'sophistic' and indeed in the use by later Chinese commentators of the term *Ming Jia*, see now Reding 1985, books 4 and 5, especially pp. 460ff (cf Graham 1978, p. 19).

2 The difficulties in using the term Feudalism in either its political or its economic applications in relation to the Chinese data are pointed out by Bodde 1956.

3 How far any of the stories relating to this episode are to be believed is not at all clear and certainly they bear the hallmarks of later propaganda. It may well be, as Nathan Sivin points out to me, that the general destruction of warfare was responsible for as many losses from the pre-Han period as any such action on the part of the first Qin Emperor.

4 These periods are only very approximately contemporary. Allowance has to be made, for example, for the fact that the unification of China took place in 221 B.C. and was comparatively durable. In the West on Alexander's death in 323 B.C. his successors divided up the territories he had conquered. While those conquests mark an important phase in the decline of the Greek city-state, the eventual rise to dominance of Rome was a gradual process.

5 Chinese mathematics and astronomy in the Yuan period may have been stimulated in part by contact with the world of Islam, an influence mediated through Central Asia, though that was only one of a series of factors contributing to this remarkable upsurge of activity.

6 Outside mathematics, the notion of verification, *yan*, is used in such contexts as that of checking a divination and in medicine in relation to the effectiveness of a treatment.

7 There is an interesting note, in this regard, in Li and Du (1987, pp. 194f.) who point out that when the *Elements* of Euclid eventually came to be translated into Chinese in the seventeenth century, some justification of its *usefulness* seems to have been thought necessary (cf. Martzloff 1980, 1981, on the Chinese reception of Euclid). A similar concern, with regard to practical usefulness, can already by illustrated in the work of Liu Hui in the third century A.D., see Wagner 1979, p. 182.

8 This aspect of Chinese mathematics is brought out forcefully in the recent work of Karine Chemla, 1988 and forthcoming, to whom I owe this point. On the possible modelling of ethical arguments on geometrical ones in late Mohist thought, see Reding 1986 and forthcoming. On further aspects of the Chinese use of, even preoccupation with, correlations and complementarities, see Graham 1986.

9 禮 . this is not to be confused with its homophone, *li*, 理 , meaning the immanent order of things.

10 Gernet 1989 provides a suggestive discussion of the implications of the contrast between Greek *logos* and Chinese *li* as the immanent order of the universe.

11 比 *bi*, see Cheng 1979, Yu 1987, pp. 57ff., 168ff. The distinction between *fu* (descriptive/expository), *bi* (comparative/analogical) and *xing* (elevated/ evocative) modes goes back to the Great Preface to the Book of Odes (*Shi Jing*) though the interpretation of all three, and especially of *xing*, is disputed among both ancient Chinese literary theorists and modern scholars: cf. also Liu 1975, pp. 109ff., Jullien 1985, pp. 67ff., 175ff.

12 Beyond the predominantly social, and often specifically moral, applications discussed in *Xun Zi*, the rectification of names may be used in other domains of inquiry too: in mathematics Chemla (personal communication) reports research in progress on the role it may have played in the search for analogies between different procedures.

13 As Nathan Sivin has emphasised to me, the topic remains vexed because the terminology used to distinguish slavery, indenture, hereditary tenantry and so on, is still largely Western. We have, once again, an example of the artificialities that arise from imposing categories derived from Western experience on the Chinese data.

Conclusion: Mentalities demystified

1 See Lévy-Bruhl 1975, p. 10: 'it does not seem admissable [sic] to us that the laws of nature should contradict themselves (the case of miracles excepted)'; p. 29:

'in our civilizations, save in the very rare case of the miracle, no one thinks that the regularity has ceased to exist'; p. 139: 'the mystical experience has for them [viz. "primitive peoples"] an objective value which it does not have in our eyes (leaving aside miracles and religious faith)'.

2 At p. 136 Lévy-Bruhl remarked that primitive men are 'never embarrassed by what we would call miracles or ruptures in the natural order' and at p. 180 said that 'nature does not admit of miracles'. But whatever Lévy-Bruhl's own position he clearly recognised that some of his contemporaries in France believed in miracles.

Bibliography

This bibliography contains details of all the modern books and articles I have cited together with a small number of others that deal directly with specific topics that I discuss. I make no attempt to list all the works that have influenced my own thinking on the subjects tackled but for a fuller (but still not comprehensive) bibliography, with particular focus on material to do with ancient Greece, the reader may be referred to my *The Revolutions of Wisdom*, Lloyd 1987a, below.

Ackerman, R. (1987) *J. G. Frazer: his life and work* (Cambridge).
Barnes, J. (forthcoming) 'Galen on Logic and Therapy', in *Proceedings of the Second International Galen Conference, Kiel 1982*, ed. F. Kudlien, forthcoming.
Bartlett, F. C. (1923) *Psychology and Primitive Culture* (Cambridge).
Beattie, J. H. M. (1970) 'On understanding ritual', in Wilson 1970, pp. 240–68.
Behr, C. A. (1968) *Aelius Aristides and the Sacred Tales* (Amsterdam).
Benveniste, E. (1971) *Problems in General Linguistics* (trans. M. E. Meek of *Problèmes de linguistique générale*, 2 vols, Paris 1966) (London).
Bernstein, B. (1964) 'Elaborated and Restricted Codes: Their social origins and some consequences', *American Anthropologist*, special publications LXVI, 6, part 2, pp. 55–69.
Berry, J. W. and Dasen, P. R. (edd.) (1974) *Culture and Cognition: Readings in Cross-cultural Psychology* (London).
Black, M. (1962) *Models and Metaphors* (Ithaca, New York).
Bloch, Maurice (1977) 'The Past and the Present in the Present', *Man* NS XII, 278–92.
Bloch, Maurice (ed.) (1975) *Political Language and Oratory in Traditional Society* (London).
Bodde, D. (1956) 'Feudalism in China', in *Feudalism in History*, ed. R. Coulborn (Princeton), pp. 49–92 (repr. in *Essays on Chinese Civilization*, edd. C. Le Blanc and D. Borei, Princeton, 1981, pp. 85–131).
Bottéro, J. (1977) 'Les Noms de Marduk, l'écriture et la "logique" en Mésopotamie ancienne', in *Essays on the Ancient Near East*, ed. M. de Jong Ellis (Memoirs of the Connecticut Academy of Arts and Sciences 19, Hamden, Connecticut), pp. 5–28.
Bourdieu, P. (1977) *Outline of a Theory of Practice* (trans. R. Nice of *Esquisse d'une théorie de la pratique*, Geneva, 1972) (Cambridge).

Bibliography

Brannigan, A. (1981) *The Social Basis of Scientific Discoveries* (Cambridge).

Brown, G. and Desforges, C. (1979) *Piaget's Theory: A psychological critique* (Boston).

Bruner, J. S., Olver, R. R. and Greenfield, P. M. (1966) *Studies in Cognitive Growth* (New York).

Brunschvicg, L. (1949) *L'Expérience humaine et la causalité physique* (1st ed. 1922), 3rd ed. (Paris).

Brunschwig, J. (1980) 'Du mouvement et de l'immobilité de la loi', *Revue Internationale de Philosophie* CXXXIII–CXXXIV, 512–40.

Bürk, A. (1901) 'Das Āpastamba-Śulba-Sūtra I', *Zeitschrift der deutschen morgenländischen Gesellschaft* LV, 543–91.

(1902) 'Das Āpastamba-Śulba-Sūtra II', *Zeitschrift der deutschen morgenländischen Gesellschaft* LVI, 327–91.

Burke, P. (1986) 'Strengths and weaknesses of the history of mentalities', *History of European Ideas* VII, 439–51.

Burke, P. (ed.) (1973) *A New Kind of History* (London).

Burkert, W. (1972) *Lore and Science in Ancient Pythagoreanism* (revised trans. E. L. Minar of *Weisheit und Wissenschaft*, Nürnberg, 1962) (Cambridge, Mass.).

Carter, L. B. (1986) *The Quiet Athenian* (Oxford).

Cassirer, E. (1953–7) *The Philosophy of Symbolic Forms* (trans. R. Mannheim of *Philosophie der symbolischen Formen*, Berlin, 1923–9), 3 vols. (New Haven).

Chace, A. B., Bull, L. and Manning, H. P. (1929) *The Rhind Mathematical Papyrus*, Vol. 2 (Oberlin).

Chakravarti, G. (1934) 'On the earliest Hindu methods of Quadrature', *Journal of the Department of Letters, University of Calcutta* XXIV, 23–8.

Chartier, R. (1982) 'Intellectual history or sociocultural history? The French Trajectories', in *Modern European Intellectual History*, edd. D. LaCapra and S. Kaplan (Ithaca, New York), pp. 13–46.

Chattopadhyaya, D. (1986) *History of Science and Technology in Ancient India. The Beginnings* (Calcutta).

Chemla, K. (1988) 'La pertinence du concept de classification pour l'analyse de textes mathématiques chinois', *Extrême-Orient, Extrême-Occident* X, 61–87.

(forthcoming) 'Du parallélisme entre énoncés mathématiques', *Revue d'histoire des sciences*.

Cheng, F. (1979) 'Bi et xing', *Cahiers de linguistique asie orientale* VI, 63–74.

Colby, B. and Cole, M. (1973) 'Culture, Memory and Narrative', in Horton and Finnegan 1973, pp. 63–91.

Cole, M. and Scribner, S. (1974) *Culture and Thought* (New York).

Comte, A. (1830–42) *Cours de philosophie positive*, 6 vols. (Paris).

Cooper, D. E. (1975) 'Alternative logic in "primitive thought"', *Man* NS X, 238–56.

Cornford, F. M. (1907) *Thucydides Mythistoricus* (London).

(1912) *From Religion to Philosophy* (London).

Darnton, R. (1980) 'Intellectual and cultural history', in *The Past Before Us*, ed. M. Kammen (Ithaca, New York), pp. 327–54.

Dasen, P. R. (1974) 'Cross-cultural Piagetian research: a summary', in Berry and Dasen 1974, pp. 409–23.

Davidson, D. (1980) *Essays on Action and Events* (Oxford).

Bibliography

(1984) *Inquiries into Truth and Interpretation* (Oxford).

Day, M. Henri (1972) *Spontaneity and the Pattern of Things. The ziran and wushi of Wang Chong's Lun Heng* (Stockholm).

Delatte, A. (1915) *Etudes sur la littérature Pythagoricienne* (Bibliothèque de l'école des hautes études 217, Paris).

Derrida, J. (1982) *Margins of Philosophy* (trans. A. Bass of *Marges de la philosophie*, Paris, 1972) (Brighton, Sussex).

Detienne, M. (1979) *Dionysos Slain* (trans. M. and L. Muellner of *Dionysos mis à mort*, Paris, 1977) (Baltimore).

  (1986) *The Creation of Mythology* (trans. M. Cook of *L'Invention de la mythologie*, Paris, 1981) (Chicago).

Detienne, M. and Vernant, J.-P. (1978) *Cunning Intelligence in Greek Culture and Society* (trans. J. Lloyd of *Les Ruses de l'intelligence: La Mètis des grecs*, Paris, 1974) (Hassocks, Sussex).

Dodds, E. R. (1951) *The Greeks and the Irrational* (Berkeley).

Douglas, M. (1975) *Implicit Meanings* (London).

Du Shiran (ed.) (1983) *Ancient China's Technology and Science* (Beijing).

Duby, G. (1961) 'Histoire des mentalités', in *L'Histoire et ses méthodes*, ed. C. Samaran (Paris), pp. 937–66.

Durkheim, E. (1976) *The Elementary Forms of the Religious Life* (trans. J. W. Swain of *Les Formes élémentaires de la vie religieuse*, Paris, 1912), 2nd ed. (London).

Edelstein, L. (1967) *Ancient Medicine*, edd. O. and C. L. Temkin (Baltimore).

Eisenstein, E. L. (1979) *The Printing Press as an Agent of Change*, 2 vols. (Cambridge).

Eisenstadt, S. N. (ed.) (1986) *The Origins and Diversity of Axial Age Civilizations* (New York).

Elvin, M. (1973) *The Pattern of the Chinese Past* (London).

Evans-Pritchard, E. E. (1934) 'Lévy-Bruhl's Theory of Primitive Mentality', *University of Egypt, Bulletin of the Faculty of Arts* II, 1, 1–36.

  (1937) *Witchcraft, Oracles and Magic among the Azande* (Oxford).

  (1956) *Nuer Religion* (Oxford).

Farrar, C. (1988) *The Origins of Democratic Thinking* (Cambridge).

Favret-Saada, J. (1980) *Deadly Words; Witchcraft in the Bocage* (trans. C. Cullen of *Les Mots, la mort, les sorts*, Paris, 1977) (Cambridge).

Febvre, L. (1982) *The Problem of Unbelief in the Sixteenth Century* (trans. B. Gottlieb of *Le Problème de l'incroyance au XVIe siècle*, Paris, 1942) (Cambridge, Mass.).

Fernandez, J. W. (1982) *Bwiti: An Ethnography of the Religious Imagination in Africa* (Princeton).

Ferrari, G. (1989) 'Plato and poetry', in *The Cambridge History of Literary Criticism*, vol. 1, *Classical Criticism*, ed. G. A. Kennedy (Cambridge), pp. 92–148.

Festinger, L. (1957) *A Theory of Cognitive Dissonance* (Evanston).

Feyerabend, P. K. (1961) *Knowledge without Foundations* (Oberlin).

  (1975) *Against Method* (London).

Finley, M. I. (1973) *Democracy Ancient and Modern* (London).

  (1975) 'The Freedom of the Citizen in the Greek World', *Talanta* (Proceedings of the Dutch Archaeological and Historical Society) VII, 1–23.

  (1980) *Ancient Slavery and Modern Ideology* (London).

  (1983) *Politics in the Ancient World* (Cambridge).

Bibliography

Forke, A. (1907) *Lun Heng, Part I: Philosophical Essays of Wang Ch'ung* (Leipzig).

(1911) *Lun Heng, part II: Miscellaneous Essays of Wang Ch'ung* (Berlin).

Fortes, M. and Evans-Pritchard, E. E. (edd.) (1940) *African Political Systems* (Oxford).

Fowler, D. H. (1987) *The Mathematics of Plato's Academy* (Oxford).

Frankel, S. (1986) *The Huli Response to Illness* (Cambridge).

Frazer, J. G. (1911–15) *The Golden Bough*, 12 vols., 3rd ed. (London).

Gagarin, M. (1986) *Early Greek Law* (New Haven).

Geertz, C. (1973) *The Interpretation of Cultures* (New York).

(1983) *Local Knowledge* (New York).

Gellner, E. (1970) 'Concepts and Society', in Wilson 1970, pp. 18–49.

(1973) 'The Savage and the Modern Mind', in Horton and Finnegan 1973, pp. 162–81.

(1985) *Relativism and the Social Sciences* (Cambridge).

Gelman, R. and Baillargeon, R. (1983) 'A Review of some Piagetian concepts', in *Handbook of Child Psychology*, Vol. 3, ed. P. H. Mussen (New York), pp. 167–230.

Gernet, J. (1982) *A History of Chinese Civilization* (trans. J. R. Foster of *Le Monde chinois*, Paris, 1972) (Cambridge).

1989 'Sciences et rationalité: l'originalité des données chinoises', *Revue d'histoire des sciences* XLII, 323–32.

Gernet, L. (1981) *The Anthropology of Ancient Greece* (trans. J. Hamilton and B. Nagy of *Anthropologie de la Grèce antique*, Paris, 1968) (Baltimore).

Gluckman, M. (1967) *The Judicial Process among the Barotse of Northern Rhodesia* (1st ed. 1955), 2nd ed. (Manchester University Press).

(1972) *The Ideas in Barotse Jurisprudence* (1st ed. 1965), 2nd ed. (Manchester University Press).

Goldhill, S. (1986) *Reading Greek Tragedy* (Cambridge).

(1987a) 'Anthropologie, idéologie et les grandes Dionysies', *Cahiers du Gita* III, 55–74.

(1987b) 'The Great Dionysia and Civic Ideology', *Journal of Hellenic Studies* CVII, 58–76.

Goltz, D. (1974) *Studien zur altorientalischen und griechischen Heilkunde, Therapie, Arzneibereitung, Rezeptstruktur* (Sudhoffs Archiv Beiheft 16, Wiesbaden).

Gombrich, E. (1972) *Symbolic Images: Studies in the Art of the Renaissance* (London).

Gonda, J. (1975) *Vedic Literature: Saṃhitās and Brāhmaṇas* (A History of Indian Literature, I, 1, Weisbaden).

(1977) *The Ritual Sūtras* (A History of Indian Literature, I, 2, Wiesbaden)

Goodman, N. (1978) *Ways of Worldmaking* (Hassocks, Sussex).

Goody, J. (1977) *The Domestication of the Savage Mind* (Cambridge).

(1987) *The Interface between the Written and the Oral* (Cambridge).

Gotthelf, A. (1987) 'First principles in Aristotle's *Parts of Animals*', in *Philosophical Issues in Aristotle's Biology*, edd. A. Gotthelf and J. G. Lennox (Cambridge), pp. 167–98.

Graham, A. C. (1964) 'The logic of the Mohist *Hsiao-ch'ü*', *T'oung Pao* LI, 1–54.

(1973) 'China, Europe and the Origins of Modern Science', in Nakayama and Sivin 1973, pp. 45–69.

Bibliography

(1978) *Later Mohist Logic, Ethics and Science* (London).

(1981) *Chuang-tzu: The Seven Inner Chapters* (London).

(1986) *Yin Yang and the Nature of Correlative Thinking* (Singapore).

Granet, M. (1934a) *La Pensée chinoise* (Paris).

(1934b) 'La Mentalité chinoise', in *L'Evolution humaine des origines à nos jours*, Vol. 1, ed. M. Lahy-Hollebecque (Paris), pp. 371–87.

Green, P. M. (1954) 'Prolegomena to the Study of Magic and Superstition in the *Natural History* of Pliny the Elder, with special reference to book XXX and its sources', Ph.D. dissertation, Cambridge.

Grice, H. P. (1957) 'Meaning', *Philosophical Review* LXVI, 377–88.

(1968) 'Utterer's Meaning, Sentence-Meaning and Word-Meaning', *Foundations of Language* IV, 225–42.

(1975) 'Logic and conversation', in *Syntax and Semantics 3: Speech Acts*, edd. P. Cole and J. L. Morgan (New York), pp. 41–58.

(1978) 'Further notes on logic and conversation', in *Syntax and Semantics 9: Pragmatics*, ed. P. Cole (New York), pp. 113–27.

Guthrie, W. K. C. (1962) *A History of Greek Philosophy*, Vol. 1: *The Earlier Presocratics and the Pythagoreans* (Cambridge).

(1965) *A History of Greek Philosophy*, Vol. 2: *The Presocratic Tradition from Parmenides to Democritus* (Cambridge).

(1969) *A History of Greek Philosophy*, Vol. 3: *The Fifth-Century Enlightenment* (Cambridge).

Habermas, J. (1978) *Knowledge and Human Interests* (trans. J. J. Shapiro of *Erkenntnis und Interesse*, Frankfurt, 1968) new ed. (London).

Hacking, I. (1982) 'Language, Truth and Reason', in Hollis and Lukes 1982, pp. 48–66.

(1983) *Representing and Intervening* (Cambridge).

Hacking, I. (ed.) (1981) *Scientific Revolutions* (Oxford).

Hall, J. A. (1985) *Powers and Liberties* (Oxford).

Hallpike, C. R. (1979) *The Foundations of Primitive Thought* (Oxford).

(1986) *The Principles of Social Evolution* (Oxford).

Hankinson, R. J. (forthcoming) 'Galen on the Foundations of Science', in *Galeno: Obra, Pensamiento y Influencia* (Proceedings of Madrid Galen conference, March 1988), ed. J. López Férez (Madrid).

Hansen, M. H. (1983) *The Athenian Ecclesia* (Copenhagen).

Hanson, A. (forthcoming) 'The Medical Writers' Woman', in *Before Sexuality: Construction of Erotic Experience in the Ancient Greek World*, edd. D. Halperin, J. Winkler, F. Zeitlin (Princeton).

Harig, G. (1980) 'Anfänge der theoretischen Pharmakologie in Corpus Hippocraticum', in *Hippocratica* (Actes du Colloque Hippocratique de Paris), ed. M. Grmek (Paris), pp. 223–45.

Harrison, J. E. (1927) *Themis* (1st ed. 1912), 2nd ed. (Cambridge).

Hartog, F. (1988) *The Mirror of Herodotus* (trans. J. Lloyd of *Le Miroir d'Hérodote*, Paris, 1980) (Berkeley).

Havelock, E. A. (1963) *Preface to Plato* (Oxford).

(1982) *The Literate Revolution in Greece and its Cultural Consequences* (Princeton).

Bibliography

He Shaogeng (1983) 'Method for Determining Segment Areas and Evaluation of π', in Du Shiran 1983, pp. 90–8.

Heath, T. E. (1921) *A History of Greek Mathematics*, 2 vols. (Oxford).

Heinimann, F. (1945) *Nomos und Physis* (Schweizerische Beiträge zur Altertumswissenschaft 1, Basel).

Henderson, D. K. (1987) 'The Principle of Charity and the Problem of Irrationality', *Synthese* LXXVIII, 225–52.

Herzog, R. (1931) *Die Wunderheilungen von Epidauros* (Philologus Suppl. Bd. XXII, 3 Leipzig).

Hesse, M. (1980) *Revolutions and Reconstructions in the Philosophy of Science* (Brighton, Sussex).

(1982) 'The Cognitive Claims of Metaphor', in *Metaphor and Religion*, ed. J. P. von Noppen (Brussels), pp. 27–45.

Hockett, C. F. (1954) 'Chinese versus English: An Exploration of the Whorfian Theses', in *Language in Culture*, ed. H. Hoijer (Chicago), pp. 106–23.

Hoijer, H. (1954) 'The Sapir-Whorf hypothesis', in *Language in Culture*, ed. H. Hoijer (Chicago), pp. 92–105.

Hollis, M. (1970) 'The Limits of Irrationality', in Wilson 1970, pp. 214–20.

Hollis, M. and Lukes, S. (edd.) (1982) *Rationality and Relativism* (Oxford).

Holton, G. J. (1973) *Thematic Origins of Scientific Thought: Kepler to Einstein* (Cambridge, Mass.).

(1978) *The Scientific Imagination* (Cambridge).

(1986) *The Advancement of Science, and its Burdens* (Cambridge).

Horton, R. (1967) 'African Traditional Thought and Western Science', *Africa* XXXVII, 50–71, 155–87 (abbreviated version reprinted in Wilson 1970, pp. 131–71).

(1973) 'Lévy-Bruhl, Durkheim and the Scientific Revolution', in Horton and Finnegan 1973, pp. 249–305.

(1982) 'Tradition and Modernity Revisited', in Hollis and Lukes 1982, pp. 201–60.

Horton, R. and Finnegan, R. (edd.) (1973) *Modes of Thought* (London).

Huizinga, J. (1970) *Homo Ludens* (trans. R. F. C. Hull of 1944 German ed. (original Dutch ed. 1938)), 2nd ed. (London).

Humphreys, S. C. (1978) *Anthropology and the Greeks* (London).

(1983) *The Family, Women and Death* (London).

(1985) 'Social relations on stage: Witnesses in Classical Athens', *History and Anthropology* I, 313–69.

(1986) 'Dynamics of the Greek Breakthrough', in Eisenstadt 1986, pp. 92–110.

Jahoda, G. (1980) 'Theoretical and systematic approaches in cross-cultural psychology', in *Handbook of Cross-Cultural Psychology*, Vol. 1, edd. H. T. Triandis and W. W. Lambert (Boston), pp. 69–141.

(1982) *Psychology and Anthropology. A Psychological Perspective* (London).

Jullien, F. (1985) *La Valeur allusive. Des catégories originales de l'interprétation poétique dans la tradition chinoise* (Paris).

Keith, A. B. (1925) *The Religion and Philosophy of the Veda and Upanishads* 2 vols. (Cambridge, Mass.).

(1928) *A History of Sanskrit Literature* (Oxford).

Bibliography

King, H. (1983) 'Bound to bleed: Artemis and Greek Women', in *Images of Women in Antiquity*, edd. A. Cameron and A. Kuhrt (London), pp. 109–27.

Kirk, G. S., Raven, J. E. and Schofield, M. (1983) *The Presocratic Philosophers*, 2nd ed. (Cambridge).

Klein, J. (1968) *Greek Mathematical Thought and the Origin of Algebra* (Cambridge, Mass.).

Knorr, W. R. (1975) *The Evolution of the Euclidean Elements* (Dordrecht).

(1981) 'On the Early History of Axiomatics: The Interaction of Mathematics and Philosophy in Greek Antiquity', in *Theory Change, Ancient Axiomatics and Galileo's Methodology*, edd. J. Hintikka, D. Gruender, A. Agazzi (Dordrecht), pp. 145–86.

(1982) 'Infinity and Continuity: The Interaction of Mathematics and Philosophy in Antiquity', in *Infinity and Continuity in Ancient and Medieval Thought*, ed. N. Kretzmann (Ithaca, New York), pp. 112–45.

(1986) *The Ancient Tradition of Geometric Problems* (Boston).

Kudlien, F. (1967) *Der Beginn des medizinischen Denkens bei den Griechen* (Zurich).

Kuhn, T. S. (1957) *The Copernican Revolution* (Cambridge, Mass.).

(1970) *The Structure of Scientific Revolutions* (1st ed. 1962) 2nd ed. (Chicago).

(1977) *The Essential Tension* (Chicago).

(1979) 'Metaphor in Science', in *Metaphor and Thought*, ed. A. Ortony (Cambridge), pp. 409–19.

Lakatos, I. (1978a) *The Methodology of Scientific Research Programmes, Philosophical Papers*, Vol. 1, edd. J. Worrall and G. Currie (Cambridge).

(1978b) *Mathematics, Science and Epistemology, Philosophical Papers*, Vol. 2, edd. J. Worrall and G. Currie (Cambridge).

Lakatos, I. and Musgrave, A. (edd.) (1970) *Criticism and the Growth of Knowledge* (Cambridge).

Lam Lay-Yong and Shen Kangsheng (1984) 'Right-angled Triangles in Ancient China', *Archive for History of Exact Sciences* xxx, 87–112.

Lambert, W. G. (1960) *The Babylonian Wisdom Literature* (Oxford).

Lau, D. C. (1982) *Tao Te Ching* (Hong Kong).

Laudan, L. (1977) *Progress and its Problems* (Berkeley).

Leach, E. R. (1961) 'Golden Bough or Gilded Twig?', *Daedalus* xc, 371–87.

(1965) 'Frazer and Malinowski: On the Founding Fathers', *Encounter* xxv, 24–36.

Lear, J. (1980) *Aristotle and Logical Theory* (Cambridge).

LeBlanc, C. (1985) *Huai-nan Tzu. Philosophical Synthesis in Early Han Thought* (Hong Kong).

Leeuw, G. van der (1928) 'La Structure de la mentalité primitive', *Revue d'histoire et de philosophie religieuses* viii, 1–31.

LeGoff, J. (1974) 'Les mentalités: une histoire ambiguë', in *Faire de l'histoire*, edd. J. LeGoff and P. Nora, Vol. 3 (Paris), pp. 76–94 (trans. in *Constructing The Past*, edd. J. LeGoff and P. Nora (Cambridge, 1985), pp. 166–80).

Lesher, J. H. (1984) 'Parmenides' Critique of Thinking: the Poludēris Elenchos of Fragment 7', *Oxford Studies in Ancient Philosophy* ii, 1–30.

Leslie, D. (1964) *Argument by Contradiction in Pre-Buddhist Chinese Reasoning* (Australian National University, Centre of Oriental Studies, Occasional Paper 4, Canberra).

Lévi-Strauss, C. (1966) *The Savage Mind* (trans. of *La Pensée sauvage*, Paris, 1962) (London).

(1973) *From Honey to Ashes* (trans. J. and D. Weightman of *Du Miel aux cendres*, Paris, 1967) (New York).

(1981) *The Naked Man* (trans. J. and D. Weightman of *L'Homme nu*, Paris, 1971) (London).

Lévy-Bruhl, L. (1923) *Primitive Mentality* (trans. L. A. Clare of *La Mentalité primitive*, Paris, 1922) (London).

(1926) *How Natives Think* (trans. L. A. Clare of *Les Fonctions mentales dans les sociétés inférieures*, Paris, 1910) (London).

(1975) *The Notebooks on Primitive Mentality* (trans. P. Rivière of *Les Carnets* de Lucien Lévy-Bruhl, Paris, 1949) (London).

Lewis, G. (1975) *Knowledge of Illness in a Sepik Society* (London).

Li Guohao, Zhang Mengwen and Cao Tianqin (edd.) (1982) *Explorations in the History of Science and Technology in China* (Shanghai).

Li Yan and Du Shiran (1987) *Chinese Mathematics: a Concise History* (trans. J. N. Crossley and A. W.-C. Lun) (Oxford).

Libbrecht, U. (1972) *Chinese Mathematics in the Thirteenth Century: The Shu-shu chiu-chang of Ch'in Chiu-shao* (MIT East Asian Science Series, 1, Cambridge, Mass.).

Liu, J. J. Y. (1975) *Chinese Theories of Literature* (Chicago).

Lloyd, B. (1983) 'Cross-cultural studies of Piaget's theory', in *Jean Piaget: an Interdisciplinary Critique*, edd. S. Modgil, C. Modgil, G. Brown (London), pp. 27–41.

Lloyd, G. E. R. (1963) 'Who is attacked in *On Ancient Medicine*?', *Phronesis* VIII, 108–26.

(1964) 'Experiment in early Greek philosophy and medicine', *Proceedings of the Cambridge Philological Society* NS x, 50–72.

(1966) *Polarity and Analogy* (Cambridge).

(1975a) 'Alcmaeon and the early history of dissection', *Sudhoffs Archiv* LIX, 113–47.

(1975b) 'The Hippocratic Question', *Classical Quarterly* NS xxv, 171–92.

(1978) 'Saving the appearances', *Classical Quarterly* NS xxviii, 202–22.

(1979) *Magic, Reason and Experience* (Cambridge).

(1983) *Science, Folklore and Ideology* (Cambridge).

(1987a) *The Revolutions of Wisdom* (Berkeley).

(1987b) 'The Alleged Fallacy of Hippocrates of Chios', *Apeiron* xx, 103–28.

(forthcoming) 'Aristotle's zoology and his metaphysics: the status quaestionis', in *Biologie logique et métaphysique chez Aristote*, ed. P. Pellegrin (Paris).

Loewe, M. (1968) *Everyday Life in Early Imperial China* (London).

(1974) *Crisis and Conflict in Han China 104 B.C. to A.D. 9* (London).

Loraux, N. (1980) 'Thucydide n'est pas un collègue', *Quaderni di Storia* XII, 55–81.

(1986) *The Invention of Athens* (trans. A. Sheridan of *L'Invention d'Athènes*, Paris, 1981) (Cambridge, Mass.).

(1987) 'Le lien de la division', *Le Cahier du Collège international de la philosophie* IV, 101–24.

Luhrmann, T. (1986) 'Witchcraft, morality and magic in contemporary London', *International Journal of Moral and Social Studies* I, 77–94.

(1989) *The Persuasions of the Witch's Craft* (Oxford).

Lukes, S. (1970) 'Some problems about rationality', in Wilson 1970, pp. 194–213.

(1982) 'Relativism in its place', in Hollis and Lukes 1982, pp. 261–305.

MacIntyre, A. (1970) 'The idea of a social science', in Wilson 1970, pp. 112–30.

Malinowski, B. (1922) *Argonauts of the Western Pacific* (London).

(1935) *Coral Gardens and their Magic*, 2 Vols. (London).

Mansfeld, J. (1988) 'Philosophy in the service of Scripture', in *The Question of "Eclecticism"*, edd. J. M. Dillon and A. A. Long (Berkeley), pp. 70–102.

Martzloff, J.–C. (1980) 'La compréhension chinoise des méthodes démonstratives euclidiennes au cours du XVIIe et au début du XVIII$^{e\prime}$, in *Actes du IIe colloque international de sinologie* (Chantilly 16–18 septembre 1977) (Paris), pp. 125–41.

(1981) 'Le géométrie euclidienne selon Mei Wending', *Historia Scientiarum* XXI, 27–42.

Masson-Oursel, P. (1917a) 'Etudes de logique comparée I: évolution de la logique indienne', *Revue philosophique* LXXXIII, 453–69.

(1917b) 'Etudes de logique comparée II: évolution de la logique chinoise', *Revue philosophique* LXXXIV, 59–76.

(1918) 'Etudes de logique comparée III: confrontations et analyse comparative', *Revue philosophique* LXXXV, 148–66.

Mauss, M. (1972) *A General Theory of Magic* (trans. R. Brain from *Sociologie et Anthropologie*, Paris, 1950) (London).

Michaels, A. (1978) *Beweisverfahren in der vedischen Sakralgeometrie: ein Beitrag zur Entstehungsgeschichte von Wissenschaft* (Alt- und neu-indische Studien 20, Wiesbaden).

Mignucci, M. (1975) *L'argomentazione dimostrativa in Aristotele* (Padua).

Mittelstrass, J. (1962) *Die Rettung der Phänomene* (Berlin).

Momigliano, A. (1973) 'Freedom of speech in Antiquity', in *Dictionary of the History of Ideas*, ed. P. P. Wiener, vol. 2 (New York), pp. 252–62.

(1975) *Alien Wisdom: The Limits of Hellenization* (Cambridge).

Mourelatos, A. P. D. (1970) *The Route of Parmenides* (New Haven).

Müller, C. (1930) *Die Mathematik der Śulvasûtra: eine Studie zur Geschichte indischer Mathematik* (Abhandlungen aus dem mathematischen Seminar der hamburgischen Universität 7, 2/3, 1929, pp. 173–204, Leipzig, 1930).

Mueller, I. (1969) 'Euclid's *Elements* and the Axiomatic Method', *British Journal for the Philosophy of Science* XX, 289–309.

(1974) 'Greek Mathematics and Greek Logic', in *Ancient Logic and its Modern Interpretations*, ed. J. Corcoran (Dordrecht), pp. 35–70.

(1981) *Philosophy of Mathematics and Deductive Structure in Euclid's Elements* (Cambridge, Mass.).

(1982) 'Aristotle and the Quadrature of the Circle', in *Infinity and Continuity in Ancient and Medieval Thought*, ed. N. Kretzmann (Ithaca, New York), pp. 146–64.

Mulkay, M. J. (1979) *Science and the Sociology of Knowledge* (London).

Murray, O. (1987) 'Cities of Reason', *European Journal of Sociology* xxviii, 325–46.

Nakamura, H. (1960) *The Ways of Thinking of Eastern Peoples* (Tokyo).

Nakayama, S. (1984) *Academic and Scientific Traditions in China, Japan and the West* (trans. J. Dusenberry) (Tokyo).

Nakayama, S. and Sivin, N. (edd.) (1973) *Chinese Science: Explorations of an Ancient Tradition* (Cambridge, Mass.).

Needham, J. (1954–) *Science and Civilisation in China* (Cambridge).

(1956) *Science and Civilisation in China*, Vol. 2: *History of Scientific Thought* (Cambridge).

(1959) *Science and Civilisation in China*, Vol. 3: *Mathematics and the Sciences of the Heavens and the Earth* (Cambridge).

(1969) *The Grand Titration: Science and Society in East and West* (London).

Needham, R. (1972) *Belief, Language and Experience* (Oxford).

(1978) *Essential Perplexities* (Oxford).

(1980) *Reconnaissances* (Toronto).

(1987) *Counterpoints* (Berkeley).

Neugebauer, O. (1975) *A History of Ancient Mathematical Astronomy*, 3 vols (Berlin).

Nylan, M. and Sivin, N. (1987) 'The First Neo-Confucianism: an Introduction to Yang Hsiung's "Canon of Supreme Mystery" (T'ai hsuan ching, c. 4 B.C.)', in *Chinese Ideas about nature and society*, edd. C. LeBlanc and S. Bladen (Hong Kong), pp. 41–99

Ohnuki-Tierney, E. (1984) *Illness and Culture in Contemporary Japan* (Cambridge).

Olson, D. R., Torrance, N. and Hildyard, A. (edd.) (1985) *Literacy, Language, and Learning* (Cambridge).

Oppenheim, A. Leo (1962) 'Mesopotamian Medicine', *Bulletin of the History of Medicine* xxxvi, 97–108.

Osborn, E. (1981) *The Beginning of Christian Philosophy* (Cambridge).

Osborne, R. (1985) *Demos: The Discovery of Classical Attika* (Cambridge).

Ostwald, M. (1969) *Nomos and the Beginnings of the Athenian Democracy* (Oxford).

(1986) *From Popular Sovereignty to the Sovereignty of Law* (Berkeley).

Owen, G. E. L. (1986) *Logic, Science and Dialectic* (London).

Parker, R. C. T. (1983) *Miasma* (Oxford).

Parry, J. P. (1985) 'The Brahmanical Tradition and the Technology of the Intellect', in *Reason and Morality*, ed. J. Overing (London), pp. 200–25.

Peet, T. E. (1923) *The Rhind Mathematical Papyrus* (London).

Peyre, H. (1973) *Renan et la Grèce* (Paris).

Piaget, J. (1929) *The Child's Conception of the World* (trans. J. and A. Tomlinson of *La Répresentation du monde chez l'enfant*) (London).

(1930) *The Child's Conception of Physical Causality* (Trans. M. Gabain of *La Causalité physique chez l'enfant*) (London).

Pingree, D. (1981) *Jyotiḥśāstra. Astral and mathematical literature* (A History of Indian Literature vi, 4, Wiesbaden).

Pocock, J. G. A. (1972) *Politics, Language and Time* (London).

Pollner, M. (1987) *Mundane Reasoning* (Cambridge).

Popper, K. R. (1962) *The Open Society and its Enemies*, 2 vols, 4th ed. (London).

(1963) *Conjectures and Refutations* (London).

Bibliography

Porkert, M. (1974) *The Theoretical Foundations of Chinese Medicine* (Cambridge, Mass.).

Putnam, H. (1981) *Reason, Truth and History* (Cambridge).

(1983) *Realism and Reason: Philosophical Papers*, Vol. 3 (Cambridge).

Quine, W. van O. (1953/1961) *From a Logical Point of View* (1st ed. 1953), 2nd ed. (Cambridge, Mass., 1961).

(1960) *Word and Object* (Cambridge, Mass.).

(1969) *Ontological Relativity and Other Essays* (New York).

Radin, P. (1938) *Primitive Religion: its Nature and Origin* (London).

Rawski, E. S. (1979) *Education and Popular Literacy in Ch'ing China* (Ann Arbor).

Reding, J.-P. (1985) *Les Fondements philosophiques de la rhétorique chez les sophistes grecs et chez les sophistes chinois* (Berne).

(1986) 'Greek and Chinese categories: a re-examination of the problem of linguistic relativism', *Philosophy East and West* xxxvi, 349–74.

(forthcoming) 'La Pensée rationnelle en Chine antique', *Chroniques de Philosophie* vi, *Institut international de philosophie*.

Reichardt, R. (1978) ' "Histoire des Mentalités". Eine neue Dimension der Sozialgeschichte am Beispiel des französischen Ancien Régime', *Internationales Archiv für Sozialgeschichte der deutschen Literatur* iii, 130–66.

Renan, E. (1935) *The Memoirs of Ernest Renan* (trans. J. Lewis May) (London).

(1948) *Œuvres complètes*, ed. H. Psichari, Vol. 2 (Paris).

Renou, L. (1964) *Etudes védiques et pāṇinéennes*, Vol. 12 (Publications de l'Institut de Civilisation Indienne 20, Paris).

Rey, A. (1930) *La Science dans l'antiquité*, Vol. 1 (Paris).

(1933) *La Science dans l'antiquité*, Vol. 2 (Paris).

Reymond, A. (1927) *History of the Sciences in Greco-Roman Antiquity* (trans. R. de Bray of 1st ed. of *Histoire des sciences exactes et naturelles dans l'antiquité gréco-romaine*, Paris, 1924) (London).

Richards, I. A. (1936) *The Philosophy of Rhetoric* (London).

Ricoeur, P. (1977) *The Rule of Metaphor* (trans. R. Czerny with K. McLaughlin and J. Costello of *La Métaphore vive*, Paris, 1975) (Toronto).

Robin, L. (1967) *La Pensée hellénique des origines à Epicure* (1st ed. 1942), 2nd ed. (Paris).

Romilly, J. de (1975) *Magic and Rhetoric in Ancient Greece* (Cambridge, Mass.).

Rorty, R. (1980) *Philosophy and the Mirror of Nature* (Princeton).

Ruben, W. (1954) *Geschichte der indischen Philosophie* (Berlin).

(1971) *Die Entwicklung der Philosophie im alten Indien* (Berlin).

(1979) *Wissen gegen Glauben. Der Beginn des Kampfes des Wissens gegen den/das Glauben im alten Indien und Griechenland* (Abhandlungen der Akademie der Wissenschaften der DDR, Abteilung Gesellschaftswissenschaften, Jahrgang 1979, Berlin).

Rubin, V. A. (1965–6) 'Tzu-ch'an and the city-state of ancient China', *T'oung Pao* lii, 8–34.

Salmon, M. H. (1978) 'Do Azande and Nuer use a non-standard logic?', *Man* NS xiii, 444–54.

Sambursky, S. (1962) *The Physical World of Late Antiquity* (London).

Bibliography

Sapir, E. (1949) *Selected Writings of Edward Sapir in Language, Culture, and Personality* (Berkeley).

Sapir, J. D. and Crocker, J. C. (edd.) (1977) *The Social Use of Metaphor* (Philadelphia).

Sato, T. (1986) 'A Reconstruction of *The Method* Proposition 17, and the development of Archimedes' Thought on Quadrature, Part I', *Historia Scientiarum* xxxi, 61–86.

(1987) 'A Reconstruction of *The Method* Proposition 17, and the development of Archimedes' Thought on Quadrature, Part II', *Historia Scientiarum* xxxii, 75–142.

Scarpat, G. (1964) *Parrhesia: storia del termine e delle sue traduzioni in latino* (Brescia).

Schuhl, P. M. (1949) *Essai sur la formation de la pensée grecque* (1st ed. 1934), 2nd ed. (Paris).

Schwartz, B. I. (1985) *The World of Thought in Ancient China* (Cambridge, Mass.).

Scribner, S. and Cole, M. (1981) *The Psychology of Literacy* (Cambridge, Mass.).

Searle, J. R. (1969) *Speech Acts* (Cambridge).

(1979) *Expression and Meaning* (Cambridge).

Seidenberg, A. (1960–2) 'The Ritual Origin of Geometry', *Archive for History of Exact Sciences* i, 488–527.

(1974–5) 'Did Euclid's *Elements*, Book I, develop geometry axiomatically?', *Archive for History of Exact Sciences* xiv, 263–95.

(1977–8) 'The Origin of Mathematics', *Archive for History of Exact Sciences* xviii, 301–42.

Shirokogoroff, S. M. (1935) *Psychomental Complex of the Tungus* (London).

Shweder, R. (1982) 'On Savages and other children', *American Anthropologist* lxxxiv, 354–66.

Sivin, N. (1978) 'On the word "Taoist" as a source of perplexity. With special reference to the relations of science and religion in traditional China', *History of Religions* xvii, 303–30.

(1985) 'Why the Scientific Revolution did not take place in China – or didn't it?', in *Transformation and Tradition in the Sciences*, ed. E. Mendelsohn (Cambridge), pp. 531–54.

(1986) 'On the limits of empirical knowledge in the traditional Chinese sciences', in *Time, Science, and Society in China and the West*, edd. J. T. Fraser, N. Lawrence and F. C. Haber (Amherst), pp. 151–69.

(1987) *Traditional Medicine in Contemporary China* (Ann Arbor).

(1988) 'Science and Medicine in Imperial China – the State of the Field', *Journal of Asian Studies* xlvii, 41–90.

Skorupski, J. (1976) *Symbol and Theory* (Cambridge).

Smith, A. M. (1981) 'Saving the Appearances of the Appearances: The Foundations of Classical Geometrical Optics', *Archive for History of Exact Sciences* xxiv, 73–99.

(1982) 'Ptolemy's Search for a Law of Refraction: A Case-Study in the Classical Methodology of 'Saving the Appearances' and its Limitations', *Archive for History of Exact Sciences* xxvi, 221–40.

Smith, W. D. (1979) *The Hippocratic Tradition* (Ithaca, New York).

Snell, B. (1953) *The Discovery of the Mind* (trans. T. G. Rosenmeyer of *Die Entdeckung des Geistes*, 2nd ed., Hamburg, 1948) (Oxford).

Bibliography

Sperber, D. (1975) *Rethinking Symbolism* (trans. A. L. Morton) (Cambridge).

(1980) 'Is Symbolic Thought Pre-rational?', in *Symbol as Sense*, edd. M. L. Foster and S. H. Brandes (New York), pp. 25–44.

(1985) *On Anthropological Knowledge* (Cambridge).

Sperber, D. and Wilson, D. (1986) *Relevance: Communication and Cognition* (Oxford).

Staden, H. von (1975) 'Experiment and Experience in Hellenistic Medicine', *Bulletin of the Institute of Classical Studies* xxii, 178–99.

(1989) *Herophilus: The Art of Medicine in Ptolemaic Alexandria* (Cambridge).

Stange, H. O. H. (1950) 'Chinesische und abendländische Philosophie', *Saeculum* i, 380–96.

Sternberg, R. J. (ed.) (1982) *Handbook of Human Intelligence* (Cambridge).

Sternberg, R. J. and Powell, J. S. (1983) 'The Development of Intelligence', in *Handbook of Child Psychology*, Vol. 3, ed. P. H. Mussen (New York), pp. 341–419.

Szabó, Á. (1964–6) 'The Transformation of Mathematics into Deductive Science and the Beginnings of Its Foundation on Definitions and Axioms', *Scripta Mathematica* xxvii, 27–48a and 113–39.

(1978) *The Beginnings of Greek Mathematics* (trans. A. M. Ungar of *Anfänge der griechischen Mathematik*, Vienna, 1969) (Budapest).

Tamba-Mecz, L. and Veyne, P. (1979) '*Metaphora* et comparaison selon Aristote', *Revue des Etudes Grecques* xcii, 77–98.

Tambiah, S. J. (1968) 'The Magical Power of Words', *Man* NS iii, 175–208.

(1973) 'Form and Meaning of Magical Acts: A Point of View', in Horton and Finnegan 1973, pp. 199–229.

(1990) *Magic, Science, Religion and the Scope of Rationality* (Cambridge).

Thibault, G. (1875) 'On the Śulvaśutras', *Journal of the Asiatic Society of Bengal* xliv, 227–75.

Thomas, K. (1971) *Religion and the Decline of Magic* (London).

Thorndike, L. (1923–58) *A History of Magic and Experimental Science*, 8 Vols. (New York).

Todd, S. (forthcoming) 'The Purpose of Evidence in Athenian Courts', in *Nomos*, edd. P. Cartledge, P. Millett, S. Todd (Cambridge).

Turner, T. S. (1973) Review of J. Piaget, *Genetic Epistemology* and *Le Structuralisme*, *American Anthropologist* lxxv, 351–73.

Turner, V. W. (1974) *Dramas, Fields and Metaphors* (New York).

Unschuld, P. U. (1985) *Medicine in China: A History of Ideas* (Berkeley).

Van Fraassen, B. C. (1980) *The Scientific Image* (Oxford).

Vennemann, T. (1975) 'Topics, sentence accent, ellipsis: a proposal for their formal treatment', in *Formal Semantics of Natural Languages*, ed. E. L. Keenan (Cambridge), pp. 313–28.

Vernant, J.-P. (1962/1982) *The Origins of Greek Thought* (trans. of *Les Origines de la pensée grecque*, Paris, 1962) (London, 1982).

(1965/1983) *Myth and Thought among the Greeks* (trans. of *Mythe et pensée chez les grecs*, 2nd ed., Paris, 1965) (London, 1983).

Vernant, J.-P. and Vidal-Naquet, P. (1988) *Myth and Tragedy in Ancient Greece* (trans. J. Lloyd of *Mythe et tragédie en Grèce ancienne*, Paris, 1972, and *Mythe et tragédie deux*, Paris, 1986) (New York).

Vickers, B. (ed.) (1984) *Occult and Scientific Mentalities in the Renaissance* (Cambridge).

Vidal-Naquet, P. (1967/1986) 'Greek Rationality and the City' (originally 'La Raison grecque et la cité', *Raison présente* II, 1967, pp. 51–61), in *The Black Hunter: Forms of Thought and Forms of Society in the Greek World* (trans. A. Szegedy-Maszak of *Le Chasseur noir: Formes de pensée et formes de société dans le monde grec*, Paris, 1981) (Baltimore), pp. 249–62.

Vlastos, G. (1975) *Plato's Universe* (Oxford).

(1988) 'Elenchus and mathematics: a turning-point in Plato's philosophical development', *American Journal of Philology* CIX, 362–96.

Vovelle, M. (1982) 'Ideologies and mentalities', in *Culture, Ideology and Politics*, edd. R. Samuel and G. Stedman Jones (London), pp. 2–11.

Vygotsky, L. S. (1962) *Thought and Language* (trans. E. Hanfmann and G. Vakar) (Cambridge, Mass.).

Waerden, B. L. van der (1961) *Science Awakening* (trans. A. Dresden of *Ontwakende Wetenschap*) 2nd ed. (New York).

(1974) *Science Awakening* II: *The Birth of Astronomy* (Leiden).

(1980) 'On Pre-Babylonian Mathematics, I, and II', *Archive for History of Exact Sciences* XXIII, 1–25 and 27–46.

Wagner, D. B. (1978a) 'Liu Hui and Tsu Keng-chih on the volume of a sphere', *Chinese Science* III, 59–79.

(1978b) 'Doubts concerning the attribution of Liu Hui's commentary on the *Chiu-Chang Suan-Shu*', *Acta Orientalia* XXXIX, 199–212.

(1979) 'An early Chinese derivation of the volume of a pyramid: Liu Hui, Third Century A.D.', *Historia Mathematica* VI, 164–88.

Walker, R. L. (1953) *The Multi-State System of Ancient China* (Hamden, Connecticut).

Wasserstein, A. (1962) 'Greek Scientific Thought', *Proceedings of the Cambridge Philological Society* NS VIII, 51–63.

Watson, Burton (1963) *Hsün Tzu: basic writings* (New York).

Whorf, B. L. (1956) *Language, Thought and Reality* (New York).

Wilbur, C. M. (1943) *Slavery in China During the Former Han Dynasty* (Chicago).

Wilson, B. R. (ed.) (1970) *Rationality* (Oxford).

Wilson, J. A. (1962) 'Medicine in Ancient Egypt', *Bulletin of the History of Medicine* XXXVI, 114–23.

Winch, P. (1958) *The Idea of a Social Science* (London).

(1970) 'Understanding a Primitive Society', in Wilson 1970, pp. 78–111.

Winternitz, M. (1927) *A History of Indian Literature*, vol. 1 (trans. S. Ketkar) (Calcutta).

Wittgenstein, L. (1979) *Remarks on Frazer's Golden Bough*, ed. R. Rhees (Brynmill).

Wu Wenchun (1983) 'The Out-in Complementary Principle', in Du Shiran 1983, pp. 66–89.

Yu, P. (1987) *The Reading of Imagery in the Chinese poetic tradition* (Princeton).

Ziff, P. (1972) *Understanding understanding* (Ithaca, New York).

Index

171

Index

Rome 11, 110–11
Rubin, V. A. 125

Sapir, E. 136
scepticism 11, 110, 113–14, 118–19, 130
Seidenberg, A. 74, 99–102, 104
Shirokogoroff, S. M. 44
Simplicius 80–1
Sivin, N. 111, 114, 117, 122, 154 n.3, 155 n.13
slaves 59, 123, 131
Socrates 66
Solon 60–1
sophists 36, 48, 86, 96, 109, 142, 154 n.1
Soranus 54–5
Sperber, D. 19–20
stasis (political faction) 47, 64
statics 29, 43, 56, 87, 90, 93
Stoics 109, 119
Śulbasūtras 98–104
surgery 45–6, 49–50
syllogistic 21–2, 74, 77, 88, 119
Szabó, Á. 82

Tai Xuan Jing 108
Tambiah, S. J. 41, 54
technology 52, 110
temple medicine 31, 52–4, 57, 70
Tertullian 24
Thales 60–1, 80, 83
Theaetetus 85
Theodorus (mathematician) 85
Theodorus (writer on rhetoric) 76

theology 24, 141
Thibault, G. 99, 101–4
Thorndike, L. 70
Thucydides 23, 45–7, 62–4, 67
torture 49–50, 59
tradition 10, 20, 26, 29, 34–5, 50, 53, 58, 63–5, 68–71, 73, 94, 111, 114–15, 130, 133–4, 141, 143
tragedy 65–7
truth 12, 20, 45–7, 74, 84–6, 96, 126–9

univocity 18–19, 21, 25, 89

Veda 74–5, 98–104
Vernant, J.-P. 36, 66
Vickers, B. 3, 92
Vidal-Naquet, P. 36, 66
vivisection 29, 43, 56

Wang Chong 111, 113–15, 127
Whorf, B. L. 136
writing 112, 125–6, 132; *see also* literacy

Xun Zi 114–15, 128–9

Yan Tie Lun 122
Yin Yang 108, 116–18, 126

Zhuang Zi 108, 115, 119, 123
Zi Chan 125
zoology 88–9
Zu Geng 114

174